Produced by Ana Noyce at Artini Press
AnnaNoyce@gmail.com
CircleInsights.com

To Jodi my dearest friend all my love

For my Mother Donna who taught me to always finish what I start.

Table of Contents

Introduction

There are those times in our lives that our Spirit calls to us and our soul feels the strong need to answer. For most it is something that is not only life changing but deeply fulfilling when we finally let go and follow the call. It is when we ignore our soul's purpose that life becomes stagnant and painful. This is what is called soul sickness.

A Journey into the Sacred Heart is a personal account of a quest to find healing with the discovery that the seat of the soul rests in the heart chakra. It was upon this pursuit that I became deeply aware that healing comes from our sacred connection to both the physical and spiritual world bringing back into balance this human condition.

This odyssey that I would like to share with you is broken up into four parts in a series of stories of a life experience. Part one is about The Awakening where nothing makes any sense, only to find it all makes perfect sense. These chapters are about a journey of self discovery and acceptance of the self while learning about the path that one is on in this lifetime.

The second part, Recognizing The Journey, focuses on understanding that there is a process of learning how to build and renew trust within the self and honoring the sacred relationship of the Spirit. It is about knowing when you are on your path.

The third part of the book is about Discovery and Learning which is the knowing that comes from the life lessons in the physical plane being connected to the spiritual plane.

The fourth part, The Teachings, are stories about moving into a place of expansion to where one can look back and see the journey from a much broader perspective.

The intention of this book is to give hope to anyone who is beginning to honor their own personal journey in understanding and expanding their awareness.

Side note: It is important to note that the book does not follow chronological order as it is an account of stories that create a patchwork of experiences that piece together a network of life lessons. After contemplating how to present my account of personal experiences I finally consulted with my

Spirit team and they offered the advice that since in the spirit world time is of no relevance as it is on the physical plane I might consider to start in the middle moving forward and backwards. I remembered then that when we access our Akashic Records we do start in the middle and we have the ability to move in the past, present, and future possibilities which make up a conglomerate of lifetimes and experiences. However there was an effort to stay in the linear time frame as much as possible.

Part I
The Awakening

"Like all births there is a great deal of pain, but completely worth all the effort. Spiritual awakening is no different"

Ana Noyce

Chapter One: The Journey

The Crisis

When I stepped off the airplane in Albuquerque, New Mexico, on a bright, sunny day, I had no idea I was in a spiritual crisis. I didn't even know what a spiritual crisis was. All I knew was that if someone even smiled at me I would break down in hysterics, wailing from the depths of my soul. Then my body would start to shake all over and eventually go numb. I would have no thoughts or feelings for a while until the next episode. When I was in a place to ask myself what was going on, the words "Soul Sickness" came from somewhere deep inside me. Something was seriously wrong with me, but I didn't know how to fix it.

The plane ride from DFW Airport was short but a slow torture for me. I tried desperately to keep to myself, with my eyes drawn down towards the floor, for fear of making eye contact with anyone. One act of kindness would send me spiraling down into hysterics. My sunglasses were used as a physical shield from others seeing my bloodshot eyes after hours of crying. For most of the ride I pretended to be asleep or engaged in my book in which the words made no sense to me. At one point in the trip, I discovered that the book was upside down, as I was trying desperately to decipher the words. Nothing around me made any sense.

At the airport, my mother Donna waved, greeting me in the baggage claim area. Her smile and her simple "hello" brought big tears gushing out of my eyes, falling onto my shoes, surprising me as they splattered on the floor. There was no end to the flow of water that seemed to pour from my eyes as the emotional flood gates burst open. Once again, sobbing, gasping, and swallowing huge breaths of air took hold of my body, leaving me feeling completely helpless. People around me stopped to watch, then turned away, as if they were afraid they might catch what I had. We grabbed my bags and made a quick exit out the door, heading for the car and a box of Kleenex.

My mother had driven three hours to pick me up to take me back to Taos, New Mexico, where she lived. I had called her only a few days earlier and asked if I could come for a visit. She later confessed that she knew something was going on but it wasn't until she saw me that she realized the extent of what was happening to me. My husband, Steve, and our two children knew I needed to get out of town and take a break. Even the pastor at the church where I worked gave me his blessing to go.

I went back home to Taos to heal, but what did that mean? I had already spent a week visiting with my mother trying to allow myself time to figure out what was happening but as the week passed I was still at my wit's end. It wasn't until a few days before I was scheduled to fly back and hadn't made any progress, that I knew I was still in no shape to go home. Desperately I started to search the Internet for a counselor or healer in Taos who could help me knowing I was there for a reason and was going to make the trip count. Then I came across the website for Golden Willow Retreat Center, which focused on grief therapy. What struck me was that the symptoms for grief fit me like a glove. I was grieving! But what was it that I was grieving?

As luck would have it, I was able to make an appointment the next day to talk to Ted Wiard a counselor, who, I later learned, was the founder of the retreat center. I didn't know what I was in for, but somewhere inside me there was a sense that it was a step in the right direction. There, in my own excitement over learning that I was grieving, I made a small connection to find some peace within myself. If I could find what was causing the grief, then maybe I could overcome what was happening to me. Help was on the way.

Ted's office was on the outskirts of town. My mother drove me there, offering to come inside if I needed her. I told her I was okay and reluctantly got out of her pickup. For a brief moment, I felt very small and insignificant, as I walked the few steps up to the door. I had some fear of what I would find on the other side, not to mention what I would find within myself. I nervously opened the door and stepped inside, where I was greeted by a woman whom I came to know later as Mirabai Star another healer and known author. She asked me my name while seeming to sense my nervousness. She engaged me in polite conversation about Taos as she tried her best to put me at ease, handing me the usual information and paperwork to fill out.

As I waited patiently for my appointment, a heavy vulnerability set up inside my bones and seemed to permeate out through my skin into the room. I tried my best not to think about the tears that were welling up behind my eyes waiting for any opportunity to escape. Time seemed to slow down drastically as I sat there in my own purgatory plotting a path toward the outside door. That option never arrived. I was eventually led down a big hall to a small office where I was greeted by the counselor.

What struck me the most about Ted was that he had really blond hair, which was rather unusual for Taos. He also had an accent that sounded like he was from the beaches of California. For some reason this put me at ease as we began to talk. I discovered that he was a minister who had come into grief counseling after losing his family through illness and tragedy.

As a minister he understood my delicate predicament of working on a church staff. As we sat there talking, words began to spill out of my mouth. Surprised, I listened to myself as I felt my heart opening up. I began explaining to the counselor that somewhere I felt that I had lost my spiritual connection with God. Tears rolled down my cheeks, leaving streaks on my blouse as I continued to talk.

I explained that I was following all the rules. I was a member at a church and sat on the church staff. I went to both services and sang in the band. Even with all of my participation in the church, the only thing I could feel was complete emptiness. Inside, the emptiness was a feeling of being starved, which only fueled my frustration with my situation. Somewhere deep within me I had lost my soul connection to my true spiritual path. I had also lost all trust and integrity in myself. I had lost who I was created to be, as I had blocked myself from speaking my truth, for fear of being judged. I felt that I had no right to express what I was experiencing and that I had come to this place in my heart where I believed I had no personal power or will.

After we talked, I felt strongly the need to discover that part of myself which had been sacrificed. That was when we discussed my spending the week at the Golden Willow Retreat Center. The conversation brought hope into my heart, and later I made the phone call home to my husband and my children, about staying at the retreat.

Thus began my spiritual journey to find my way back to my soul's true path and my personal connection with my Creator.

Golden Willow

The retreat center was not at all what I expected. To be honest I am not sure I knew what to expect. I was still in a state of emotional torment.

My mother drove me out to Golden Willow on a beautiful afternoon a few days after scheduling with the counselor. On the ride out to the retreat, I had mixed emotions and some trepidation about what I would discover about myself. The one thing I could conclude was that it was my chance to either face myself or to ask for a prescription to numb the pain to stop the emotional outbursts. I knew that I had to move through my deepest fears or I was not going to be able to go on.

The ride to the retreat was bumpy and slow as we made our way along a winding dirt road and up a few hills to the top of a mesa, my mom's old pickup truck seemed to magnify the sound of the rocks that spat out from under the rubber tires, flying off to the sides, and rolling down into ditches etched in the sides of the road. Once we were finally on a flat surface, we moved away from the valley below, towards a fork in the road that split into a long driveway where we could see a house.

I choked back tears that came out of nowhere as we drove up to the house and were greeted by two big dogs who had been sitting in the shade next to some trees that surrounded the house. Hummingbirds darted in and out of feeders hanging off the roof. As I stepped out of the truck I could feel wet dog noses probing my hands, greeting me eagerly, looking for attention. The dogs smelled my clothing, quickly deciding if I was interesting or had something for them to eat. Mom swung her door open and my new friends scattered, running to the other side of the truck to see what she had for them as a small offering.

Glancing around at the house, I spotted a small path that led from the driveway to the front porch. Once again I found myself reluctantly trudging up to an unfamiliar door and knocking. In that instant fear shot through my heart, and part of me left my body, floating somewhere on the outside of myself, looking for comfort with the two dogs who had followed me to the porch. All that was left standing was a half-empty shell waiting to be greeted by whomever or whatever was on the other side.

To my relief, a young woman in her mid-twenties with dark hair answered the door. She greeted me and my mom with a smile and let me know that she had been waiting for my arrival, as she invited us inside. I could feel that other part of me that had vacated come slowly back as I walked into the room. We entered the hallway leading to the living room and the kitchen. From there I could see that the house was larger than I originally imagined. She then took us on a small tour through the house and showed us the room that I would occupy. She handed me an itinerary with the schedule for the upcoming days during my stay, along with papers to sign. She paused for a brief moment as if she had forgotten something, then added when lunch would be served, then turned to make her exit.

I stood there looking at my mother, trying to hold back the flood of tears that bubbled to the surface. I dug my fingernails into the palms of my hands in a desperate attempt to stop the tears from making me feel like a fool. She looked at me and quickly mentioned we should get my bags. I followed her back outside to the pickup as the entourage of dogs followed us from the porch. She handed me my bags, hugged me while saying goodbye, then turned around to get into the truck. I watched for a few minutes as the old, white pickup made its way down the long driveway. Filling my lungs with air, and sighing, I turned around and hauled my bags to my room, leaving two very disappointed dogs waiting for my return on the porch.

I went to my room and chose a bed next to the window. Throwing my bags on the bed I began placing my things in the chest of drawers to feel more at home. The room I stayed in had several beds with a combination of old Mexico and New Mexican flavor. I had been informed that I was the only guest in that room during my visit. After settling in, I read the paperwork and signed the rest of the forms. It was getting close to noon, so I decided to wash my hands in the bathroom that was located between my room and the next. I went out to explore and see who else was staying at the retreat. I entered a small hallway that led me through another living space that opened out into the main living room.

Eventually I found my way to the kitchen and was greeted by my hostess who offered me a wonderful and healthy lunch. It seemed I was the only one there, and after visiting with her I found out that she was expecting someone else the next day. We talked for a while, both of us enjoying each other's company. Then I had to go and get ready for my session with the counselor, so I returned to my room.

From what I read on the forms, I would be meeting with the counselor two to three times a day for the next five days, plus body and soul work. Okay, this was Taos and I had come home to heal, but I was still nervous about what was to come. Consoling myself I grabbed my Archos 604 and started to watch a movie recorded on my new video player that my husband had just bought for me.

The Sessions

When the time came, my hostess found me in my room and summoned me to follow her to another room off of the living room. Once inside, I couldn't help but notice two narrow windows where the light trickled down, showing dust particles as they danced in the sun. A big white sofa and an easy chair sitting at an angle made the room look more inviting. The walls were decorated in Native American art, which seemed to be appropriate to me since we were in New Mexico.

A tall, slender woman who seemed to be a little older than me stood up and introduced herself as my new counselor. She shook my hand and then motioned me to the couch. I sat down on the farthest side, wanting only to be in my own space.

For two sessions that day, we went into my childhood traumas of illnesses and old wounds. She guided me through my subconscious, finding the keys that unlocked the old records of the past deep within. Several times I burst into tears and didn't know why. When the tears came, deep sadness spread through my body like a flood filling me up. Overwhelming tears took over my whole being, then, as quickly as it came, I dropped into a state of utter calm. I felt it move through me, taking over, and all tears ceased. I didn't seem to have any control of my emotions or what was happening, as my body responded to my grief.

Still, after a day of work, we were no further from where we were when we began. I went back to my room and started to shake uncontrollably. My temperature seemed to drop as I grabbed blankets while my teeth chattered. I tried desperately to keep warm. It stopped within an hour, and soon after I fell into a deep sleep.

Following breakfast the next morning I went for a walk, exploring the grounds and looking for the company of my two dog friends, who were very eager to accept the small tokens of leftovers from my breakfast. Pleased with my gifts, they accompanied me to the other side of the house to watch the magpies chattering to each other. Looking down at my watch, I realized it was time to go back. The dogs, with wagging tails, escorted me back to the porch and watched me intently as I went inside.

From somewhere inside the house I could hear deep sobbing. When I saw my hostess in the living room she informed me that my session would be late. I was good with that, as I was in no hurry to begin. With this news, I decided to return to my room and finish my movie while waiting for my time with the counselor.

After a while, I was escorted back to the room where my counselor was waiting for me. Our morning session began a little differently than the ones before. This time she wanted me take a few moments to close my eyes and go inward, to see if we could find another key to fit into the lock of my subconscious. Then she gave me some art supplies and told me we were going to do an exercise. I was first going to do a meditation where I would close my eyes, and go within my heart and see what was locked up inside it. Then, when we finished, she wanted me to draw what I saw. This was certainly different.

Feeling that I had nothing to lose, I let myself relax as I followed her instructions listening to the tones in her voice. I closed my eyes and dropped my awareness into my heart. To my surprise I could feel a sinking sensation inside of my body, as if I had left my brain and was falling down into a long tunnel. The sensation reminded me of Alice in Wonderland as she fell down the rabbit hole.

Eventually I did land and found myself in complete darkness, realizing her voice had faded away completely and I was alone. I did a quick check to see if I was okay and found that I was still fully aware of where I was within myself. I waited for what seemed like some time, until a small light started to open up in the dark. The longer I watched it the brighter it became. Finally I could see where I was. My awareness became very acute as my focus began tracking something in the distance. All of a sudden, like a bullet shooting out of a gun, I was up close, and in vivid clarity I could see something enormous which resembled a black pearl. The sound of a heartbeat pulsed in rhythm as energy radiated from the pearl with what looked like orange and blue lighting bolts shooting out in all directions. In an instant it all transformed, bursting into a beautiful flower with thousands of petals on it. It was an "Ah!" moment.

As I stood there completely mesmerized, I heard the counselor's voice pierce through the vision, and I lost all sight, dropping back into darkness. I could hear her voice, and I followed it back, as my awareness of my body took over. After a moment, I opened my eyes and felt extremely exhilarated. I could see my counselor sitting in her chair. She asked me how I was. I told her I was all right and started to draw what I had seen in my vision.

After I drew what I had seen the counselor reminded me that part of my program that week at Golden Willow was to also have several sessions with body-workers. She asked me if I knew anyone in Taos that I wanted to work with. I told her about my mother's friend Jean who did some kind of body-work by laying of hands without touching the body. Seeing the counselor cock her head to one side, I started to fill her in on what I meant.

I began with my story of visiting my mother in Taos last spring. I was having allergies from the construction at the church where I worked and it had turned into a big sinus infection, so I took some time off to see mom. Flying and getting on a bus with people on a three-hour ride from the airport in Albuquerque did not help at all. By the time I got there, I collapsed and was miserable. My ears had closed up, along with my nose, which made me agitated.

Mom finally said, "You know, Ana, I have this friend, who is known as a healer. She might be able to help you." I was taking some medicine that I got from the drugstore which didn't seem to help. At that point I would have done anything.

"Okay," I said as I blew my nose for the millionth time, feeling like it was going to fall off.

She called her friend Jean to come over. To be honest, I didn't know what to expect. I just wanted some or any relief from my state. I remember she came over, and my mother introduced me. They began to chat about their regular day-to-day activities, just catching up. Standing there listening, I felt a little confused when she pulled up two chairs in the middle of the room, facing the same direction and then motioned for me to sit down in one of them. Then she sat behind me. I was thinking at the time how ridiculous that seemed, when she placed her hands behind my head and on my neck while still visiting with my mom.

I wondered why on earth my mother would subject me to the silly idea of working with this woman, when a warm rush of heat started to run through my head and into my sinuses. I felt it run down through my nose and also my ears as they began to open up. I could hear and breathe all at once. Then as I sat there, the warm heat began to flow though my chest and into my lungs that had been fighting for breath. They started to relax allowing the air to fill them up. My body stopped fighting for air and accepted the aid in relief. Jean worked on me for ten minutes without missing a word of her conversation with my mom. Then she stood up and said goodbye, leaving to do other things on her list for that day. I remember looking at my mother in wonder as she was smiling back at me. I was still not really sure what had just happened.

That night I went to bed and slept for the first time in weeks, a very sound and deep sleep. When I awoke I asked my mom for Jean, the healer's, number and scheduled an hour session with her. I didn't know what she did, but I was now a true believer.

I met her at her home, where she did her work, the next day. As I laid on her table thinking, "What am I doing?" she brought out a crystal bowl and struck it several times with a mallet over my body. Each time it was hit the bowl made a sound like a thud. "Okay, okay, Lets get on with it," I thought as she did this, not knowing where this was going.

All she did was lay her hands on my feet and sometimes a few inches above my body as she worked her way up to the top of my head. She would tell me as she moved and worked what she was doing. I never felt invaded, or uncomfortable. To my amazement, my body began to relax again, and I started to fight off sleep. After Jean finished she got out her crystal bowl again and struck it. It was amazing! The sound had changed from a thud to a clear bell sound, and I could feel the vibration of the bowl ring though my whole body. I could feel it and knew where I felt it inside, as my body began to tingle as though it was vibrating with the bowl.

The counselor smiled at me when I finished my story asking if I had Jean's number.   She promptly wrote it down in her book of notes. She then reassured me that she was going to call that afternoon and make arrangements for me to see her.

We took a break for lunch after our session, and I noticed this time I was not unbearably cold or shaking. I opened the window in my room to catch the afternoon breeze. I laughed at the black and white magpies talking and playing in the tree next to the window. They were so funny chattering at one another. I called to one of the birds who seemed to be talking directly to me. He heard me call and flew to the window, cocking his head from side to side. "Oh," I thought to myself, "you want to visit." I asked him politely about his day and what he was doing. He looked at me curiously and made his way almost inside the window as he kept a close eye on me. I walked up to him, chatting away as he made no signs of leaving. I was only a few feet from him when I leaned down to get a closer look at him. My nose almost touched his head, but he didn't seem to be afraid. He just watched me, silently drinking me in with his beautiful eyes. A knock on the door shattered our connection, and the voice of my hostess moved me back into the moment to let me know lunch was ready. I only glanced at the door for a second, but when I looked back, my friend was gone.

Straightening back up, I grabbed my sweater on the way out and was immediately hit with an aroma of something that smelled absolutely delicious on the other side of the door. It was all I could do not to skip as I followed the smell all the way to the kitchen.

Crazy, or Not?

That afternoon I was bored waiting for the next session, so I picked up a magazine that was lying on the coffee table in the main living room. It was called "The Light of Consciousness." It was the 2007 summer edition that had an article about flower essences. I have always loved flowers and felt the need to read something that I could identify with. The article talked about something called the Chakra System and how the chakras affect the body. I guess what shocked me the most was how the colors of the seven chakras matched the colors from my drawing of my vision. What I saw and experienced within myself that morning was described very clearly in the article. "Could this be real?" I thought. The counselor never mentioned chakras?

As I sat there reading the article over and over, trying to absorb it into my brain, the woman who was in the session came out. I could see tears from her blood shot eyes. She then made her way to the couch and sat down as the counselor went to get her a glass of water. That was when I saw the man. He was standing behind her with his hands on her shoulders as if trying to comfort her.

Startled, I blinked, realizing that that was no man. I was seeing a ghost. I could see right through him, as if he were made out of a haze, yet there he was. He seemed to pay me no mind as I watched him standing there with a loving expression on his face while the counselor was making sure she was okay. I couldn't help staring at them out of curiosity. Desperately, I tried to turn my gaze so as not to be rude. After a few minutes, to my relief, the counselor motioned for me to follow her to the room. I quickly brushed past the couple, noticing that our presence didn't seem to sway him in the least. He was so intent on the woman. I couldn't help wondering who he was as I walked into the other room.

I sat there in the room thinking I was crazy when the thought hit me that now was the time to find out if I really was. As soon as I had that thought, fear shot through me like electrical shocks exploding throughout my body. Fear of doing something wrong and then the emotion of guilt crushed my heart, causing me to gag as I opened my mouth to speak.

I decided instead to take a step back and share with the counselor my discovery and what I thought the colors meant. I think she was a little surprised at the direction we were going as I shared with her about the chakras, colors, and what they meant. Then out of nowhere I blurted out, "I saw a man standing by that women only he was a ghost!" There! It was out in the open and I couldn't take it back. I had just exposed myself. I cringed inside, waiting for the lecture of how crazy I was.

Instead the counselor listened with intent as I went into detail about what I had seen. Then she asked if I would be willing to share with the woman who was crying. I was shocked! No, mortified! The woman would only think I was evil or crazy! "No," I said bowing my head and wanting to crawl under the couch. The counselor smiled, and she shared with me a few stories as we continued to talk.

I was surprised to see the lady who was crying at the dinner table that evening. I didn't mention anything about what I had seen, since I was afraid of her response. We had polite conversation over another good meal. Since we only just met, neither one of us mentioned the reasons why we were there. Later when we moved into the living room, I decided to speak up. I knew it was now or never, so I tensed my whole body up readying myself for the anger or disgust that I was sure was coming my way. I took my time and explained that the counselor wanted me to share something with her. I told her about what I had seen that afternoon and the man who was with her. To my relief, instead of looking at me like I was insane she grabbed me and hugged me. She shared that she had just lost her husband and couldn't cope with the grief. Her smile lit up the room and she quickly got up to share the news with our hostess. I was still not sure what just happened and went into a daze of shock. I felt myself trying to shut down, not knowing how to handle her reaction.

The next day I met with the counselor for our morning session. I was not looking forward to it, as we were touching on some things in my past that I was unsure about. As we started I confessed what had occurred after dinner the night before with the lady and her husband. She asked what I thought. I told her I had mixed emotions about what had happened. In one way, I was happy to help the lady, and in another I was afraid that I was doing something wrong. This brought up a question from the counselor, "Why would you think it was wrong?"

I sat there, looking back on my early childhood, thinking about how much I was in communication with the spirit world. I explained to her that I started to experience the world of spirit when I was extremely young. My earliest memories were of being in my crib after my mom put me to bed and feeling people standing around me. Sometimes I could hear them talking to each other. I know that my parents thought I was having night terrors or nightmares at that time. There were so many nights that my parents spent trying to console me back to sleep. I was always afraid of the strange people who came into my room, which became a challenge.

The counselor asked me what I was thinking, and what came was the memory of often being sick. My father used to cry when he told stories of going to the doctors offices and emergency rooms when I was a toddler. He and my mother were not sure that I would pull through. Pneumonia was one of the common illnesses of my childhood. It was during those times I would feel myself floating or hovering over my body going off somewhere that I couldn't remember.

I explained my history to the counselor. I was adopted at the age of three months. It was a closed adoption so I wasn't given a lot of information about my biological parents. What I do know is that they were Mexican American, and my mother was sixteen. My father was also very young and as soon as I was born, I was put up for adoption in an agency in Fort Worth, Texas.

My adopted parents were wanting to start a family and were excited to hear that I was up for adoption and that I was Mexican. My mother wanted desperately to adopt a child who was of a different race, and since that was in the 1960s, it was not a common occurrence. My father, A. Kelly Pruitt, was a well known western artist and my mother, Donna, was his manager. Together they worked as a team to create an art business. My family had a working ranch in Presidio, Texas, right next to the Mexican border, and an art gallery in Taos, in the early 60s, and 70s. During the fall and winter we would live on the ranch where my father would retreat to do his art work and write. Then we would go back to Taos to sell art in the spring and summer. Eight years after they adopted me, my little sister, Angelique, was born. We call her our miracle baby. She is and always has been a bright light in our lives.

When I talk about my dad I often think of him as a Buddhist cowboy. He was a working cowboy with hat and all. He was also very spiritual. In his early years he studied Buddhism. Then later he went on to spend some time with the Native American Indians learning what he could. My mother, on the other hand, was a Christian Scientist at the time, so I must say my upbringing was a little different.

My parents divorced sometime after I was nine. My mother, sister, and I settled down in Fort Worth. My life changed dramatically after that. The counselor stopped me and asked what I meant by that. I told her that it was during that time that I started to become friends with many Christians. By the age of thirteen I accepted Christ into my heart. That same year my mother married my step-dad, Ken, who was also a Christian. Then a few years later my mom and sister became Christians.

During this time I spent the summers with Kelly traveling and living in tepees wherever he went to sell his art. He was always in and out of my life, but when I did spend time with him, we would talk about the earth, nature, and animals. He loved to tell stories that were handed down from other cultures and would often try to educate me in my own spiritual walk. As I was growing up, I took many of the stories as just that -- Stories.

I can see now, looking back, that my father was trying to teach me a path. However it just didn't fit into with what my friends had shared with me about religion and the church when I was at school. Even as a young child, I remembered, I just wanted to fit in. Becoming a Christian didn't stop the encounters. As an older teen, the visits and visions started to come in a lot stronger. I also started to be aware of both the angels and what I came to know as the shadow people as my experiences grew. I didn't have to do anything to make contact; it would just happen on its own.

I told the counselor that it was my experience with a dark entity that eventually led me to having an exorcism at the age of nineteen. She stopped me and asked me to go back. "Exorcism?" the counselor asked.

"Yes," I replied, "an exorcism."

"How did that make you feel?" the counselor asked.

Looking down at the floor, trying to bring that memory back, I noticed that my right leg was bouncing up and down. I could feel my nerves taking control. This only made me more nervous about what I was going to share with her. I slowly started to explain, as the memories seemed to gather around my head.

By that time in my life, I had a lot of fear of judgment from others. All through my teens I was in and out of a state of denial of what was happening to me. I was also very determined to live a normal life, or what I thought was normal. I kept it at bay the best I could, trying to ignore it. The few times I brought up the subject of the supernatural, it was not received well by my friends. Most thought I was joking or playing around. Others told me not to even go there. It was fine as long as I kept myself distracted, which was easy during the day but the night was just something I endured as my fear seemed to fuel it.

This all came to a head by the time I was in my first year of college. It started one night when I was home for the weekend. I might even go so far as to say that the experience was some kind of visitation that got out of hand. This went a step further than all the rest of my encounters. As I started to tell my story, a motion caught my attention. I saw out of the corner of my eye a mockingbird diving off the roof and disappearing into the grass. For some reason it startled me and I forgot what I was saying. The distraction from the past was a relief, but the counselor redirected my attention. Finding the memory, I continued on.

I was having trouble with an entity that had attached itself to me, making its presence known when I started to go to sleep. When I turned the lights off, I could see it in the corner of the room, sitting there watching me. It looked like an outline of a large man but appeared to be darker than the darkness in the room. Quickly I would jump up and turn on the lights. I couldn't see it in the light, but could feel it was still there. I discovered if I turned the lights off and allowed my eyes to adjust to the darkness, the outline would reappear. I spent many nights with the lights on, only to feel deep anger and pure hatred bearing down on me as I lay there. I was constantly in my own hell and terror all night.

It didn't matter if I slept with the lights on or off; it was there. I would lie there for hours, afraid to drift off to sleep, losing the battle, only to awaken feeling its weight bearing down upon my body, holding me down. I couldn't move or scream. All I could hear was a silent screaming inside my head. I could see the outline of a man in a dark shape with its hatred for me trying to enter my body as it pushed the breath out of my chest with its weight. If I was home, away at college, or at a friend's house; it would always find me when it was time to go to bed. It happened over and over for months, until I finally couldn't take it any more and confessed to my mother that I was terrified and being tormented by this dark, angry entity.

My mom sought help at a local church and found these ladies called "God's Handmaidens." I remember the day they came. They knocked on the door, and there was nothing out of the ordinary about them. I must admit that I was a little worried, not sure what to expect. I was desperate and tired, wanting relief from the night attacks. They sat down with us, and we told them what I was going through. They then explained how they worked. The women would sing religious songs while sweeping the house with their voices, clearing the rooms of dark entities. Then they would sing over me, clearing me of the attachment.

It was beautiful as they serenaded us, moving through the house, singing in unison. I had never experienced anything like it. It felt good. Then finally they made their way to my upstairs room and stopped. Mom and I followed close behind as they moved into the room.

One of the ladies let us know there was something there and then asked me to lie down on my bed. I didn't know what to think, but did as I was told. They gathered around me and held hands over me, singing several songs. It felt nice, and I was at peace. Then they spread out and went through my room singing at the top of their voices. When it was done, they stopped and paused, giving thanks in prayer.

They gave us strict instructions to go through the room and throw away any objects that I might have gotten just before the attachment came, or any items that might open a doorway. Then, saying goodbye, they left. Mom and I went upstairs and cleaned out my room, doing exactly what they said. That night I rested without an attack. I was free until I was a lot older and married. Then it all started over again. This time I was sleeping in bed with my husband when I awoke with a feeling of anger bearing down on me. As I watched I could see a shape of a man darker than the darkness of the room coming in from the corner of the ceiling making its way toward me.

Fear instantly shot through my body. I knew very well the outcome of this visit. I could feel a heavy pressure bearing down on my chest wanting full access to my body. I saw and felt him hold me down. Sheer terror took over my brain as I couldn't move or scream for help, for my husband who was only an inch away from me. I couldn't even bend my finger to touch him, although I was fully aware he was that close to me. All I could feel was helplessness of the reality of my fate sinking in as I felt the entity bearing down on my chest wanting full access to my body. I fought with every ounce of willpower that I had, trying desperately to keep the dark entity out.

It wasn't until the next morning that I was released from being paralyzed and able to wake up my husband. Crying, I told him about what had occurred during the night, as I shook in fear of it all happening again. The only evidence of the attack was the sweat that drenched my nightgown and soaked our bed where I was pinned down.

This all happened a few weeks before passover and I was scared to death. I knew I had to do something to protect myself and my family. I had just watched the movie "The Ten Commandments" and remembered the part where they took the sheep's blood and spread it over the door, so death would pass over it in the last part of the plagues of Egypt. I didn't want any part of the blood, but I had olive oil.

I decided first to pray in every room. I asked for help to remove all ghosts and entities. Then I took the olive oil and prayed, asking for it to be blessed. Next I went all through the house and the attic drawing crosses on the frames above all the doors, windows, and the fireplace in the house with the intention of sealing them off from the spirit world for a year. It worked! In fact it worked so well that no one bothered us for that whole year. I ended up doing this during Passover each year for a few years as a ritual to keep any unwelcome entities out of the house and away from my family.

I finished the story and looked up at my counselor, who sat there quietly taking notes. She paused, then started to lead me into a discussion of the effect the ritual had on my family and me. As I sat there talking with her, I suddenly realized that in the past I had always been very careful about whom I shared my experiences with and that I was now starting to feel very vulnerable. I was not sure anymore where the boundaries were and when I had crossed them. The lines had become blurred in the open sharing of my experiences with the counselor. I started to feel a slow feeling of shock creeping up inside of my body and all through me. Then out of nowhere may body started to shake uncontrollably from within, right down to my inner core. My mind shifted somewhere into a private purgatory as fear of exposing myself took over. I noticed that somewhere deep within I was also feeling the freedom of speaking my full truth to someone. All connections of my body, mind, and soul split off into different directions. I understood in that moment that I didn't know how to pull myself back together.

The counselor stopped then and explained that I was learning how to carry and accept, my inner truth. It would take some time, but eventually my body, mind, and soul would discover the healing pattern of integrating back together when I spoke my truth openly. My job was to recognize what was happening and to allow the natural process of healing to begin.

Within a few minutes, the shaking stopped. A feeling of peace flooded in, rushing through me and over my skin. I felt a connection deep inside my cells within my body. I was soothed by an inner calmness. I took a long breath, letting the air fill my lungs to their full capacity. On the out breath, I let go of any anxiety that I was holding. As I let it all sink in, I knew I was going to be okay.

We finished the session, and I slowly dragged myself back to my room for a nap. I was exhausted, and sleep overtook me. I had no control over it but felt happy to fully surrender to it.

Soul Sickness

When I finally awoke the next morning, I found myself in an unfamiliar place. It took me a few minutes to remember where I was. An overwhelming emotional feeling of rawness hit my body once I got my bearings. I knew I was working on something that had to be taken care of so I could move on, but I was not looking forward to the work ahead. I lay there on my side for a few minutes, thinking of what I had shared in confidence with the counselor. I consoled myself, trying to let go of any guilt, still wondering where all of this would lead. The sun hit the windows and the entire room brightened as sunbeams danced in the air. Watching the rays of light streak across the room, I began to accept that I was now on a new journey in my life and that the time had come to discover what was locked up deep inside myself. I knew somewhere within the sacredness of my heart was the answer for my own healing and my soul's purpose.

By the close of my stay at Golden Willow, I discovered that grief does not have a quick fix. It is something that one must work through, allowing the self to have the luxury of the experience. Not only was I grieving my soul, but I was also learning that my mind was preconditioned by a program that I created within myself to live in the world where I wanted to be accepted. I had done such a good job of suppressing my emotional fears of being judged that the scars were now interwoven within the cellular structure of my physical body. Somewhere within me was an old tape that could be triggered into a blindness of fight-or-flight mode when encountering the spirit world. My attempts to override the program without understanding the whole process were the source of my emotional breakdowns. That was when the shaking would start as the body tried to bring itself back into balance with the mind and soul.

I also learned that healing soul sickness is finding those missing pieces that have been scattered. Not only was I to find the pieces, but I was to work on reprogramming my mind and body. The goal was to heal the old wounds, so they no longer amplified the emotional triggers that sent out scrambled signals threatening my well being. The only setback was that the solution was within the scattered pieces. Taking a step back, I could see the puzzle and the task that was laid out before me. The key was hunting for the missing pieces without knowing what to expect. I knew then: this was not going to be an easy task. I was not even sure where to go to look for all the pieces.

Finding those scattered parts is integral to a personal journey of recovery, and to starting the healing process. Once the procedure is set into motion, genuine self discovery and resolution take place. This process allows you to bring back into balance the mind, body, and soul and helps to restore peace as a complete being. Somewhere I had lost my way of feeling whole. I experienced small fragments of myself drifting about or hiding from myself, which only created the feeling of loss and hopelessness. It was time now to be okay with allowing myself to become whole again.

I had learned that week to share more openly about my experiences with those I trusted. Like water dripping from a leaking faucet, memories from my past trickled in. I knew many keys were still missing that fit other locked doors within myself. All the same, the keys were only misplaced, and with each session I gained more confidence in finding them.

After my experience at Golden Willow, I discovered I was grateful to have had the opportunity to find what was lost and jump-start my own healing journey. All in all, I had to learn to be loving, and more accepting of myself.

I still felt raw inside as my hostess drove me back to Taos and dropped me off at my mother's art gallery. I don't remember a lot of the drive. I was somewhere deep within myself, trying to fit the pieces back together. I did recognize a spark of hope, and I could live with that. I finally had something to hold on to.

I can only look back with a smile, knowing now that I was about to embark on a personal pilgrimage of self-discovery.

The Medicine Man

A few days after my return from the retreat to my mother's house in Taos, a friend of mine named Chris arranged for me to meet with a medicine man thinking it might help my healing to ask some questions of him. I still had so many things to ask and not nearly enough answers. My friend, who was an artist, showed up at my mother's art gallery in the mid-afternoon. We walked a few doors away to another gallery where we were going to meet with the medicine man. I could feel myself becoming nervous. Tears began to escape once again, beyond my control. My friend gave me a few moments to compose myself as he slipped out to the porch located behind the gallery, which overlooked Taos Mountain. He and the medicine man talked while they waited for me to get myself together.

I finally got my nerve back and dried my tears. This time I noticed they were not the same tears that fell a few weeks ago. Checking in with myself, all I could say was that I felt very raw and exposed. What was I going to do? I had to go back into my life, except I was me but not me. I was different and yet still not sure who I was. I slipped out to the porch where my friend introduced me to the medicine man.

The first thing he said to me was, "Life is an adventure and a learning experience. You are here to learn and not to judge yourself or others for the experiences." My friend used that as his cue to leave and excused himself. I was left to fend for myself.

Looking around, I saw a chair with a pillow on it and pulled it closer so I could face the medicine man and still see the mountains. The air had cooled down a little. The small breeze was more than welcome as it brushed up against my skin. I asked him how he came to be a medicine man, and he shared his story with me. He asked about me, and I told him how I had come to Taos and about my stay at Golden Willow. Finally I asked him point-blank when I would know that I was healed. He looked at me and smiled then said, "The path to healing is a journey that never ends. It changes with us as we grow and learn from each of our experiences." Not the answer I wanted to hear, but I did think about what he was saying.

We sat there in silence for a while, looking out at the view of the mountains. The medicine man asked me out of the blue, what did I think about death? Startled, I was not sure why he asked me that question. But I searched my brain for an answer. The first thing to pop up was my cat's death just a few years before. I had to admit that I was not prepared for death on the mental level and that I did not understand what it was like to let go. I asked him if he would like to hear my story. He waved me on to speak, so I began.

My beautiful cat Buddy taught me the lesson of loss when, after nineteen years of being my pet and animal child, she was ready for the other side. She had cancer and was in the last stages of the illness. I knew it was time when I saw her struggle just to get up, so I called the veterinarian and scheduled a time to let her go. My dear friend Stacy, who used to work for a veterinarian's office, knew how attached I was to my cat and went with me to hold my hand and let me cry. Buddy took her last breath with a huge purr and was gone as I held her, watching the life leave her eyes. I had never watched a loved one take their last breath before. I was at once devastated and horrified.

My friend held me as I cried huge tears that drenched her tee shirt. My eyes were so puffy I couldn't see. The vet let me know that if I was not ready to take my cat, they would be happy to hold her body in the freezer so that my husband could bring her home to bury. I left trying to deal with my grief and a broken heart from losing her. I was so grief stricken that no one, not even my co-workers, wanted to be around me. My boss, the pastor at the church where I worked, let me take the rest of the week off.

My husband Steve got off work early and picked Buddy up to bury her in our yard. I didn't have the heart to watch, so when he was done, he asked if I wanted to see her resting place. I followed him out into the yard and he pointed to a spot a few feet from our fence. I realized that the lawnmower would have to mow over her when he did the yard, so I asked him if he would move her to my flower bed so that she would not be disturbed. He dutifully dug her up, knowing how distressed I was, and buried her in the flower bed. I felt happy that she was at rest and that no one could mow over her memory.

I went to bed normally that evening, only to awaken from a dream at about two in the morning, fully aware of the darkness and the absence of my cat. I had this huge urge to dig her back up, thinking that it was all a mistake and that she was very much alive when we buried her. I woke my husband up from his peaceful sleep, crying that it was all a mistake and that we needed to dig her up because she was gasping for air under the ground. My poor husband talked to me, trying desperately to ease my fears. He said that if I still felt the same way in the morning he would go out and dig her up to check to see if she was alive. He said that considering she was frozen when he picked her up he was pretty sure she wasn't alive.

I had nightmares all the rest of the night. As soon as dawn broke, (yes, you guessed it!) I asked Steve to dig up our cat. He did, and held the box up and let me know that she was not moving inside. I was good for the day and made it through the next night. The next afternoon, I had this horrible fear that she was alive and gasping for air. Steve came home during his lunch hour and once again dug up Buddy to show me that she was not moving and that she was very much dead. I dealt with my grief the rest of the day but woke up in the middle of the night again with nightmares of my cat needing my help.

Once again I woke my husband from a deep sleep. I was in tears and wracked with terror that we had buried my cat alive. He begged me to let him sleep and said he would dig her up in the morning if I could calm myself, and that he would prove that she was dead. As soon as the sun touched the sky, I was up with the shovel, asking him to help me dig her up. This time he stomped out of the house angrily to dig. He pulled her box out of the ground and moved to open it. I screamed, mortified. He shook the box, telling me that if I wanted to open it, I was free to do so. He placed it in the ground and stomped off. Perplexed at his actions, I stood there wondering what had gotten into him.

My son Mason had gotten up early that morning, wondering what all the ruckus was outside. He came out to where I was standing, looking at the gaping hole in the ground and Buddy's box next to it. Shaking his head back and forth, he said, "Dad is really angry."

I said, "I know... I'm not sure why?"

My son replied, "Well, he is just tired of digging up Buddy."

It was as if a light bulb flashed in my brain saying, "Crazy!" I realized that I had flipped, lost it, and that I was being insane. My denial of the death of my cat had pushed me too far.

"Oh," I said, and burst out into tears. I cried and cried, but it was a great release. I finally let go of my beautiful cat and all the grief that I carried for her loss. After the cry I went back inside and apologized to my husband, and asked if he would once more place my beloved cat in the ground. He did, and I let her rest in peace.

A few days later, I noticed that my other cat Allie was acting strange, so I went to see what was causing her distress. I caught a glimpse of a gray cat running past me and around the couch. Buddy was gray, and Allie was orange. On another day, I was sitting in my bedroom writing an email when something scampered across the room and darted under the bed. My orange cat followed in hot pursuit and chased the shadow of the gray cat out from the other side of the bed and into the living room. She was back! Buddy had come back!

A few years later, Allie also left on the journey to the other side. For another year I had two ghost cats chasing each other around the room and jumping on the couch. My daughter also saw them and often made comments about seeing them playing. On another occasion, an intuitive friend dropped by to visit. Out of the blue, he asked if I had an orange cat just as she jumped into his lap, then took off running. Laughing, I had to confess to him about my cats that stayed with us and kept me company. One day I noticed that I had not seen them in a while. They were gone.

After I finished recounting my "Buddy" story, the medicine man asked me again what I thought about death. While I tried to think about his question, another experience popped in my head. Scrambling for an answer, I started to tell him of my experience on an airplane. He seemed intent on listening, so I continued.

When I was eighteen, my mom and step-dad had saved up all year to take our family on a week's vacation to Jamaica. Not only were we getting to go, but my little sister and I each got to invite a friend! I can't even tell you how much fun we had. My parents seemed to spare no expense.

As we started to explore the island and run around, I thought to myself that for some reason I was supposed to be there. I had a flashback of my music teacher in fourth grade teaching us a song called 'Mary Ann' about Jamaica. I knew then in my heart that someday I would be going there. There was no doubt, only a knowing that it would happen.

Like all trips, ours came to an end. As we sat on the plane waiting to take off, my friend fell asleep. I had some time to myself to look around the cabin, since we were all scattered throughout the plane, each of us in different sections.

In that moment I became afraid of the plane taking off. Panic and fear washed over me. I felt like I had jumped into a swimming pool in the middle of winter. An icy cold feeling moving through me froze my bones down to my inner core.

Then, as quickly as the fear took hold of me, I felt a strong, invisible presence wrap itself around my body. As it did, a light prickly energy started moving slowly through me. The fear that had gripped me was replaced with a warmth that spread throughout my body, allowing me to finally relax. I felt a sense of calm and peace, as though I had just discarded a cold wet blanket and replaced it with a warm dry one. A sensation of unconditional love moved through me, saturating my whole being. A full knowing came to me that everything was going to be all right.

The plane started to taxi down the runway, and as it lifted into the air, I was in a mental and physical bliss. Then I heard very clearly, "This is what it will be like when it is your time to leave this earth. Don't be afraid." The words brought no fear. I knew without a doubt that this experience was the way things worked with the transition into the next world.

I sat there watching the medicine man after finishing my story. I waited for a reaction of some kind as he sat very still with his eyes looking out over the spectacular view outside the gallery. The sun began to set, giving off rays of pink, orange, and gold mixed with deep blues and purples. I took advantage of the silence to ask myself what I thought about death. Then I repeated his question out loud and spouted out the answer, "I don't know. I think I am confused!"

The medicine man replied without taking his eyes off of the sunset, "Soul sickness is about the separation of three parts trying to put themselves back together. Ana, your journey of awakening has begun. You have an adventure ahead, of finding your way back to your own beginning. Remember too that energy is neither good nor evil, it is only energy. It is the intent of the person that makes it good or evil." After saying that, he got up and stretched, wished me well, then walked down the steps of the porch and departed.

"Wait," I thought to myself, "I have so many questions. I am not sure what it all means." But as I sat there, I said nothing, only straining my eyes as I watched him make his way down the road to disappear behind the buildings. I was afraid to let him out of my sight. I was alone again, sitting by myself on the porch as the coolness of the breeze crept up into my bones. I sat there with my teeth chattering, not sure I even knew what he was talking about.

A Gentle Courage

It has been a while since I sat there on the porch behind the gallery with the medicine man, staring off at the sunset wondering about what I was going to do. The counselor told me once, "It was like opening the door for a caged tiger who had forgotten what it was like to be a tiger. Now it was time for the tiger to decide whether to stay in the cage or learn to walk in freedom as a tiger."

I still had so many questions. At the same time, I didn't even know what it was I wanted to ask. I was not even sure how to find someone to answer them or how to look for a teacher. The only thing I could do was to make my way home and trust what my counselor told me, which was, "When the student is ready, the teacher will come." I have discovered this to be true, not only on the physical level, but also the spiritual level. Our Creator and the angels open up the heavens and the universe for us when we ask for help. A teacher on the physical and spiritual level will appear to guide the process of spiritual growth.

The true challenge is trusting the teachers that show up in your life to help you learn, rather than sitting silently in a box, afraid of making a wrong choice. Your whole life experience is really up to you and what you decide to take away from it.

Chapter Two: Remembering the Spirits

A Sign

Part of our learning process involves remembering that we are not alone in the world or in the universe. There is so much more to this world than we could ever imagine. As we become more aware, we start to experience things that prove this. I know this to be true from my own experiences.

After I returned from my spiritual crisis in Taos, I was still unsure about admitting that there was really something out there -- guardian angels or spirit guides -- keeping watch over us in our lives. I spent the first week sleeping before I prepared myself to go back to work at the church.

When I returned I found a card on my desk from a lady who asked me to call her when I got back from my trip. Stella talked to me about spiritual gifts without any fear, and for the first time in a long while, I had someone to talk to. We soon became fast friends.

A month later she became my mentor. She came to my office and invited me to a weekend mediumship seminar at a retreat center called "The Crossing" in Austin, Texas. The teacher John Holland could communicate with the other side. Stella was very persistent not giving me a lot of room to say no. Finally I agreed to go, making it my mission to prove, once and for all, that this was all in my imagination, so I could go on with my life at the church.

The teacher for the weekend, I learned, was a renowned psychic medium and spiritual teacher. The timing was coincidental. A few weeks before the trip, my mother called to tell me that one of my friends in Taos had committed suicide. I was devastated. I spent the weeks before the seminar crying in shock and disbelief. By the time I made the trip to Austin, I was angry with my friend for taking his life. It was all that occupied my mind for the three-hour drive out to the healing center, where I planned to meet up with my mentor.

In the car, I ranted and raved out loud at my friend, telling him that since I was going to this seminar, he better show up. I had a few things to say to him face-to-face. I could feel his presence in the truck but pushed him away with my anger.

Once I got settled in at the retreat center, I met up with Stella and her mom, who had come with her. That evening after dinner we attended a free demonstration by John for the general public.

The room was packed. Three hundred people showed up! I had never seen a medium work with an audience and I was really not sure what to expect. Still angry with my friend, I told him once again that he better show up or this was it! I was mad! Then our teacher got on stage and explained how he did readings with large groups. I was skeptical.

John said, "I have someone who is pushing his way to the front of the line, wanting to speak to someone here tonight who's name begins with the letter A. Anne, No! Ana?" As I realized what was happening, fear shot through me like a launched rocket. I found myself afraid of talking to this medium, in front of all these people. I lost all nerve and started to plead silently with my friend to stop the communication. I had changed my mind. I told him I believed he was there and was sorry for being so angry.

Then John said, "Oh, he is moving away and now he is gone." Grateful, I thanked my friend for not calling me out in front of everyone. That night when I said my prayers, I spent some time talking to my friend. I let him know I was not angry with him any more and wished him well. I could feel him leave after we made peace. I knew he had come to say goodbye and let me know he was going to be okay. I could feel his concern and love for me as we parted.

The next morning, I met with Stella for the seminar. Maybe there was something to all of this. But even with the experience from the night before, I was still feeling cautious and on-guard. When John our teacher had us do a meditation, my energy began to shift once again. In the meditation, we asked if there was an angel or guide around us. We then asked for the guides to please give us proof that they existed by showing us something close to our hearts that only we would know.

Meditating is not something I enjoy doing. It is a lot like pulling teeth for me. To this day I can't seem to make myself sit quietly long enough to let go of my thoughts. If I am lucky to even get still enough to be quiet I will drop off to sleep as soon as I sit down. But since I was there in the group, I went though the motions. I asked silently to be shown a sign that the angels and spirit guides existed. Anything to move on so that we could finish and go to lunch. I was starving and getting tired of sitting there listening. Then John dismissed us for lunch and a little free time, giving us time to process what we had just learned. After we finished eating I told Stella that I wanted to stop by the little bookstore by the cafeteria before we went back to finish the second half of the class.

Stealing some time to myself, I indulged myself in the freedom of being surrounded with books. I read the covers of each book I passed. In the corner of the store, a necklace caught my attention. I gazed at it in complete shock. Right in front of me was the design I had drawn for the counselor when I was asked to go deep inside of my heart at Golden Willow. That was something personal with symbols that had a lot of meaning to me. What a coincidence! I Immediately grabbed up the medallion necklace and threw it to the back of the old shelf. I sulked back to the seminar. I was hurt and upset. How could anyone steal my design? I had not shared it with anyone except the counselor. It was personal!

The first thing our teacher asked when we started the seminar again was, "Did anyone receive a sign, or something from their angel or guides, that told them that they were real?" Oh no! I forgot! I looked at Stella, and felt the color drain from my face. I realized the necklace was from someone who knew who I really was, deep within. I couldn't wait to get back to the bookstore.

As soon as we were released from the class, I ran to the bookstore and quickly dug through all the jewelry to find the medallion necklace with my design. When I found it again, I took the time to really examine it. When I turned it over, there were words stamped on the back that read, "Guide This Woman." Amazed, I bought it and later restrung it to wear close to my heart. It was a gentle reminder I was not alone.

Years later I moved past having to wear my necklace every day as a reminder. But now I am always aware of a soft inner voice that lets me know that I might want to pay attention. I am not always good at listening, but there is still hope.

The Call

After I returned home from the seminar, I began to work on my own recovery. I started by listening to a CD that I bought at the seminar called

"Tapping Into Your Inner Confidence & Personal Power." [1] It was a guided meditation and another step in my journey. I was learning how to accept myself and the spiritual gifts I was given, even though I still wanted to fit in. As I followed the path to piecing myself back together my idea of what I thought was normal was not matching up to what my heart was calling me to do. This confusion continued to cause a split in who I was. I began to cry all over again when I realized I wasn't satisfied with my position as the Fellowship Director at the church any more. I had to resign. When I got the courage to talk to the pastor, he offered me the opportunity to run a healing ministry for the church. Now that sparked my interest! Drying my tears, I agreed to stay, and I accepted the challenge.

Someone on staff suggested that I go to Los Angeles and investigate a program that was being taught at Saddleback Church on healing and recovery. My husband thought it would be a wonderful experience for me. To back me up, he funded the whole trip, since it was a new ministry and there was no money in the church account to pay for it. He suggested that I take a friend with me -- someone who might want to help me build the ministry when I returned -- since I was not used to traveling alone.

I asked my friend Sonya, whom I had met at the church, if she would join me and see what she thought about the program. She agreed to go. The dates of the training just happened to be on the week of my birthday. I was a little sad to be away from my husband and kids, but my little sister was living there, so I would have the opportunity to see her for my birthday.

Exhausted after the long flight, we finally got to the hotel and stopped moving for a while. We were so grateful it was clean and had plenty of room to move around that I didn't pay too much attention to the spirits that hung out in the room. I brought up the subject of the ghosts when we were heading off to bed. Sonya was one of the few who really knew about what I saw. It was nice that she wasn't afraid, so I was happy to share with her what the ghosts were doing those few nights we stayed at the hotel.

The training at the church was amazing. Three thousand people attended that week-long conference. We sat wherever we could find a seat but there was enough space for all of us. Like many trainings, we were taken off to small groups and then brought together to one big group where we would compare notes. Sonya and I usually split up to absorb more information, in order to organize the ministry from a broader perspective when we returned home.

On one of the last days of the training, we scattered all over the beautiful campus for lunch. Sonya and I sat on the steps of one of the buildings, enjoying our lunch, when we overheard a couple sharing their story about their teenage daughter, who had been diagnosed with cancer the week before. It was a heart-breaking story and all of us there were touched by the couple and what they shared. I heard a voice very clearly from somewhere inside of me say that the daughter would be healed from the cancer in the next few months and would go on to live a long life. The message was so strong it made me uncomfortable. I kept thinking I needed to tell them, but I was afraid to approach the couple with all the people around. The idea came to me to make a bargain that might get me off the hook. I told the voice that if I was meant to tell the couple, we would run into them again. I figured it was a safe bet we wouldn't run into them. I felt better and finished my lunch, then went with my friend to find a seat for the big gathering, where I shared with her what I had heard.

In the middle of the gathering, I excused myself to use the restroom. I skirted around people and went out of the main building to find the public restrooms. When I arrived at the facilities, I saw the sick girl's mother washing her hands. I ran into a stall and closed the door between us so I didn't have to see her. She was gone when I came out. "It must have been a coincidence," I thought, brushing it aside. I made my way back into the main building to find my seat. As I sat, I caught a glimpse of the couple sitting only a few rows away from us. "No, that couldn't be," I was thinking, "that is too strange." On our way out the doors to find our small groups on the campus I ran smack dab into the father, almost knocking myself down. "No way!" I thought. I continued to see them. They were assigned to my small group. Each time we met, I chickened out.

By the end of the day, my nerves were shot. Sonya suggested we skip out on the last big gathering and go to an early dinner, since it was my birthday. I jumped at the chance. I wanted to have some fun while we were there.

After returning to our hotel, Sonya pulled out of her suitcase what had once been a nicely wrapped package. The TSA had torn it open for inspection at the airport. She apologized for its condition. I could see she had tried to fix it. She gave me her gift. Delighted, I opened it up to find two books. The one that caught my attention was about Reiki. I had heard the name before but had no idea what it was. I examined the book and gave her a big hug, knowing that I had just received something really special.

The next day we went to meet with my little sister Angelique, and she made a big deal out of my birthday. It was so nice to be with my sister and my dear friend on my birthday. My sister took us out for dinner at a sushi restaurant, where we got to meet her boyfriend. He later became her loving husband and best friend.

The next morning, I found myself in the kitchen alone with my sister, having coffee, while my friend was busy in the other room packing. I told my sister about the couple and how I had chickened out. I had it in my head she was going to give me some sympathy for having to deal with such an experience, but surprisingly, she reacted very strongly in the other direction. She made it very clear that this gift was something I had run from most of my life and that it was time to step up and not be afraid any more to share with others. If I was getting messages, there was a reason. I knew that repeatedly running into the couple meant that I had something they needed to know. I had not been true to Spirit, to the couple, or to myself.

My friend came back into the kitchen. Catching the tail-end of the conversation, she agreed with my sister that it was time for me to learn to be accepting of myself and to become more serious about the gift that was calling for me. After our discussion, we got our suitcases packed and loaded into the rental car, said our goodbyes, and hurried off to catch our plane back to DFW. I still had a lot of thinking to do about what was happening in my life and the changes it would bring into my future.

I knew one thing for sure: My little sister doesn't speak out unless she really means it. With all that I had learned, why was I still trying to sabotage myself? Did I need faith, or did I just need to trust in myself and Spirit? I didn't have any answers.

Reiki

My husband was delighted to have me home, and I quickly shared with him all that I had learned. After catching up with the kids, I went back to our room to unpack. I found my two new books. I knew that I needed to read the Reiki book and see what it was all about. From what I understood, Reiki was an energy that channeled through the hands and came from Source to promote healing in the body. Because of my religious background, I was still a little nervous about the metaphysical nature of the book and continued to approach it with caution. I found it to be an easy read, and was done within a few days. I still was not sure how I felt about it, so I searched for more books about Reiki at the bookstore and found another to read.

By the time I finished the second book, I was convinced that I also needed to find a teacher but where would I start to look for one? I began with an Internet search and found some teachers in California and other states, but no one anywhere close. Steve was concerned about our budget, so I needed to find someone affordable in the area. I gave up the search, thinking that it was a lost cause and soon forgot about it.

Just a few days after giving up the search, I received a Continuing Education magazine in the mail from the University of Texas at Arlington. Advertised in the magazine was a class on Reiki, taught by a Reiki Master Teacher. The class was well within our budget! I signed up immediately to take the class. I was starting to think that maybe there was something to that old saying, "There is no such thing as coincidence."

I found myself excited and eager to go to the class. Even with all my reading on the subject, I was still not sure what to expect, or if I needed to prepare myself for the class. I just showed up with a pen and a pad of paper, in case I needed to take notes. When I sat down with the other students waiting for our teacher, my mind started to play thoughts coated in fear. I was not sure if Reiki required more expertise in other skills than what I possessed. I could feel the anxiety creeping its way through my body.

That all went away when our teacher came into the room pulling a small suitcase behind her. Our teacher Holli Blackwell was not at all what I would have imagined to be a Reiki Energy Master. She immediately put us all at ease with her bubbly personality, which spilled over into the room as she unloaded her suitcase. I watched out of curiosity as she pulled out a candle, matches, and other odds and ends. She formally greeted the class and took the roll. I sat there trying to get my bearings, all the while checking out the reaction of the other students. Everyone seemed to be in the same place I was, wondering what to expect from this interesting teacher. I decided not to bolt for the door. Like a cat waiting for the toy mouse to move, I wanted to see what would happen next.

Our teacher asked us to share our personal interests in Reiki. I told about my experience with Jean the healer in Taos. As we went around the room and shared our thoughts, dreams, and fears, I came to understand that I had a lot in common with the other students. As it turned out the first class was really just an introduction and we were instructed to get a textbook [2] at the University store. We soon discovered it was an excellent guide which helped to inspire lots of in depth class discussions.

In that class I met three friends Amy, Caroline, and Linda who shared similar experiences as I did growing up. I was fascinated and excited to find people in my own backyard who wanted to share with me as much as I wanted to share with them. There was no judgment, only a huge relief that we had found each other. This friendship continued even after the Reiki classes and they became some of my dearest friends. We began the learning adventure together and continued to grow and support each other on our journeys.

On the third day of the Reiki class our teacher had us line up our chairs back-to-back. Holli announced that she was going to perform our first Reiki attunement. Happy to be on the same journey with my newfound friends, I lined up my chair with the class and sat down. Our teacher instructed us to close our eyes, and turned off the lights. I could hear soft music playing from somewhere in the room as I wondered what to expect next. Holli told us to keep our eyes shut until she told us to open them.

My mind wandered in many different directions. My thoughts separated off to some events that had happened at our staff meeting earlier that day. Anger took over me as I remembered the heated conversations in the meeting. Just then, I felt the teacher place her hands on my head. It took just a moment for the anger to funnel through my body like a whirlwind and out the soles of my feet. The anger was gone. Startled, I searched for it, but I only felt heat rising up in my heart dissolving all my anxiety at losing that emotion. A sense of peace and calm flooded my body, and I relaxed.

Still closing my eyes, I noticed that I could see my thoughts in high definition. Everything was extremely sharp and clear. I had always seen my thoughts and dreams in color, but had no idea I had been looking at them through a haze. Images were very defined to the smallest detail. Psychedelic colors burst into my mind, causing me to choke up with tears. It was all so beautiful. I felt as though I was wearing glasses for the first time and could finally see, only it was all happening inside of me.

"Strange..." I thought, wondering why this had happened. Holli lightly touched my hands and my feet. A mass of energy shot up and down my entire body within seconds. It seemed to clear out the muck that had been stuck inside of me. Before I could entirely comprehend what had just happened, I suddenly became very aware of the direction of the blood flow pumping through my veins. My cells tingled, and I felt my whole body sighing, as if taking a breath of fresh air, even within my cells.

"How could this be?" I thought to myself. My body had been struggling to breathe all this while until now. "What is going on?" I could feel oxygen move through me and I realized that I had been cleansed of toxins that had somehow polluted my body on many levels: Mental, cellular, emotional, chakra, spiritual, etc.

Our teacher told us we could open our eyes. When I tried to find my friends, hoping to make eye contact and validate what just happened, most of the class still had their eyes closed, taking their time coming out of the attunement.

Finally, Amy opened her eyes and looked at me with a huge smile on her face. I not only saw her joy: I could feel it. The emotion hit me like a wave that vibrated through me, settling deep down into my bones. She beamed love back at me. A strong sensation of peace surged through the whole room.

After class my friends and I compared notes only to discover that we all had different but similar experiences. I felt drunk. Waves of energy surged through my body. I could feel everything around me.

I started home around nine o'clock in the evening. I was having trouble. Colors were bursting off of the lit-up storefront signs, blinding me as I drove past them. Traffic lights danced with colors and made geometric designs that reflected on the roads and in the air around them. I was almost too distracted to drive, but I eventually arrived safely home and fell into bed, exhausted. I slept like there was no tomorrow.

I awoke with the feeling that something special had happened the night before. I continued to feel a sense of peace as I went about the rest of my week.

I enjoyed that class so much that I continued to take all the class levels with our teacher. I went on to receive my Master Teacher's certifications in both Usui and Karuna® Reiki. Today Reiki remains a vital part of my life.

The Sixth Sense

Now I want to go back several years, before I began working at the church and had the crisis. It was the summer of 1999. I was home washing dishes when I received an excited phone call from my little sister. She had just seen the movie "The Sixth Sense" and needed to tell me all about it. She explained that it was like living with me when we were growing up. After hanging up, I wanted to see the movie also. I had not even heard of it before her call. We went with two good friends. I was amazed at how accurate it was. The movie described what I went through with my own fear more closely than any movie I had seen before. The way the ghosts tried to communicate was very similar to my experiences.

I couldn't stop talking about it as we left the theater. I had to buy the movie on DVD and watch it repeatedly. It made me feel like someone out there really understood what it was like growing up like that. For the first time in my life, I started to tell a very few close friends about my experiences. A few of my friends believed me and were fascinated by it. Some thought it was funny and made fun of me in public social gatherings. A few were afraid of it and were sure I was doing something wrong.

I have learned over years of experience that a lot of my encounters as a child were not negative. My fear caused me to perceive those experiences as scary. Many of them came across as very needy, clingy, or angry. Even the angels, who always came across very loving and gentle, made me afraid because I didn't understand why they were coming. Later on, when I learned how to communicate with the angels and guides, I learned discernment.

I understand now why I was frightened all the time. I learned that my fear created an energy field that attracted the lower energy ghosts who fed on or were addicted to those lower emotions. It was kind of a catch-22 where my fear, like that of the little boy, attracted that which terrified me.

Amnesia?

In one of my earliest childhood memories, I kept thinking I had amnesia. I knew I had come from somewhere else, before being born on this earth. I used to wrack my brain trying to remember where I had come from and why I couldn't remember. Later, in my teen years, I would have flashes of memories of somewhere else, where there was all this white light. When I saw a small glimpse, I would catch myself trying to hold on to the memory, but I always lost it when I focused on it. The only thing that would stay with me was a feeling of calm, that I had remembered something and that it was real.

Another memory that I have always had is choosing which gender I wanted to be in this lifetime. This memory stands out for some reason. I don't know why I remember thinking about the perks of each gender and finally choosing to be a girl. Girls got to wear different kinds of clothing and have their hair and makeup done. These things seemed to be more important than being a boy. I also knew if I were to choose the female gender, I would meet my husband, and we would start a family.

Somewhere around the age of three, I was afraid of the dark. To comfort me, my mom used to tell me that God was everywhere. But instead of calming my fears, she only increased my anxiety. At the time, I had no concept of God and was already being visited in my crib by ghosts. I have vivid memories of spending countless hours terrified under my covers, waiting for the morning to come.

One day, I caught my father's attention when he saw me hiding under my blanket. (He used to tell the story to anyone who would listen, smiling with amusement) He observed me for a little while before finally asking what I was doing. I peeked out from under the blanket with wide eyes and told him. "God is everywhere!" Laughing, he explained what my mother meant by everywhere.

As a small child, when someone would mention God, I tried to picture in my mind an image of what God looked like. My parents told me that he was both male and female, so in my young mind I tried to imagine what both genders at once would look like. It was so much easier to think of God as a man walking in the heavens.

As an adult looking back now, I can see that as a child I was trying to fit my parents' image of God into human form. Now, having had the experience of projecting out of my physical body and merging with All, I see that God does not fit so neatly in a box.

My Dad and His Strange Ways

My father Kelly used to give talks and lectures about spirituality that he learned through his teachers and his own travels. When I was growing up he spent a great deal of time and effort in trying to verse me in some of them. Most of the time I understood and would follow his direction, but a lot of the time I was not sure if he was just making up something to keep me occupied or entertained.

Once, when I was eight years old, I was gathering rocks to place around the fire in the tepee we were living in for the summer. It was a warm day, and I was getting tired of lugging big rocks around. I started dropping them on the ground just to hear the thud they made when they hit the earth. Observing my actions, my father stopped whatever he was doing and came over to me. He said that I shouldn't drop the big rocks on the ground. He explained that I needed to respect them, as they were rock people, and had their own consciousness.

"What?" I exclaimed. I could not comprehend the idea of rocks as live beings! They were inanimate objects subject to my will. I thought that he must have rocks in his head.

I noticed him studying the expression on my face. He smiled as he appeared to read my thoughts. After a moment, he picked up a rock and cradled it in his hands. He explained that the rock beings, along with everything else in the universe, were conscious, but not in the way human beings or animals were conscious. He waited for me to mull this over in my head. It was not my fault, he continued, that I was not aware of this, because I was asleep. In fact most people were asleep and unaware of this state of being.

I knew very well that I was wide awake. Somewhere in that statement I felt insulted. He was nuts. I immediately went into a rant that he didn't understand the meaning of being awake. The tirade only lasted for a few minutes before I realized that he was not arguing back. He had squatted down listening to me go on with a big grin on his face, waiting for me to finish.

I stopped ranting to see why he thought the whole thing was so funny. I was very serious about my argument and knew perfectly well that he was really wrong. I wanted him to stop teasing me like it was all a big joke. I stood there with my feet firmly planted in the ground, ready for him to argue. He then asked me if I was finished.

I wanted to tell him "No," because he was wrong. But I told him "Yes," only to see why he thought I was asleep. Then he asked if I wanted to hear the rest of what he had to share. I could feel my pride stuck somewhere in my throat. I was hurt, but I was curious to know why he thought I was asleep and why he thought the rocks were conscious.

He started by saying that to be awake in this world is about knowing and respecting all things living and non-living, including the rock people. He went on to explain that everything in the universe is alive because the truth is that all that exists around and within us is created out of one conscious mind. We exist within a dream of our Creator, whose one thought connects all things. Since we are part of this one dream from this one consciousness, all things are conscious. I later came to understand the dream to be the mind of God.

At the age of eight, my mind couldn't handle this. I just stood there rolling my eyes, thinking that once again my father had gone off the deep end. I had nothing to say. I waited impatiently to be allowed to finish my task of building the rock circle in peace so I could go off and play with the ranch animals. But my father didn't let me off that easy. He still had more to say. He let me know that he knew that I was not ready to hear the words he had shared. He told me that someday I would understand and remember what he was trying to teach me.

He said that the purpose for me gathering the rocks was to place them in the middle of the tepee to guard the fire. He gave me the ridiculous task of asking the rocks permission to use them in our tepee to guard the fire. "Why would I have to now take the extra time to talk to a rock when I could just gather them up and finish the job a lot quicker?"

My dad watched my expression as I was thinking, and he said, "Just see what happens if you try." I took the first rock and held it in my hand. I asked it in a silly voice if it wanted to guard the fire. It said nothing to me, so I put it down and picked up the next one. This went on until I had made the rounds with all the rocks that I had gathered.

I reported to my dad in triumph that none of them had anything to say. He just shook his head slowly and said, "They speak to you and you cannot hear the answers. You are still sleepwalking and you don't even know it." He told me to go on, dismissing me. He would finish the job later because he knew that my heart was not in it. I watched him as he slowly got up, dusting his pants off, and walked away, mumbling to himself. I was still not sure if I had won the argument or lost it. I didn't know what he meant by saying that I was asleep. All I knew was I was eager to go in the opposite direction, towards the barn, to find a mama cat who had given birth to some kittens a few weeks ago.

Sometimes I went with my dad when he gave lectures about the "Warrior's Way." Besides his recognition as an artist, he was also known for his teachings and talks about following a spiritual path.

Most of my childhood memories are of my dad talking to me. He told stories about learning how to focus on personal power and the mastering of the self. He used to meditate. Meditating seemed to be something he always brought up to see if I had mastered it. He would ask when we got together, even when I was older, if I was taking time to practice meditating.

The one thing I enjoyed the most about my youth was working with the animals on our ranch, both domestic and wild. My dad taught me how to communicate by being aware and moving my energy levels to certain points, so as to not cause the animal fear or distress. To me this was pure magic. He would instruct me, and I would see the animal respond to the energy almost immediately. I learned how to change my body language and the tone of my voice when I worked with the animals so that they trusted me.

My father also taught me how to use my thoughts to send out suggestions to an animal, using the energy from my emotions to push them out into the animal's energy field. This energy would then be reciprocated by the animal, which helped me to understand its energy pattern and allowed me to bond with them. We spent time watching their reactions closely so that we could change the way our signals were being sent out. By doing this, we no longer seemed to be a threat. Horses, dogs, and cats were my favorites, although we would also go out and use the techniques with the animals in the wild.

Once when I was about seven, we were at the ranch in Presidio, Texas. My father took me to an old barrel that looked a lot like the one we burned our trash in. As we walked toward it, he hit the side of it, and it echoed with a noise that sounded like a rattle. He asked if I would look inside, and when I did, I saw a rattlesnake. I jerked back, feeling afraid. He watched my reaction, and then he said, "It is your choice if the animal in the barrel is to live or die." He explained that the snake was living on our ranch, and it felt like this was his home. The dilemma was that we felt the same and that one day we may meet again, only the next meeting could be tragic for one of us. The snake had a place in this world to live and to do what snakes do. Should we let the snake live, or kill it? Either way, he wanted me to make the decision.

I knew in my heart that even though I was terrified of the rattlesnake, I didn't want my father to kill it. I told him with some hesitation that I wanted it to live. He looked in my eyes and smiled. "Okay," he said, "Tell you what: we can relocate the snake to another part of our ranch. That way we all can live in peace."

He used a long hoe to put the rattlesnake in a large cardboard box. I could hear the snake and felt its fear mixing with my own. We got into Dad's pickup and drove away from the house and barn. When we stopped, he unloaded the box from the truck and placed it on the ground. He squatted right in front of the box. I stood on the other side a few yards away.

When the box was opened, the snake was coiled to strike. It was angry and afraid. Then my father did a strange thing. He started to talk to the snake, telling it that it would be okay and that no one would harm it. He let it know that we understood it had a purpose and that we honored its part in this world. The snake seemed to understand what he was saying and stopped rattling. Then, to my surprise, it unwound itself and came out of the box, moving in front of my father without fear. It went on into the brush and into the desert. I didn't know what to say. I watched my dad pick up the box and place it in the truck. We got in the truck and drove to the house where my mother was waiting for us to have lunch.

I spent a great deal of time riding horseback on trails with my dad, tracking animals by examining their prints. I learned that when we got close enough to an animal I could open up my heart and energy fields to locate them. That served me well when I went searching for kittens that had been hidden away by their mother.

He told stories about the rock people, cloud people, trees, snakes, spiders, and all of the elements. We spent time watching bugs, and learning about their social patterns and how they fit in with nature. He told wonderful stories from other cultures about creation and how the universe worked. Some nights when it was cool enough, we took our sleeping bags and slept in the back of his old pickup on an old dirt road. He would tell me about the stars and their patterns in the night sky. Often there were stories about the stars that came from the Greeks, Romans, Native Americans, Aztec, and other cultures that he knew about.

My father was very interested in spiritual and healing energy. He used to show me how to lay my hands on animals and people to move energy to help speed up healing. I thought all this was to amuse me and keep me out of trouble. I have memories of falling asleep with the lights on during his lectures and him waking me up when it was time to go. It took me years to discover what a blessing I had to learn about working with energy and communicating with animals and nature around me. It is now a part of me and my healing work.

My father liked to tell stories about medicine men and how they traveled in spirit form. One day, when I was eight years old, I closed my eyes for a moment while I was reading on my bedroll in the tepee. I found myself astral projecting. I was not asleep but I was not in my body. I could see my body lying on my bedroll as I floated somewhere close to the door. Curious, I went around the circumference of the tepee looking at all the personal things that were hung up on the sides: animal skins, peace pipe, silver concho belt, blankets, beaded vest and leather coats. I discovered that I could navigate myself around the tepee with just my thoughts so I changed direction and drifted towards the fire in the center and looked at the circle of fireplace rocks close up.

I heard the door rustling. A lady came in, and was talking to my father. She seemed to be interested in looking around, and they were discussing the traditions of the tepee. My dad came in halfway behind her before he noticed I was on my bedroll. He dropped his voice, thinking I was asleep.

I heard him let the lady know that she could come back and see the tepee when I got up from my nap, and they started to turn around to leave. I floated over to her before she could leave and waved my hands in her face to let her know that it was okay for her to look around, but she didn't seem to notice me. I stuck my face next to hers and still she did not see me as she walked out the tepee opening.

I could hear my dad and the lady talking about going to lunch, He was deciding if he should wake me up. I saw my father come back into the tepee and walk over to where I was sleeping. When he called my name, trying to wake me up, I felt a pull drawing me back towards my physical form. The next thing I knew, I was opening my eyes and was fully inside of my body, looking at my dad as he was asking me if I wanted to go for lunch. Later, when I had time to talk to my dad, I told him what I did. He chuckled to himself and commented that I should explore astral projecting more often.

My father taught me the tradition of the tepee: When a person enters a tepee, he or she follows the path around the inside perimeter, completing the circle once around. My life has always followed this pattern, too. Tradition holds that one follows the path of completing the circle once around the inside of the tepee. I may walk the path many times, but each time I always come back to where I began, only a little wiser. The crisis in Taos brought me back to these memories of my father, which I had long since buried. "Welcome to learning to remember that which you have forgotten," the medicine man said, "It will be a life-long journey as it is with everyone. Only now, you are awake."

Some might call my father different. He followed the path of the Warrior's Way almost his entire life. My journey took me on a different road as got older, and we rarely saw each other. When we did get together, we always picked up where we left off, as though no time had been lost in between.

Now, as an adult, I am finding that all of what I learned in my life can be applied to healing and teaching. Instead of following the Warrior's Way like my father, I resonated more with the shamanic path of the Adventurer whose focus is on unconditional love.

As a teenager, I decided that it would be best for me to forget all of my father's teachings so that I could move on to a different path. My biggest fear was that if I didn't forget, I would not fit into the world that I wanted so desperately to be part of. I didn't know how detrimental that decision would be on my physical and spiritual well-being. I discovered later that I can't hide from who I am. Like a lot of teens I thought I had everything under control.

The Third Eye

After I took the mediumship seminar at The Crossing with my mentor Stella, I practiced seeing auras. That is when my third eye really became developed. I started to see without it just being spontaneous. At the time, I had no concept of how quickly it would evolve. Within a few weeks, my experiences grew as my eyes began to adjust to the energy that moved through and around rooms.

One day I was practicing, and my thirteen-year-old son Mason came in the room and asked me what I was doing. I told him I was learning how to see auras. He looked at me funny, then said, "Oh, you mean all those colored lights that are around people." I asked him if he saw the colors. He replied, "Yes, I see them all the time, but it's just my eyes playing tricks on me." This made me laugh.

It was a perfect example of what my teachers had always said: We all can see but have forgotten or thought it was only our imagination.

I started to see energy in various colors and shapes. Eventually I discovered that I could see multiple colors in a person's auras. I had to learn what it all meant. What good is having a gift if you don't understand how it relates to everything? I had learned in the seminar that the colors of the chakra relate to our moods, so I decided to start there. I attended chakra workshops in Dallas and I bought books about the colors of chakras and aura fields. I wanted to know it all. I discovered how it all connected and was amazed at what I learned about human beings and energy. I embraced the whole experience of seeing and understanding how it all fits together and began a journey that would permanently shift my view of the world. I had a lot of ground to cover.

Emotional Energy

Now, just for fun, I would like to mention a little about vibrations, and how they effect us, and what we are sending out which includes emotional energy. You may ask, "What is emotional energy?" "Why it is the energy that you feel in your body that is attached to an emotion!" I like to use love as the example of feeling like you are on "cloud nine." When you are in a well balanced love you feel good all over. If you are out of balance you may feel obsessive or out of control. Emotions affect our bodies and our brains.

All emotions have energy that make our bodies chemically react to someone or something. When it happens, you can feel this energy move through your body. If you are aware at the time, you can even pick up on what part of the brain is being triggered when it happens to you. Emotional energy can also affect the way people perceive us as it sends out a frequency that can impact their personal radar. On a more personal level when we feel an emotion it sends out a vibrational signal to the body causing us to blush, feel nervous, tense up, feel afraid, etc... This energy can be so powerful because it motivates us to move and change things either in a small or large way.

Emotions cause invisible energy waves that move through the body, sending out signals which affect our physical body. When this happens we send out vibrations that can affect the situations we are in. If these signals are negative you may feel uncomfortable or upset if you are on the receiving end of them. A very strong emotion can sway or cause damage to a situation or person. An example of this is walking into a room where a fight has just taken place. You may feel uncomfortable in that room or around the people who had the fight. If you are sensitive you may even pick sides. On the other hand, emotions such as unconditional love can cause the receiver to feel really good. If someone is projecting unconditional love, people will be attracted to them and want to be around that person. Either way these emotions are sending out signals.

When I was a little girl and living on a ranch, my father taught me how important these energy waves of emotions can be. They affect both people and animals nearby. I learned that if I carried fear in my heart it would start to permeate through my skin and would be immediately sensed by the animal, causing a reaction. If there was trust and love in my heart the animal sensed that and would react to the emotional vibrational waves that I was sending out. I soon learned that I could control my emotional vibration by being aware of myself and the signals that I was sending out.

Through working with the ranch animals on a day-to-day basis, I learned that what I carry in my heart is also picked up by the hearts of other living creatures. I found this to be true later on working with others as I grew up. As multi-dimensional beings people and animals pick up the invisible waves of energy though their bodies and try to process them so they can react. This is also where if you are aware of the energy coming in you can ask, if it is yours or someone else's? A lot of the time we carry someone else's emotions or fears. Then there are those times when we also project our own emotions and fears onto others. The point here is to be aware of what really belongs to you.

The Breath of God

The word 'spirit' in Latin means breath. I love that. For me it really describes what happens when I am touched by the presence of the Holy Spirit.

When I was sixteen, I was working at our family patio store one day with my grandmother Mary, who was in an unhappy mood at the time. Her frustration that day seemed to be directed towards me. No matter what I did, I only seemed to aggravate her more. I was tired of trying to please her. I was mad at her and was on the verge of stomping off, ready to call it quits, when out of nowhere I felt a warm sensation spread over the top of my head and move across my brain from the inside. In that instant, I felt a strong feeling of knowing assert itself inside my mind, followed by unconditional love permeating my whole being. A tingling sensation swept out of my body and over my skin expanding through the air around me.

The whole experience was like a soft breeze blowing through me. The anger immediately evaporated. I could see into her heart and feel the pain that she carried that day. I remembered we were upset with each other, but when I searched, I couldn't find the anger that had been there. The anger that I felt was truly gone, and I only felt compassion and understanding for my grandmother, which saturated my inner being. I knew that something unusual was happening to me, but I didn't know really why.

Out of the blue, she stopped and took a few seconds to study me. I knew that she knew that something had changed within me. I saw her shake her head like a chill went through her, and then she smiled and pulled her anger away from me. She stopped scolding and started to change her tone and the way she was talking to me. It was like she understood that I was not going to be an obstacle and was there to support her. I told her that I loved her, and she said she loved me too. We both went about the rest of our day feeling that something was very special between us.

I never lost that feeling for her the rest of my life. What happened that day was recorded in my cells. As long as she lived, whenever we were on the verge of disagreement, anger was never in the equation. People always knew we had a unique bond, but they never knew how special it really was. We always understood each other. Even in the separation of death, we are still connected.

Looking back on this experience, I understand now that we not only have a connection on the physical plane, but we are also connected to our higher selves on the spiritual plane. This is the part that never forgets what it is like to be connected and to know God. I call this connection, the "Breath of God" because it is like a breeze that is always moving in and around us. It is a part of us.

In that moment that I was angry with my grandmother, I was able to connect to my higher self, which understands that we are all created out of the one consciousness of unconditional love that only comes from God. When my higher self opened up, so did hers, and I was able to feel her experience. Since I was connected and open to my higher self, I only had unconditional love for her and her higher self, knowing that we are part of something much bigger than our experience on this earth. When there is nothing but love, there is no room for anything else.

I know that even with these experiences, we have things that we are here on this physical earth to participate in. In the trials and tribulations of emotions, in our relationships with ourselves and others, we learn. It is just part of our life experiences and education. Truth be known, the "Breath of God," is always present, even when we think we can't see or feel it.

The Knitting Story

"I don't get it," my friend Robin said as she pounded the table with her hand. "I don't believe that the table is alive!" Toward the end of our lunch, the conversation had turned to my knitting experience, a story that I shared with her a few months prior.

I was knitting by the fireplace in the living room of my house when a feeling of gratitude, love, and peace swept all through my being and shot me out of my body. In an instant, I found myself hovering just a few feet above the crown of my head. From there, I could see my body sitting, holding the knitting needles, as well as the whole room all around me. I quickly checked to see if I was okay and realized that my thoughts were not coming from my brain still down in my body. I was intact, fully conscious and thinking without my brain.

I felt the weight of all my worries and concerns discarded like dirty garments dropping to the floor. I was suddenly aware of each worry as it landed somewhere down near my physical body. I had not even been conscious of these concerns wearing me down, but I certainly could feel the release and freedom from them as they dropped away. I became highly attuned to everything around me moving like light particles, and I recognized that everything was created out of those particles. It was all saturated and created out of unconditional love that belonged to one conscious mind. With that, I understood without question that I was connected to everything and everything was connected to me. I was only a tiny part of this consciousness, which was a whole.

I cast my attention down to the table and all the things on it that I thought were just things. An understanding swept through me that it too was conscious and alive. It all came from the one true source, which was God. Nothing was separate, and everything was one. We were all a part of the mind of God. Then suddenly, I was aware that it is a lie and an illusion that we are separated from the Creator.

I wondered: If everything is created out of one consciousness which is alive, filled with unconditional love, why do we think we are separate? My father Kelly was right. I understood in that instant that even the things that we think are just inanimate objects are created out of the same fundamental building blocks when you break them down to the Source, God, which is alive and well. The full knowing hit me then. I was and I am always in the mind of God, our Creator, or what some have also called the Universal mind. I am a thought from our Creator, just like everything else that exists.

I recognized that I was a part of something much bigger than myself. I knew without a doubt that I could merge completely into the All, just by expanding my thoughts. As I explored the idea, my thoughts moved like water. They flooded the space around me, moving past the outside of the room toward the house next door. I could hear the thoughts of my neighbors next door simultaneously, and I could comprehend everything they were thinking, or even saying to each other out loud.

This was exciting. I decided to expand my thoughts over our entire neighborhood. I could hear the thoughts and conversations of everyone who was home that day. I could hear and process what they were saying at the same time. I heard and understood each conversation individually, without effort, as though I was listening to each one. It hit me. This is how God hears all of our prayers at once. Wow, I had always wondered how God did this.

I became curious and decided to try to expand my thoughts over all of Arlington, Texas. With this single thought, my awareness exploded like a hotline, and again I was able to process a few thousand thoughts and conversations simultaneously. I was excited about what I was doing. I realized it was really happening.

"Wait," I thought, "this is not normal." Fear came flooding in, and instantly I felt myself crammed back into my body. Fear and doubt had caused my fall from grace.

Shaken by the experience, I spent years trying to understand the event and why I felt changed. I came to understand that God, our Creator, is so much more than what we could ever imagine. I know that there is not one single person, place, or thing in the universe that is ever separated from the one consciousness of God. I have heard the question, "Are we the drop of water or are we the ocean?" I always thought this was silly but now I can answer in full confidence that we are both.

Furthermore, while the table was not alive in the way that we think of things being alive in this world of physical matter, the energy and the source from which it was created is very much alive and full of the living consciousness of God the Creator. The true shift is having to think outside of the box and leaving behind the old thinking that the world is flat. My father used to quote the ancients to me: "We are all living inside the dream of the Creator." Now, I have a great understanding that God is something much greater than I ever imagined. God is omnipotent.

Chapter Three: Lost "Living in the Petrified Forest"

Being Sensitive

Being overly sensitive can often be described as too much information coming in all at once. Sometimes it feels like every pore and cell in the body is taking in information too quickly to comprehend all that is going on at that time. The skin starts to hurt and becomes very sensitive, even to the air. Other people's thoughts become rough as sandpaper, causing irritation all over. The eyes ache in response to light and sound. Then the body starts to shake from deep within its core.

Many people experience the feeling of lifting out of the body or losing the connection to the physical plane. When this happens, it is best to find a quiet space to sit or lie down and let it pass. Work on staying grounded in the body: Hold one's energy within the body, relax, and allow the body to adjust to the energy that is passing through it.

I have discovered that over-sensitivity happens when there is too much energy work being done at one time. The body is learning to process higher energy frequencies and trying to adjust to holding higher vibrations. As our bodies are an extensive system of connections and meridians, the excess energy makes it feel like all the circuits are being blown out. The process can be quite a shock to the physical body and the mind as it tries to pinpoint why flooding of energy is happening.

When we start to process higher vibrations on a higher spiritual level, the energy affects our physical bodies. This happens when we have old baggage that needs to be released or cleared out, so we can hold or move into those higher vibrations. That is why over-sensitivity feels like things are out of control as we let our emotional, physical, and spiritual bodies move into alignment with our higher selves.

I once had an experience with over-sensitivity where I was lucky to be with my Akashic teacher Jodi Lovoi in a small class. She was able to lead me out of the situation by talking me through it with her voice. Instead of words, all I could hear were the different frequencies in each word that came out of her mouth. The tones in Jodi's voice led me through a breathing exercise that helped me focus and brought me back into balance, so that my physical body could handle all the energy that was moving through me.

Even with her help, I took some time to feel comfortable back in my own body. It was a strange experience: My mind and consciousness split from the reality of what was happening to my body. All I could do was move through the experience as best as I could, trying to find the balance between the mind, physical form, and spirit as they tried to integrate a new alignment.

After that experience, my senses were extremely heightened. I began to experience both the physical and the astral worlds as though they were meshed together. My mind was still able to discern this world from the other, but I was able to see the other side a lot clearer, as though it were right here in this plane of existence.

I felt fine when I left the class and drove home. When I pulled into my driveway, I saw people walking around the neighborhood. Some people take walks at night, so I thought nothing about it.

As soon as I walked into the door, I bumped into someone. I was very tired and said, "Excuse me." When I stepped into the kitchen I noticed that there was a bunch of people standing and walking around. Alarms went off in my head and I wondered whether my husband was throwing a party in my absence. But then I realized this was not a party, but a gathering of people from the other side.

These ghosts were not like the transparent spirits I normally saw. They had full, solid bodies. Their clothes from another time gave them away. No smoke, no shadow figure, no light, no darkness, just people like me hanging out in the kitchen.

I walked to the bedroom and saw my husband Steve sound asleep. People were congregating in the room and standing next to our bed. I checked on my kids; they were asleep. Most of the activity was in the bedroom and the kitchen.

"Great," I said out loud. "Not up for this. I need to take a bath and go to bed." A few of the ghosts followed me into the bathroom, and I asked very politely for them to leave. I was at least glad they couldn't sneak in without my seeing them.

I took a quick bath watching the door to make sure I was alone. I did my nightly grooming ritual then headed off to bed.

As I walked into the bedroom, I could see lots of people standing around the bed. Exhausted, I moved past them, telling them good night, then climbed into bed and closed my eyes. There really was not much else I could do. I was just too tired to work with crossing them.

The next morning, I woke up and found that everyone had left, like nothing had happened. I looked all through the house and found no one. I told my husband the whole story about my experience in the class and what I had seen the night before. He listened intently as he drank his coffee, then he gave me a hug and got up to get ready for work. What could he say?

Two Weeks of Silence

During the first few weeks working at the church in my mid-thirties, I learned very quickly that I was picking up on other people's feelings. It got so bad that I asked God to spare me and help me stop feeling others. In a way this was just a jest, as I was still very much in denial that I could really feel what others were feeling. A few days later, I was sitting in my office at the church when I realized that I had not been picking up on what the staff and congregation around me were feeling. I somehow felt very strange, almost like I had gone numb. I felt dead inside: nothing, void. I couldn't even feel my own emotions.

The whole experience was very odd. I had to admit that I needed to feel again. Once again I cried out to God and asked to be back to normal. All I knew was if there is hell on earth, I had found it. Over a period of about two weeks, little by little I began to feel more like myself. I started to pick up on what others were feeling. I discovered that it isn't good to get caught up in other people's emotions and carry their life along with mine. Climbing a spiritual mountain is harder when carrying all that extra weight around.

Empath: Feeling Others

After the two weeks of silence, I really started to take more notice of how it felt when someone walked into a room and how I was affected when they were with me and when they left. I soon discovered a pattern. If they were mad, I was mad. If they were upset, I was upset. If they were excited, I was excited. Often I could not tell where their feelings started and where mine ended. It was one big huge ball of emotional confusion when I examined what was happening.

I soon learned that by being conscious of what was going on, I could identify when things got out of hand. I would then excuse myself, run to the bathroom (hoping no one was there), and do an assessment of my own emotions. I would ask myself first if I was okay. If I was, I would continue asking what I was feeling. Then I would think of the person who was in my office visiting and try to assess what they were feeling when they came in. I discovered that no matter what they were feeling when they walked in, by the time they walked out, they could be fine, but I would be under the table, taking on whatever emotions they came in with.

By doing the assessment, I learned that their mood swings had nothing to do with me. I was just picking up the feelings of the other person. One Sunday I walked by a lady on my way into church and had to run into my office as I burst into tears. Later, after the service, she was in the pastor's office crying. I had already done an assessment and confirmed the sadness was not mine, so when I saw her I was not surprised. Soon, I found myself staying on-guard, as I had no idea what gamut of emotions would walk through the door and lay me out flat.

In my own quest for healing, I found others who had the same experiences. They called it being "empathic." From there, I learned that empaths are good at feeling what others feel, and will often carry emotions that belong to others. In some cases, an empath can even go as far as picking up on another person's illness, thinking it is theirs. This can be a problem if someone doesn't know they are an empath.

Later on, my Reiki teacher Holli taught us that being an empath is a natural gift. You can use the empathic energy in a positive way when you work with people. We used it to check in on a client to see how they were doing during the Reiki session. After that, we had to cut off the empathic connection, so as not to be overwhelmed with clients' emotions or illnesses.

My training in Reiki taught me how to keep myself from picking up other people's energy, and how to protect myself, so that I can be more effective as a practitioner. I sometimes catch myself off my guard when I leave the house to do errands. When this happens, often I get hit with overwhelming emotions or feel something physical, and I have to discern if what I am experiencing is mine. If it is not mine, I use my prayers of protection to not be involved with what others are feeling while I am out.

Empathic energy is more of a blessing than a burden when you learn to work with it and understand it. I meet many people who are overwhelmed with situations because they don't know they are empathic. Truth be told, we are all empaths, but some of us are not aware of it. Some people have blocked it because they didn't like the way they felt. The empathic energy that we carry is a true gift when it doesn't take over our lives. We can live with it in balance.

Looking For The Messiah

Before I really understood the full meaning of the knitting experience I chose to work at the church. The main reason was that somewhere in my mid-thirties I had started a search for the Messiah. I had a lot of questions and wasn't sure where to begin.

When I decided to seek out answers at the church we had been attending a staff position opened up for the Fellowship Director. I thought about it and felt very strongly that there was no better way to find God and serve than to work at a church. Deep within myself, I was really looking for another experience to find that amazing feeling of being whole and a part of everything.

Soon after starting at the church I traded in the search for a personal connection with the Messiah for the idea that good works get you into heaven. Later I recognized the hollowness and turned anger on myself for selling myself and my family out. I did not follow my intuition to leave when I knew that I wasn't going to find my connection there.

I could still feel a pull within my own heart: Somewhere God was reaching out to my soul. I was having some spiritual experiences, but I couldn't hold on to energy patterns for long periods of time. Each time I had a connection, it would quickly fade. This only made me more frustrated, and I started to feel an emptiness inside of me. My dear friend Amy was appalled when she met me at a luncheon for an event outside of our church. Though we rarely saw each other, she could see that I was getting sick. She begged me to make a decision that wouldn't rip my soul in half. My stubbornness to make a difference and find God in a physical place such as the church only made me dig in my heels even more. I didn't understand that spiritual connection is not a religion but rather the mind, body, and soul as it merges into the Creator as a whole. The spiritual connection is not something that you find in a physical place, but only within the sacred heart of the whole. I was lost.

That saying by Samuel Taylor Coleridge, "Water, water everywhere but not a drop to drink,"[3] best describes the madness of the illusion of separation. This feeling of being separated from God creates a crisis within the soul. No matter how many people are all around, the feeling of isolation – being different and apart – can be huge. This same blind illusion cuts us off from feeling connected to ourselves and to our Creator. But in truth, we cannot be separated from something out of which we are created.

Loss Of Integrity

One thing you learn when you compromise yourself is that you lose faith in your own integrity. I discovered this as I continued to deny what I experienced on a spiritual level, because it didn't fit into others' expectations on the physical plane. This was a constant repeating theme in my life: finding validation from what others believe. The fear of being different was strong. I bring this up, because loss of the integrity is part of the process of learning that something is seriously not working in your life. The loss always seems to rip apart any belief system you want to hide in.

After I confided to my friend Amy about my loss, her reply was that she was so happy for me. I couldn't believe my ears! I was angry! She went on to point out that my awareness of my loss of integrity was a huge reminder that I was stuck. Simply put, somewhere I had strayed too far off my path. Her words hit my heart like a well-aimed arrow. I had to eventually acknowledge that I was afraid of finding my way back. Out of fear and sheer stubbornness, I had kept my head down, only to continue down a path that led me into more darkness.

Breaking this pattern is harder than it seems. Old beliefs are hard to let go, especially if you are conditioned to not want to see what has changed. We all believe in something, and many people can't really tell why. Those people often do things a certain way, and that is the way it is always done, period. End of story. Why question it, even when you are in pain?

I discovered that God and the universe doesn't really work that way. Healing is a process of constant motion, whether we understand it or not. When you decide on your own that you are going to go with the rest of the herd and do not recognize the highest good for your soul, there is a major conflict within. Our spirit is always connected to the Source. That is when you hear your whole being crying out, "Wrong way!"

Once again I found myself at the crossroads, dazed and confused.

A Broken Heart

Out of desperation and not knowing what to do with my struggle in working at the church, I decided that I needed to get away before the Thanksgiving holiday. I found on the Internet a class on teaching how to communicate with animals. It was all about animals who carry loyalty and unconditional love in their hearts when treated well. That was something I was so desperately craving. My husband agreed that I needed to get away, so I signed up for the class and drove to Austin for a four-day retreat.

The people whom I met at the class were all kind-hearted and happy to be there. We all shared our love for animals and had great conversations. One morning, one of my new friends asked if I would like to go on a trail hike before the class started. "Yes," I told her, and off we went after breakfast. On our way back, we walked by a building on the property for meditating.

The big stone gate was open, and out of curiosity, we found our way into a courtyard. Lush green ivy covered the walls as fountains played a symphony of music that seemed to echo through the air. As we wandered around, we ran into another lady coming out of the main building who was also attending our class. She looked at me and asked, "Why is your heart so broken?"

"Oh, you are wrong," I answered. "My heart isn't broken. What do you mean?"

"You have a large hole in your heart chakra and a feeling of emptiness inside," she blurted out.

I had not told a soul about the pain in my chest or the hollow feeling I had there. How could she know? My friend came to the rescue and changed the subject, seeing I was uncomfortable. The woman soon left us, and we continued to explore enjoying the morning. As we moved on, I felt like someone had knocked the wind out of me, so I kept quiet.

A few days later, I cried for three hours as I drove back to meet with my family. My heart was broken in two, and I had no idea why. Or so I thought.

Sight

During this time, my sight began to blossom. My clairvoyance was growing stronger, and I was starting to confide more and more with several of my friends at the church. I even shared with our pastor, who was surprisingly open to my new sight. I was still very cautious about whom I shared with, so as not to scare people. But it was freeing to be able to talk to others about what I saw.

One of my favorite things to do was to watch people in the congregation on Sunday mornings, because of all the beautiful colors surrounding them. Human beings are rainbows of light which is a beautiful sight to behold. Since there were so many people, I started to practice softening my gaze while I was listening to the Sunday sermon. At first I only saw a little bit of color, but after a few weeks of practicing, my clairvoyance just burst open one day, and I could see many layers of color around people. As my eyes made the adjustment, I began to catch glimpses of what looked like the light beings who came to see me once. I could also see shadows and swirls that looked like water vapor moving off of people. Then, I saw images of ghosts around the people, mixed in with the colors.

Behind the altar and around the room I could see extremely tall, gigantic beings that glowed with a brilliant golden light. Their light seemed to stand separate, and yet mixed in with the colors of people's auras. This made life so exciting! I couldn't help stopping whatever I was doing to watch. Three-dimensional symbols began to appear on top of people's heads. I had no idea what they meant or why they were there. Then someone would whisper or talk to me, and I would lose what I was seeing. This experience taught me that I could intentionally set my gaze to see by softening it. Later on, I discovered that my sight would open up spontaneously. This caused a slight dilemma. I needed to find the balance so that I could control the sight. I soon found it hard to be with someone because of the distractions that would open up in a room.

Even my own children started to tease me, calling me the "crazy lady." Sometimes when we were engaged in a full conversation, I would see a ghost, angel, or colors, and walk away to investigate. Sometimes I even started to talk about what I was seeing, losing track of our conversation all together. My 15 year old daughter made it very clear that I needed to get this under control. She said it was creepy. A few of my friends noticed that I was struggling to keep my new sight under control. Sometimes they asked me to share what I was seeing. In those times, I was always happy to give the details of the colors of light and energy beings filling up the room. I did eventually learn that I could turn it off.

Seeing is not all about light. I saw a dark side too. Sometimes I saw something that looked like black smoke hanging around people or moving through the air. One afternoon I was working on some paperwork for an event at the church, and happened to look up. I saw what looked like a large, dark form of smoke moving past my office doorway through the hall towards the other offices. Curious, I jumped up to get a better look, knowing somehow that I was not on its radar. I peeked at it outside my doorway and watched it float slowly down the hall. It stopped and lingered at the doorway at the end of the hall: the pastor's office. The smoke seemed to be waiting on someone or something. It didn't seem to notice me. I continued to watch, unable to take my eyes off of the image , and tried to decide how I would describe this to my husband when I got home. Suddenly it moved backwards toward me, but it stopped halfway between me and the door. That was enough to scare me. I went back quickly to my desk and pretended I was busy. After a while I got the nerve to look out the doorway again, but it was gone. There was no trace that it was ever there. I grabbed my things and went home in a hurry abandoning any work that needed to be done.

During the last year that I worked at the church, I saw this happen in that same hallway, three other times in broad daylight. The last time I didn't go to my doorway to look out. I just watched the dark smoke pass, knowing it was not about me. Lots of people go in and out of the pastor's office, so it could have been interested in anyone, but I decided I didn't want to know.

A Visit From The Divine

One morning in the spring of 2008, I found myself coming out of sleep into a dreamy, half-sleep and half-awake state. (Since then I have learned that this state has a name: "twilight.") As I lay there on my bed I scanned the room. My husband was still sound asleep.

I noticed two extremely tall figures emitting pure light standing on my side of the bed. I was startled at the sight of them so I closed my eyes in the hope that they would disappear. When I opened my eyes again they were still there, patiently waiting for me to acknowledge them. As I lay there watching, not sure what to expect, I finally asked them why they were there. One of them handed a picture frame to me and said, "Look at this." I took it in my hands and gazed.

At first the frame was empty. Then, as I watched more closely, I saw myself working in the church, running around, very busy. One of them pointed to the picture, and I heard, "See this?" I nodded in response, and then I heard, "This is not what it is about." Instantly, the frame went blank. I saw myself again in the frame. This time I was at   The University of Texas at Arlington, where I was taking a jewelry class. I was busy working on my newest project and seemed very happy. Again, I heard, "See this?" I nodded, then heard, "This is not what it is about."

"About what?" I thought. "What are they talking about?"

Then the picture went blank and started up once more, showing me by myself at home, cleaning and working around the house. The voice said, "See this?" I waited and finally nodded and heard a third time, "This is not what it is about."

They took the frame away from me. I heard a strong voice that didn't belong to the other two, coming from behind me, where our headboard is. The voice said, "Ana, come with me and let me show you what it is all about."

Okay, that was it! Fear gripped me, and I said, "No!"

There was a pause of silence, and then I heard in the same firm but loving voice, "Ana, let go of these things. This is not what it is all about. Come with me and I will show you what it is all about."

"No!" I said to them. "I will not go with you. I am perfectly happy where I am and with what I am doing! Let me be!"

The two beings by the bed chimed in together, "She is not ready."

I heard the voice from the form that I couldn't see say, "Get her ready."

I wondered, "Ready? Ready for what?" Then the two beings faded from my sight.

I turned over immediately, woke my husband Steve, and gave him a full account of what had just happened. I told him they wanted to get me ready, but for what? My mind raced. I thought, "Oh no, I am going to die. Oh, they want us to move far away. Are we all going to die? What is going on?" Steve spent a few hours calming me down. Finally I was able to move past my fears enough to get on with my day and my life.

Within a few months of the incident, my jewelry professor Fred and I seemed to have become a little distant in our friendship. In fact, the experience made me realize that it was time to move on. I decided not to sign up for another course in jewelry at the university.

I know that the Creator has a plan, and we are all a part of it. I know

now that fear and comfort can stop us from making a necessary change. Change is something most human beings do not like doing. But amazingly, when we are far off the path, the Divine will intervene and set us straight.

Chakras/Light Bodies

I won't bother you with details of all the operations I underwent to repair my body from the age of twenty until my mid-thirties. I had eight operations for various reasons. Looking back, and knowing what I know now, I see that fear had a lot to do with my physical ailments. Fear can be a major factor in blocking the emotional senses, but it also interferes with the natural energy flow in our physical form. Fear is stored in different parts of the body until it is dealt with. While it is held, fear can cause physical or emotional illnesses within those body parts. A good example is a heartache from having your heart broken which can put stress on the physical heart, causing heart problems if it is not released.

After my spiritual crisis and allowing myself to relearn about energy, I discovered that I was blocking not only many of my memories, but I was also causing myself to be sick. My discovery of chakras and how they influence the auras and light bodies turned out to be an enormous blessing in my life. They were the first few keys on my keychain. Chakras not only aided my physical healing, but also unlocked old doors within my subconscious.

As it turned out, Reiki also played a big part in allowing me to release my fear of working with energy. It gave me the courage to once more feel the energy working in my own body, and I soon discovered that my brain wanted to get involved in learning what was going on. I started to read all the books I could on chakras and how energy worked. I attended any workshops I could find in the area on chakras.

The information I learned helped me tremendously. Not only could I feel the energy, but I also could process in my mind how it was working in my own body. Slowly, old memories of the teachings that my father shared with me started to come back, and I began to apply some of the techniques to healing. I started with refocusing my attention inward towards the different areas of the body.

As the whole chakra system started to unfold itself before my eyes, I discovered just how important a part they play in our whole well-being. I learned there are hundreds of chakra points in the physical body – too many to discuss for now -- but I would like to mention the seven major chakras in the physical form. These chakras will be further discussed in Chapter Ten under "Clearing Chakras."

The first chakra is Root Chakra, located at the base of the spine near the tailbone. The chakra is the Sacral, which rests two inches below the navel. The third chakra is located in the Solar Plexus, in the ribcage area above the navel area. Then you move to the fourth, which is the Heart, located in the center of the chest over the sternum. The fifth chakra is called the Throat Chakra, located in the throat area. Then you have the Third Eye Chakra, located in the middle of the forehead, just above the eyebrows. Finally, the Crown Chakra is located at the very top of the head.

Different chakra points in the physical body help different energy fields that maintain the body and organs. When these energy points are healthy and balanced, they spin like a pinwheel in a clockwise motion. When something is wrong in the body, the energy points spin too fast, too slow, or get gummed up (stuck). Emotions can affect your chakras, causing an imbalance in the body. By knowing your chakras and how to maintain them, you can learn a lot about your body and the blocks which cause sickness.

The human body is a miracle. Not only do you have the chakras located inside the body, but you also have energy bodies stacked on the outside of your physical body, creating an energy field around you. These light bodies are also known as the aura of the person when seen. There are many of them, and I am only going to mention a few.

The energy body closest to your skin is named the Etheric body which is connected to the first chakra. It curves around the shape of your physical body. The rest of the energy bodies are egg-shaped and build on top of the Etheric. The Emotional body surrounds the Etheric body and is connected to the second chakra, followed by the Mental body linked to the third chakra. The Astral, Etheric Template, Celestial, and Causal bodies surround these, attached to the fourth, fifth, sixth and seventh chakras respectively. These light bodies each contribute to the health and maintenance of the physical body.

By working with these different energy fields, an energy practitioner may open up both the physical and the inner and outer body energy fields, thus releasing any harmful influence and allowing the body to bring itself back into balance and harmony. One thing to remember is that free will plays a huge part of this process. If it is not written in a soul contract (which will be discussed in Chapter Eleven), the practitioner can help the patient find balance within the body to bring in healing. If the patient is not willing or is blocking the healing, it can be a huge challenge for both the client and practitioner to work together as a team. It is a full team effort on the part of the client, practitioner, and the spiritual realm to bring the body back into harmony with the mind, body, and spirit.For example, a traumatic experience can cause illness and create a block that affects the emotional body by breaking down the light bodies. Think of it like a row of dominoes that fall in a line as they make their way through the body, jamming up the chakras. This, in turn, sends a warning signal to the brain that something is wrong and records the experience within the cells. The communication within the body tells the cells that life is not okay when triggered by an experience outside the body.

Emotional fears send out energy signals throughout the light bodies and chakras in waves. When this happens, a new program is then recorded with the message of "fight or flight" in the physical body. The new program then creates confusion in the cells, causing a war within the body, throwing it all out of balance when triggered by certain experiences. People often wonder why they don't get better sooner. We are not treating the whole person on the mental, physical, and spiritual level. We humans are complicated and multi-dimensional.

On the other hand, our bodies are created to heal themselves. Healing can be more successful when a person maintains balance between the mind, body, and soul in connection with the Source. This knowing causes the brain to carry a signal, released through the emotions, sending an energy wave that has permission to rewrite the program to change the old message of illness within the body and cells. This new signal removes the blocks within the chakras and light bodies, creating balance. When this happens, the new signal gives the physical body, mind, and spirit permission to heal and open up to the natural course of energy and flow, for healing to occur on all levels.

Another thing to remember is that the language of the physical body is light. You are created out of light, and when you move into this light, you find that the light is created out of unconditional love. When we are out of balance, our cells and our brains are confused with the emotions that cut us off from our natural flow and from the light from our Source which is God. Our own fears create a sense of separation from God, others, and ourselves, making us vulnerable to illness.

In my case, the energy that was harmful to me was fear. I was not allowing myself to be as I was created to be. I had to learn that I was okay and that part of my reason for being here was to communicate openly with the other side. I had to come to a place in my life where I was at peace with myself and not afraid of being condemned. The war within myself tore me up physically, emotionally, and spiritually. It caused blocks on all levels, created sickness in my body and eventually led me to have eight operations before the age of thirty.

What others might think of me had to be of lesser importance than what God was doing in my life. I had to let myself step out of my fears into trust, knowing I was cared for. I had to know that being in the light leaves no room for the darkness to hide. This was my challenge and my journey in this life. I started down a new path to work with different teachers both from the physical realm and the spirit realm.

Spirits, and Ghosts Everywhere

One thing that always strikes me as funny is that people think that they have to go to a haunted spot or have a special ceremony to make contact with ghosts or spirits. That is just not true. The door between our world and theirs is right where we are. The dimensions are all layered on top of each other. This allows ghosts to have access to other worlds, and realities, all with a single thought. Our world is no exception.

Once, when I was attending a rehearsal dinner for a wedding party, my friend Sonia leaned over to ask if we could get together sometime and call in some ghosts. This made me look up, soften my gaze, and survey the room. I could see the angels and earthbound spirits that were gathered around different people at the party. Turning to my friend, I explained that earthbound spirits, which I call ghosts, and other kinds of spirits are all around us. Some of them are interested in us, and others have no clue, just wanting to do their own thing. The room was packed not only with us, the physical beings, but also many from the other side. As I looked once again, I could see some of them joining in our celebration, hanging out with different guests as people talked and told stories.

Another time when I was recovering from a great loss in my life, my dear friend invited me over to her home to keep me occupied while I was grieving. I convinced her that I was fine and needed to go home to try to get my life back into some semblance of order. I was alone that evening. My husband Steve was out of town for the week and the children were away at summer camp. Later that night I found myself crying in bed, letting go of all my emotions, when I had the feeling that I was being watched.

As I stopped to dry my tears, I began to look around the room, opening my awareness. I could see ghosts peeking at me from behind doors and from corners of the room. When I shifted my gaze up towards the ceiling, I could see some floating above, hanging out behind the top of the frame of our four-poster bed, watching me with great compassion and curiosity.

I saw six ghosts hanging out watching me. I could see and feel them all, each one sympathetic to my sorrow. Knowing that they did not intend to harm me and seeing that some seemed to want to comfort me, I closed my eyes and fell asleep. The spirits were compassionate about what I was experiencing and in their own way, they were there watching over me. My friend Jenny called to check on me early the next morning and woke me up. I told her what happened to me the night before. I told her how I was able to finally get some sleep and that I knew I was going to be alright. I felt very supported and not at all lonely in my grief, as the ghosts were there helping and comforting me.

A large majority of the population seems to feel that ghosts are a sensation or a curiosity. One of my biggest heartaches is seeing books and programs about ghosts in which people try to catch them on film by aggravating them so they will perform. Because of my own personal experiences with the other side, I have a great compassion and respect for these beings that are lost or are choosing not to cross over, for whatever reason.

In many cases, they do not find the portal or passageway that leads them to where they need to go, so they hang around in places that only confuse them and keep them away from where they need to be. Some of them get angry because they are stuck, or just go milling around causing problems for the living. My biggest hope for those who are able to communicate with the other side is that they use their gifts and talents to help those beings cross into the light, where they are loved and wanted.

It is important to assist those who are trapped or lost, who are in great need for someone to help them make contact, so that they can reconnect with their angels, guides, and loved ones who can move them on. This process not only helps the ghosts but the living as well. I have shed many tears as I have learned the stories of those who are lost and need to find their way home. I have the honor of working with a team of angels, guides, loved ones, and animal spirits to help lost souls as they cross into another dimension. Each experience is just as unique as each person living on this planet.

Hiding From Myself Again, "Slumming"

My in-laws were celebrating their 50th wedding anniversary, and for the big event they had rented a villa in Italy during the summer. They invited all of their children and their families to join them in the celebration for two weeks. It was a wonderful gift for all of us, and we were all excited to go. At this time I was reaching my third year working at the church and had been spending long hours there. The timing was great. I needed to get away to clear my head again.

It was a relief to go. However, in the back of my mind I was a little worried, since I was becoming more aware of how sensitive I was to people's energy and was seeing light beings and auras around them. Adding to my distress, all my memories from Italy at the time had to do with nightmares from my childhood that were starting to come back in vivid recollections. I wasn't sure if I could control the nightmares or how I would react. My husband and I had a talk about these fears, and we decided to work together as a team: If I became uncomfortable, he would help me get through it.

I discovered in those two weeks that Italy was a whole different experience for me as an adult with some training, instead of as a child with no clue what was happening to me.

The villa was beautiful and secluded, a distance from a little village, with its own staff. The best part was that we had it all to ourselves.

During this time I started to have encounters with ghosts. When we got there our parents told us to explore the villa and choose which room we wanted. As we walked through the corridors and visited the rooms we ran into white smokey mist and dark shadows hanging out through the hallways and inside the rooms. I even made an acquaintance with a monk from sometime in the 14th century who liked to follow me around. For some reason he would often make an appearances in my tub when I was bathing. He was not really interested in me; he just wanted to talk. Through my spiritual gifts, I could see and hear him very clearly. It didn't matter that he spoke Italian, as his words converted to a language I could understand telepathically. He seemed to know this, and it only encouraged his frequent visits in the bathroom, which made me extremely uncomfortable. Finally after shooing him away countless times and asking for a little privacy, I gave in and let him talk. Neither one of us was good with boundaries.

The nightmares began soon after we arrived. I saw monks being tied to posts then burned alive, screaming in agony. It was horrible and nothing like watching a movie. I was there with the monks, desperately trying to untie them and free them from the fire. The sting of the hot fire scorched my skin. The smoke mixed with tears blurred my vision, making the task much harder to do.

The dreams were so vivid that I would wake up trembling, trying to remember where I was. The smell of singed hair and smoke filled my lungs while my heart beat like it would burst from my chest. Feelings of defeat and powerlessness flooded my body, leaving me exhausted in my own sweat. The monk who visited me was among them in the fire. He was so young, in his late teens. My heart broke for what he had to endure with the others. No one should ever have to go through that.

Other ghosts moved through the villa, but they did not have much contact with me. They scattered when they noticed me watching them. I tried my best not to be too nosy.

Sometime in the middle of our stay, I got this feeling of dread. One morning while I was drinking my tea, a cold shiver shot up my back. I knew something was happening with the pastor at the church. I knew in my gut that he was upset with me, but what it was, I didn't know. Then, the feeling moved somewhere outside my body and stopped as if waiting for me to absorb it. Not really knowing what was going on, I waved it away, but the feeling kept hitting me. Finally I found a guest computer in the hallway. I looked frantically at my email to see if there was any news from the church. There was nothing. The only emails were from my family and friends back home, wishing us well.

A few days later, I was coming down the stairs by myself when I had a flash of my work environment at the church and heard very clearly, "Why are you slumming?" I knew the voice of the angel who is often around me.

"Slumming? What?" Did I hear that correctly? "What do you mean?" I asked.

Then I heard, "Why do you waste your time?"

That was all that was said, leaving me to mull it over, not knowing what it was referring to. I didn't know then, but my life was about to change in more ways than one within the next few weeks.

After recovering from jet lag from our trip to Italy, I came back to work at the church, knowing that something was not right. In fact, my life became a nightmare as I tried to integrate back into my work. Things were not working out, even as I tried to ignore it and continue with what I was doing at the church. The relationship I once had with my co-workers was broken. I had nothing in common with them anymore. I didn't have it in me to continue facing the conflict required to get the healing ministry off the ground. I was tired and ready to let go.

It has been a while since that trip to Italy. I know looking back that the angel was not talking about the congregation at the church whom I was connected to at the time. The message was about the fighting, control, and power struggles that I was participating in with my fellow co-workers. That energy was dense and far away from the unconditional love that connects us to God. To the angels and guides of the higher energy frequencies it is not logical that we should pick the road of pain to learn our lessons when we have the choice to move into the light. It is the higher path that leads us to forgiveness, unconditional love, and acceptance for ourselves and our fellow man. It was time for things to change.

The Therapist

Even with all the progress I had made, I still felt I was not able to speak my truth. There was a huge block. I knew that I needed to find that part of me that was still angry inside and let it go. I could go on and blame others, or I could look at myself and see what I needed to shift so that I could be free.

I had been traveling back and forth to Taos, visiting my mom. I was enjoying my time working on healing, with much encouragement from a support group in Taos. I was learning more about some of my relationships and my own expectations within them. I felt very accepted there. I was secure there. I was learning to express myself while being more accepting of myself and my own spiritual gifts.

When I returned home and back to work at the church, I felt out of place and was afraid to speak my truth. I knew this had to change. So, after one of my trips, I decided to follow up with a therapist to continue the work in Texas. For the first few weeks, my new therapist seemed very excited about what I had learned in Taos. Then, on my fourth visit, she said that I didn't need to work with her anymore, as I was fine in my understanding of my relationships. She even took down a few notes of the books and advice that I had received.

A year later I did finally leave my position at the church. I was crushed, so I quickly found another therapist in the area. She had been recommended and was known for working with people and their spiritual gifts. I thought this would help, since I had been speaking two different languages at once: One language from my life at the church and the other from my early childhood. Unfortunately it didn't help, as the hour was up once we finally got rolling, and the time between sessions was too long. We were not going as fast as I wanted. I stopped seeing her as I could see the progress taking years.

What did help to accelerate my healing and helped me blossom was that I poured myself into creating a healing circle. I found others who were in the same boat I was in. I hosted the circle gathering in my home with two of my Reiki friends Amy and Caroline. We invited others to come and join us in a circle where we could share, learn, cry, and talk about our spiritual gifts in a safe environment. We met once a month. The healing circle became the root of others' healing processes and mine. We soon became fast friends and knew we could call on each other whenever we needed someone to hear us.

Part II
Discovery & Learning

"I cannot go back to yesterday because I was a different person then."

Lewis Carroll, <u>Alice In Wonderland</u>

Chapter Four: A Light in the Darkness

Time To Change

There seems to be a time in our lives when we can feel the wind change directions. There is still that state of confusion of not being sure what it all means.

I want to revisit the Sunday before I left the church, as I was singing with the band during second service, I cried out in silent prayer for help and to be rescued. I knew deep down from the depths of my soul that it was time for me to leave the church, and yet I couldn't see my way out. The only thing I knew was that being on the staff was too much conflict.

Then the day came. I met a lady whom I knew from our first meeting that we had a soul contract for her to help me in case I were to get stuck in that life lesson. She was there to help me leave my position. I knew that I was so immersed in working to create the healing ministry that I didn't know how to leave. I was so afraid I would let people down.

Once again I had talked myself into staying on staff, but knew deep within my heart it was time to go. I had blocked out visits – even from the angels – and was ignoring their advice. I wanted to stay and help, even to my own detriment. Then the lady was hired to be one more source for conflict. It added the last few straws to the camel's back, which broke in half six months later.

I finally called out to the heavens in defeat and let go. My cry was not wasted on deaf ears. Help came swift and fast. My prayers were answered. I was able to leave the following Tuesday. I found the strength that day to walk into the pastor's office and resign. I learned later that the lady of my conflict, along with several others, left their positions at the church within a few months of me leaving, and a few years later the pastor left.

From this experience I learned that even the antagonists in our lives, who we think make our life miserable, are a part of the bigger plan. They have parts to play in our own spiritual growth. We need to see them as they truly are: they help us learn and move on when we need to go on to do other things. To this day I am grateful for her help.

Dark vs. Light "The Angels Wait"

All I could do was leave everything behind, because if I didn't, I wouldn't have the courage to leave. As I walked out the front doors in the middle of the day, I realized that I had nowhere to go. My life and my whole family's life was wrapped up in working, volunteering, and being at the church.

I made some desperate phone calls in the parking lot to a few friends. I wanted to let them know what happened, but I couldn't reach anyone. I drove over and sat in the parking lot across the street. My life was changing in a big way, but I had no idea where to go. I felt alone and lost.

The face of a dear friend who had just gone through something like this came to mind, and I called her. Jenny picked up on the first ring and said she was just thinking about me. Through many tears, I told her a little about what happened, and she asked me to come over and talk. As I made my way to her house, my heart started to break. I felt hollow inside, and my body went into some sort of shock. Jenny was waiting outside when I drove up. She greeted me with a smile and a look of concern on her face. By the time I reached her I had started to shake all over uncontrollably. I remembered the angels that had come to my bedside, letting me know that my life was about to change. I thought that maybe they were going to forget about me and let me be.

My friend Jenny ushered me over to a neighbor's house. The neighbor, who was intuitive, welcomed me in and started speaking. I could feel that some part of myself left my body and was somewhere hanging out by the ceiling. The neighbor reminded me that I was still healing and learning about my own spiritual gifts. She said that my own fear of being different in the church, where I couldn't allow my gifts to be utilized as they were meant to be, was causing me to be sick. She pointed out that if I wanted to help anyone else, I first had to start working on my own healing. She paused, then looked into my eyes. She let me know that I had still not made a real choice. I didn't think I knew what she was talking about until she said, "The angels are waiting on you to take the final step and make a conscious decision between the path of light or the path of darkness." Her words registered in my heart. Either way, the choice was mine. I could feel a numbness slowly working its way up my body, surrounding my inner core. Mentally, I quickly checked in on my emotions, but I couldn't find any. They were gone, and so was my connection to anything else. I had gone into shock again. I felt shattered and didn't quite know how to put myself back together again. My friend took me back to her house where she cared for me for the rest of the week.

I understand now, with a few years under my belt and looking back, what she meant. I was to choose either the path of light, where I was meant to follow what was recorded in my soul contract with my Creator, or take the path of darkness, where I would struggle in my own depths of confusion, trying to find that reconnection in my plight of healing.

I wish I could say that it only took me a few months to heal; however healing is an amazing progression of the soul, one that takes a lifetime of learning. I was battling my own struggle to accept who I was. I had chosen the path of light and dug in with everything that I had to change the mental and physical pattern of being torn in two. When I chose not to move into the darkness, I was assisted by my spirit guides and teachers who came into my life to help me hold on to the path. Thus began a journey into the heart of the sacred. For several years I fought, trying not to split in half, sinking and swimming, as I worked on forgiving myself and others and letting go of my fears.

My emotions during those years moved from deep, devout love, to intense anger with myself and my situation. My husband, children, family, and friends experienced first-hand the spiritual warfare that tore me up inside. They watched me everyday move through this struggle of light and darkness, which was hard on them too.

I can't tell the day that it all ended exactly, as it all blurs together. I remember taking a breath one day and realizing that there was no pain or feeling of separation between me and my spirit. I felt a strong peace and harmony with my connection to God. Then came a full recognition that I had made it through the storm to the other side. I knew that this was not the end of my learning, but a small victory. I began my journey as a new person back onto the path of the light.

Know When To Walk Away

When I work with people and they tell me their stories, I reassure them that they have choices. They don't have to stay in an unhealthy environment.

They have the power to leave if anything is affecting them in a negative manner. There are times when the soul has not the strength to feel safe or be a part of such energy. If we stay somewhere when we know it is time to go because we feel guilty or fearful of what we will face, that choice can lead us into a path of darkness and pain. By leaving, doors will open onto another plane and move on to higher ground. When we can move into a space of unconditional love and healing, we can shed our feelings of loss of power. We can move without being sucked into the lower energy of control and anger. The real choice is ours, and we have the power to choose which path we will take.

A Leap Of Faith, "The Meet-Up"

I was sitting alone at my desk at home, wondering what I was going to do with myself, a month after I had left my position at the church. I felt like someone who didn't have a country. I didn't know where to go. I had my Reiki friends and the healing circle, but I wanted to heal faster. I felt the need to be more connected to a larger community where I could feel safe to be myself, so I could let go of my old fears of not being a part of a congregation that attended church each Sunday.

I started a process to assess myself to see what called out to me. Surprisingly, I found that I wanted to go back to what I knew deep in my heart: spirit journeying, which is traveling through the upper, middle and lower realms of the spirit world with the astral body. I went searching for a teacher. I looked on the Internet and found a meet-up for Shamanism and spirit journeying in Mansfield, near my house. Someone would be speaking and doing a journey with the Native American drum.

I called Amy, one of my Reiki friends, and asked if she would like to go, but she was busy. I thought about it and decided I was doing this for myself, so I signed up anyway. I needed to connect with myself and find out who I was. I must admit I had a tinge of fear of stepping out in faith, but all the while I knew this was the right thing to do. I was also aware that my mind still held the fear of making mistakes. As I sorted through this fear, my heart pulled and my spirit called to me. I knew that if I didn't go I would lose my chance to see if there was really something there.

The day came that I was able to go to the meet-up and join in on the journeying. Moving into the freedom of the spirit did wonders for me. I found the transition of slipping into that place of soaring in the spirit world, which renewed my confidence in my abilities to journey. On a conscious level, I thought how wonderful it was to touch the sky and walk among the heavens. I knew in that moment I had made the right choice to come to the meet-up.

On the drive home, my mind was occupied, wondering about the other people who were there that evening. I noticed that they seemed to be working on themselves and could speak in a language that was a part of my own heart. The whole experience made me feel like I had made a small step toward going back home.

My thoughts then traveled back to the beginning of the evening. I remembered a man named Daniel D'Neuville who met me at the door. The moment I set eyes on him, I had a premonition that I would be somehow working with him in the future. I didn't want to make that connection right then, as I just wanted to see how the evening would go. I learned later on that he was a fire walker. He did come into my life later as a teacher, friend, and co-worker.

Others Like Me?

I believe that one of the hardest things that many people face when they are starting to awaken is the feeling that they are all alone in this world. Spiritual experiences are not something that we all bring up in our everyday conversation with other people. There is always that chance that others will look at you like you may be missing marbles.

In my case, I was lucky. I started to find others with similar or different experiences who could relate to what was happening to me. I knew when I returned home from Taos that I didn't want to go back to the old patterns that I had repeated over and over in my lifetime.

In the long run, by talking to others I discovered that many had gone through the same or similar experiences. I was surprised by how many stories were just like mine, and yet the people that I met were perfectly normal and sane individuals. They had all learned to live and work with their spiritual gifts. All of the people that I talked to had been doing some kind of service to help others. Many were beyond generous in sharing their gifts.

From these gentle people I learned how to accept myself and others, as we are all unique. By understanding ourselves and communicating with others like us, we can help those who are thrown off balance because of judgment of themselves or others. We can all find peace in learning acceptance and forgiveness from within when we discover that we are no different from each

The Clean and Dirty Vessel

What does it mean to be a clean or dirty vessel? It means: How many skeletons do you have in your closet? The first time I experienced Reiki was amazing. Everything just seemed to come in so clear. But the third time I went to do the Master's Class, I was confused. Instead of beautiful colors and bright images, I saw darkness and death. Every time I reached inside myself, I saw images of mass destruction. When our teacher Holly asked us to share our experiences, I was really scared. I was afraid what the others might think, so I shrunk in the corner, hoping she wouldn't call on me.

Lucky for me, we ran out of time for our class, so I didn't have to share my experience out loud.

All I could think was that something must be seriously wrong with me to have those horrible visions. As time went on, I dismissed and soon forgot them. I continued to work and pursue higher levels of learning Reiki.

It wasn't until later, that Amy who had gone through all the classes with me, explained that what happened to me was quite common. She told me that when we go through a clearing process, we begin to release all of the dense energy that is somewhere stuck in our bodies and energy fields. In my case, that energy had come out in those horrible visions of death and destruction as it left me. Reiki is known for cleansing dense energy so that a much higher and more beautiful energy of unconditional love can restore balance in the energy field and allow the body to heal.

I asked my guides what that meant, and they said, "Ana, you know what it is like to drink out of a dirty bottle? Energy is like the water. If the bottle is dirty then it will contaminate the water when you drink it. It is when you clean the bottle that the water is clear and pure. You are like that bottle. You must let go of the things that you hold on to that make the water dirty, so that when you bring in that loving energy it is pure. The key is to know that it is not a one-time fix but a lifetime of cleaning out the bottle."

When you work with energy, you must clear your own personal baggage and learn how to let go of the things that no longer serve you as you journey down the path. It is important to learn to be mindful and take time to do your own work. Clearing and cleansing is like taking a bath every day.

As long as we recognize the patterns that no longer serve us, we can work on releasing them. This allows us to move on to the next level of learning, while helping those who ask.

Evolution Of The Soul

One of the hardest things to recognize when you get in our own way in this lifetime is how you stunt the progression of your soul and the things you need to accomplish with the time you have on this earth. In this book, experiences have been shared to help remind the reader that this is one of the causes for spiritual crisis. A spiritual crisis arises when you don't allow yourself to follow your true path that was intended for you. That is why it is so important to release any fear and learn lessons, to move on to wherever you need to go in this journey of life. If you deny yourself this opportunity, you can become mentally and physically ill.

Looking back, I can see that I would have spared my body a lot of grief had I only allowed myself to follow my true path. I admit that I have never been a quick learner. My lessons in this life have been slow and hard, created out of my own fears. I have learned that God and the universe never give up on us. That is why I tell people we all get it eventually. In the midst of our struggle, spiritual intervention will come in some shape or form if we are off the beaten path.

In my years of searching, I discovered that the evolution of the soul is an amazing process, but it is often painful. Through our human eyes, transformation is beautiful yet ugly at the same time. Through the eyes of spirit, transformation is the most beautiful sight to behold. Most of us will hold on to our old fears like a dirty child grabbing hold of the door frame when being taken to a bath. Now is the time to see our evolution as an adventure of going deeper into the sacred heart of our spirit. In that adventure, we learn how to connect with our true selves, each other, and the Creator. This is a gift that is given to all of us, so we can learn and experience our own personal journeys within ourselves and Source.

Dark Side

Growing up, like many children, I was afraid of the dark. When I got older, I was afraid to confront my darker side. I knew that we human beings all have a dark side, but honestly I never wanted to acknowledge that part of myself, for fear of being weak. My father used to tell me that when he was a boy, he was also afraid of the dark, until he turned on the light and realized that there was nothing there to fear. My spiritual teachers and guides taught me that my dark side was a tool to teach me about myself, by taking the time to really examine my fears. They also said that the dark side has no power unless you feed it with fear.

When facing our darker side in a healing environment, we soon discover that our greatest fears and weaknesses can show us how we sabotage our strengths. We also discover that when we walk through our own darkness, nothing can stop us from blossoming into the light except ourselves. As long as we don't hurt others, the hardest part of the process is not judging ourselves to the point that we are unable to bear looking at our past mistakes. Our job is to learn from our mistakes and move on. We are human, after all.

I learned with great respect that the Creator has an enormous amount of love and grace for us. We are the ones who hold ourselves in a hell that we don't understand. That part of us that is afraid of who we are inside keeps us separated from ourselves, others, and our Creator. As we reexamine our lives, we find that forgiveness also plays a big part in this. Forgiving ourselves and others holds the power to move us into a different energy of healing within ourselves. In the same way our Creator continually grants us grace, we also can give ourselves grace, to become more loving and forgiving as human beings.

Body Jumping

One of the strangest experiences that ever happened to me was when I was in my early thirties, while I was driving down the highway on my way home with the kids. We were heading back to Arlington from visiting our aunt who lived in Terrell. I was listening to the radio and the kids were talking in the back seat, when I noticed a man sitting in his car with the hood up on the side of the road. I could identify with him. I knew what it was like to be sitting on the side of the road in the middle of nowhere. A few years before, my husband and I were caught on the same road when our van's transmission gave out. It was hot and miserable. Compassion welled up in my body and great empathy poured out for this person. It was during the heat of the afternoon on one of our hot Texas summer days.

The next thing I knew, I recognized our Expedition as I saw it driving past me on the highway with my kids and me in the cab. I suddenly realized that I was looking out of the eyes of the man on the side of the road. As my consciousness began to gather this information, I understood first that I was not where I was supposed to be. I knew that I was in the man's body but somehow was separate. I was still me. Next, I realized that I could taste the gum that he had just put in his mouth, and I wondered how I knew that. I had instant access to his thoughts, and I knew what he was thinking (plans for dinner, and calling his wife to let her know he would be late). His cell phone was in his left pocket. His thoughts shifted to calling a tow truck service that he had used before. I knew too that on the passenger's side of the car was his black briefcase with some accounting papers from the business where he worked. He had planned on going over some of the figures later that evening, but now it would be late when he got home. He would be too tired after a long day to do that. I could feel that he was starting to feel the heat.

All of this information flooded my consciousness within a few seconds when he looked up towards the highway. The question of who was driving my SUV with my children in it, knowing I was not there, alarmed me. With that one thought, I was back in my own body, driving my truck, looking back at the man in my side mirror, wondering what on earth was going on. I felt stunned and shaken by what had just happened. I tried to make sense of it all. I could see my two children in the rearview mirror talking to each other, playing a game to pass the time. My thoughts drifted back to the man, and I knew in a flash that he had called for help, which was on the way. Somehow I was still connected, but not like before. Wanting it all to stop, I quickly concentrated on the radio, hoping for distraction for the rest of the drive. After getting home, unsure of what had happened, I blew it off.

This kind of experience didn't just stop there; it happened again a few years later. This time I was driving alone and saw a woman on the side of the road. It happened again after that while I was taking a walk at a park. In both instances I was again aware of the other person's thoughts and feelings, and what it felt like to be in their body and still be separate from them with my own thoughts. I could even see myself out of their eyes. That was a strange sight for me.

When I think back on what happened to me, I remember that I had a sense of great compassion and understanding of what the other person was experiencing. When I have these feelings for others, I make a connection. The last time this happened, I felt myself lifting out of my body. There was a big tugging from my heart area. I felt something like Jell-O start to move out past my skin, into the open air.

I was able to call myself back. I heard myself screaming inside my head, saying, "No!" With that one command, I felt the process reverse and felt myself reenter my body, settling in. I understood then that I sometimes have some control of leaving my body and joining with someone else in theirs.

A few years later, I took a week-long class from a shaman practitioner named Hank Wesselman. I learned that he had written about his own similar, but different, experiences in his books. When I sat down to read them after taking his class, I felt my physical and spiritual bodies vibrate like a ringing bell. His account gave me validation that what had happened to me was not in my imagination.

Hank's books sparked a desire to know if others had anything like this happen to them, so I started looking on the Internet. I really didn't find a lot of information or people talking about this kind of experience. I did find many people who didn't believe that body jumping actually existed or could happen. I am here to tell you that it can happen.

Later, I met a local shaman practitioner named Gail Carswell in Fort Worth who knew others with similar experiences. She warned me that it wasn't a good idea to practice it unless trained, because the process could bring sickness into your own body from another person. I remember that at the time Gail shared this with me, she pointed out that it was also a violation of a person's privacy., because it can psychically download their thoughts and memories into yours. Merging into a host without permission is frowned upon. I left there with the respectful knowledge that I needed to be careful not to continue to practice body jumping.

A year later, I found another shaman practitioner named Serge Kahili King Ph.D. who explained in his book, "Urban Shaman" [*] that when you are in someone else's body, you match them on an energetic level. This is why I was warned, because the energy structure of the illness is a program that can be copied from the other person's energy field during the merge. This program can be reproduced in the physical body so that when you return it communicates to the cells that you have the same illness.

In King's book, he uses the term "grokking," which is a process by which shamans move their conscious awareness into animals, objects, or even human beings. I learned that this was how shamans found food for their tribe. The practice was used to locate herds that had moved to other grazing lands. I discovered that grokking was also how they helped the tribe when there was severe weather, like droughts or flooding. The shaman moved his or her consciousness into the natural elements and worked to change the weather patterns so those elements would not hurt the tribe.

The book made sense to me. It brought back some of my conversations about animals with my father. He told me when I was a little girl that we as human beings could move our consciousness into an animal or inanimate object. I used to concentrate when he was not looking, trying hard to be a cat, bird, or dog. Nothing happened when I tried to force myself to merge. In the end, I just thought it was another one of his stories. Now, I was not so sure.

What I did learn from all of my experience with grokking is that the physical and spiritual realms are held together by a thought. I learned that there are no limitations when you tap into the field. I have come to understand that this experience was the beginning of teaching me what body jumping feels like, so that there would be no question in my mind that it could really happen.

Energy Reading

One of my friends asked me if I am able to read other people's energy when I am standing close to their energy field. She had discovered that some people can tap into someone else's life just by being in the same room. I explained to her that, yes, this is possible, but it is not something that is done intentionally.

I have been practicing for a long time to not read other people's energy unless they ask me to. There is too much personal information out there that is none of my business. I used to get really bogged down and upset with people's issues, which created a lot of judgment in me that made me completely miserable.

Reading other people's energy can be blocked. If for some reason I found I was picking up information that I shouldn't know, I could ask for it to go away. If I am conscious that information is coming in, I ask if it is for me to know. There are times I get information that helps me on my own path. I have learned that experiences are just that – experiences - and the judgment of whether they are good or bad is not mine to make.

Once, I was working with Alyce my Blessings teacher to give blessings to people. I realized in my first class that information was being downloaded to me when I placed my hands on people's heads. After the first two people, I understood what was happening and asked my higher self not to allow me to receive any information during the blessings. It worked, and I was able to enjoy the moment with the next person.

I also discovered that I could access information when I relaxed and allowed myself to be aware of things outside of my everyday life. Often I do this by opening up and expanding my awareness. When this happens, there seems to be a shift connected with my thoughts that allows me to receive the information from both the physical world and the spiritual world.

I found out that other people could access what I was thinking or had stored up in my energy fields too, and some were doing it without realizing it was happening. Most people don't know that everyone can receive information.

If you find yourself in a position where you don't want someone to read your energy, the best way to block them is to send out love. This can be done by thinking of someone or something that you love. I find it surprising how many people walk around with all their information hanging out.

I have noticed that it takes energy to read other people, so a lot depends on how strong and high the connection is when you are reading. It is really nice that we can control what we receive and turn it off to enjoy our lives in the physical world without all the complications of being downloaded with other people's private business.

Energy Flow

Now here is the part that is often forgotten with our every day activities, which is the part that we learned in grade school. Everything is made up of atoms and tiny molecules. Everything buzzes and moves, whether we see it or not. Your body is able to detect the flow of energy without you being aware. In the way your heart beats without your having to think about it. It just does what it does.

Think about this: When you walk into a crowded room of people, and you begin to pick up emotions, which are raw energy, you are drawn to certain people in that room. As you talk with a person, you may find that you have a lot in common; and if you don't, you move to find someone else that seems to fit your energy pattern. This person can become a friend, romantic interest, or healing match. This energy exchange is always there.

As someone who is learning about energy, I have learned that our bodies put out a flow of energy that moves through us like the water oscillating in a fountain. It is constantly in motion inside and out. When we are healthy, it moves and flows through our bodies, restoring and repairing it. Like the blood flowing through our veins bringing nutrients to the body, energy sustains our health and vitality.

However, when our energy fields become blocked, we feel slow, sluggish, and tired, not quite ourselves. Energy can get stuck when our emotions are out of whack or we have run ourselves into the ground. Your physical body is still moving with atoms, but the energy field within and around you may be having some problems. When this happens, we are more prone to diseases. If we are already carrying a block, it can cause great distress. The goal of energy is to keep it flowing and moving though the body like it was designed to do. That way the natural flow of energy is in and out of our fields.

Chapter Five: Down The Rabbit Hole

Remembering - In The Kingdom of Our Fathers

Once, a long time ago -- long enough that most of us can't remember -- there was a land of great abundance. And in this land were beings of glowing light who honored the sacredness of the self and love. But there came a presence in this beautiful world which we will call a lie, and that lie brought doubt and fear.

It was within the intent of the lie that things began to fall apart and the beings started to lose their glowing light. One by one they swallowed the lie, and one by one they relinquished their light. And soon this beautiful kingdom fell into a darkness, where the only light that shined was created by the one who wanted the lie to spread. It was there in that darkness, the beings wandered around without the hope of light or of finding each other in the dark.

Then, one being discovered a spark. Within the spark was the abundance of healing and truth, the one part of the true light that survived the whole ordeal.

Now, in this spark there was also a glow. To look at the glow reminded you of where you came from. The glow offered forgiveness and the true meaning of hope for anyone who saw or touched it.

It was there in the darkness that a healing occurred, and the one being who had first lost his light began to understand the truth and meaning of love. Within that love there was a connection to God and where we all began. As the being picked up the spark, that now started to grow into a larger light, others came to touch the light. The world that was filled with darkness was now lit up with an enormous light.

The beings began to see again and remember what they had lost because of the lie. They also understood that the only reason they lost their light is because they believed the lie, which gave it power. The true power was understanding that it was only a lie. They moved on with what they were doing, without the constant belief of the lie.

Freedom from the bondage of darkness was achieved. The beings learned that a lie is only a lie, nothing else, and nothing more.

Pressing Into God

At different times in my life when I was younger, I used to feel this weird sensation of separation from the Creator. Even with some of my own spiritual experiences of merging into the All, I would forget over many months and years what it was like to be that connected. I found myself trying to press myself into the energy of God the Creator. It was a bit like trying to squeeze into a small locker. In those moments, all I wanted to do was experience again what it felt like to be surrounded and filled by the unconditional loving energy of God. Even all the self-sacrificing I did working at the church didn't satisfy this craving. I didn't know how to trigger this union.

Much later I learned that I was looking for the connection outside of myself. It wasn't until I completely gave up and forgot about it that I discovered once again that I was already connected. One day I was aware that I was happy. I wasn't having that feeling of loss. When I started to explore my own self-awareness, I heard the voice of my spirit guide, that I have grown to love, "Ana, you have learned that God the Creator has never left you. You stopped looking for separation, and by doing that allowed the full gift of being accepted and loved to light up within you. You must remember that you already are, and always will be, part of All that Is. By letting go you let God, who has never forsaken you."

A Visit From My Grandmother

In the summer of 2008, I got a phone call from my mother that my grandma Mary, who was in a nursing home, had passed away that morning. I was driving to the grocery store when I got the call. I turned around and drove back home in shock. She and I had been very close all my life, and I didn't know how to accept her passing. I had been in a state of grief a year before, while I was working on healing from my spiritual crisis. I had shed so many tears I felt I couldn't cry. I could feel my heart aching but wasn't sure how to comfort myself, so I went home to get into a hot tub to soak. Water has always been a comfort for me, so that was the only thing I could think of at the time.

When I was in the tub, I felt her all around me and heard her tell me that she was "okay," and not to feel sad. Her presence seemed to stay with me as my heartache started to leave my body. This was not the end, and I was going to be okay. I knew in my heart that it was time for her to go, and even though I didn't see her, I knew she was there with me. I felt her love. She was comforting me. When I got out of the tub, the grief for her had gone from my body with a full knowing that all the while she was still with me. At the funeral I didn't cry. I grieved for my family who missed her, and my heart ached for them.

The Transition Into Death

Eight months after my grandmother died, my father passed away. I was at home when my mother called me to let me know. I remember being in shock and had no feelings when I hung up, trying to gather my thoughts, which had separated and scattered. Immediately I recognized the numb feeling that had invaded my mind and body. I remembered that the healers in Taos had told me that it was a defense mechanism in my body to preserve myself when I couldn't handle emotions. I knew that if I stayed in shock too long I would end up holding on to my grief, which would cause me great pain and suffering in the long run.

I thought of a guided meditation that I had been using that might be useful to bring my mind and body back into balance. I wanted to clear the sensation of shock that had taken hold so I could process my feelings again. This was quite an accomplishment, since I don't like to meditate. I made myself reach for the CD and my portable player, which sat next to my bed. I lay down on my back and turned it on, trying to get in a comfortable position so I could lose myself in the meditation.

Eventually I was able to follow the soft voice, which led me through an exercise to relax my body. Somewhere in the middle of the CD, I must have let go. I could feel a warm tingling feeling of energy rush over and through my body, bringing a sense of peace. Just as I was about to completely surrender to my peace, I felt something like Jell-O churning inside of me, where my solar plexus is located. My full attention shot down to that area of my body. A knowing came over me of what was happening as I felt myself departing. I knew in that moment that I was beginning to separate from myself.

I was aware of myself hovering over my body just long enough to get scared as I started to move on. I thought in that moment that I wanted to know how it felt when my father left the earth. In an instant I experienced a split, as though I was a part of two halves. One part of me wanted to go and have the experience. The other part of me wanted to stay there with my body. I knew I had a choice, and I immediately called myself back. I was again aware of the Jell-O sensation merging back into my body and into my solar plexus, and I was fully conscious of my union with myself.

As I lay there, a memory hit me like a slam dunk. I remembered in full detail the time I was on the airplane, when my spirit guides wrapped themselves around me showing me what death was like so I wouldn't be afraid. All my fears of death and separation disappeared as I came out of the mediation. I understood that nothing had changed, as death is only a transition. My whole being registered the experience, right down to the cellular memory in my physical form. I could feel this information explode inside of me as I understood without question that death was really not the end-all. The whole experience was powerful for me. I knew in that moment that my mind, body, soul, and spirit were in alignment, in full agreement.

The answer that I wanted had been given to me. I now knew what my father experienced when he lifted out of his body and went on to merge into the unconditional love that awaited him on the other side. Suddenly, I burst into tears, not of sorrow but of truly knowing how beautiful the whole transition was.

In the past I had missed being aware of the whole process of astral travel, as I would project with a single thought or emotion. I soon discovered that astral projection is a little different from dying, yet it is the beginning of moving through the astral layers so that we can merge with the unconditional love and then completely with the Source. I am reminded of this quote by Rumi: "You are not a drop in the ocean. You are the entire ocean in a drop." Which is the experience of a drop of water merging into the whole ocean. This understanding was very clear as I moved into the astral world and then toward merging into the plane of unconditional love. My desire at that time was not wanting to be separated from my physical body, so I was able to quickly come back.

Later, when I was with my mother, I felt her emptiness from loss and mirrored her grief. Experiencing my emotional body, I understood that this was a part of the physical experience. This plane of existence is wonderful, as we are able to experience with our humanness and with our emotions. But the fear of death never came back. I understood how it works once we move out of our bodies.

A few months after his death, I connected with my father by accident. Now, he comes in and out of my life more than he did when he was alive. Soon, with that connection, the feeling of being left behind disappeared.

Knowing Just Enough To Be Dangerous

A few years after my crisis in Taos, I was visiting my Reiki friend Amy one evening, and we were talking about ghosts. She was telling me that she was experiencing some very strange phenomena in her home. As we talked, I heard loud knocks on the floors and the walls. I told her that I had some experience with ghosts. I was starting out in helping clearing houses with one of my friends who did this for a living, so I offered to help. As we continued to visit, the bookcase in her room started to wobble, and I could feel the pressure in the room change. The air felt very thick and suffocating. We tried to ignore it and continued to talk about what we could do to clear the energy. Eventually, we saw a dark form, that looked like black cigarette smoke, forming by the door, emanating an intense feeling of hatred that invaded the room, making us feel very uncomfortable.

We both looked at each other and were about to get up to move the energy out, when the phone rang. It was her husband with car trouble, needing to be rescued right then. Both of us were relieved, not really knowing what we were going to be dealing with in the clearing, and also glad to have an excuse to leave the house. We quickly parted and went our separate ways.

That evening we had one of our Texas electrical storms with lots of lighting and thunder but no rain. It was late as I drove off in my little car, and there was not a lot of traffic on my drive home. While I was sitting at a red light waiting for the light to turn, a lightning bolt hit the sky, creating a loud crack that resonated through the car. When I looked up, I noticed what looked like lightning traveling horizontally through the power lines. I remember thinking, "How strange." The signal turned green, and I went on my way. While I was driving, the lightning bolt seemed to be keeping up with my car as I made my turns, following me through the electric lines. I knew this was not at all normal, and a sense of fear engulfed me as I went into high alert.

Finally I made it to the interstate, feeling somewhat relieved to have lost whatever it was that seemed to be tracking me. When I exited onto the little road that took me to my street, I had this deep feeling of dread. Sitting at the light, waiting to turn over the bridge, I saw the lightning again, moving horizontally over the electric lines, making its way in my direction. As I drove on I realized to my horror, it was following me again, making the same turns I made on my way home, disappearing as I entered my driveway.

Panic seized me. I knew enough to know that I had to cover my home, family, pets, and anyone that I knew with protection. Energy follows thought, and a single thought of a loved one would put them in jeopardy. Whatever was terrorizing my friend at her house had decided to follow me home. Instantly I started to pray, asking for help covering everything, all the while feeling the intense anger and hatred surrounding my car. I made myself step out of the car and run into the house. It was following me in hot pursuit. I could feel it staring me down, and the hairs on my arms and neck stood on end. I ran into the master bathroom and turned on all the lights, even the ones in the bedroom where my husband was sleeping. He was sound asleep and didn't wake up. Quickly, I changed into my pajamas, still feeling eyes piercing down on me.

Making my way to bed, I turned off the lights. I jumped next to my sleeping husband and got as close to him as I could. As my eyes adjusted to the darkness of the room I could see a darker shape taking form, standing right next to my side of the bed. Pure hatred beamed directly towards me, sending a chill up my spine. I knew that I was going to be attacked and wasn't sure how to prevent it.

That was when I heard a faint beating sound out of nowhere. I checked to see if it was my heart but realized it sounded like it was more in my head. In fact when I focused on it, the sound seemed to be coming from inside my ears. "But how is that possible?" I remember thinking. As I lay there listening, I recognized it to be the beating of my medicine drum. I shifted my gaze to where I kept the drum. I could just make out its shape hanging there on the wall next to my desk. Then a full knowing swept over me and I knew in that moment that the thing -- whatever it was -- couldn't touch any of us.

I couldn't believe it, but my drum had come to my aid when I cried for help. I looked back at the dark energy, still feeling it staring at me with deep hatred, but I knew the rhythm moving through the air was holding a sacred space for me and my family. After that, the whole experience was like watching an angry predator acting out behind steel bars at the zoo. I knew I was safe, so I turned over and went to sleep.

The next morning when I awoke, the dark energy was gone. I went through the whole house searching for it, but there was no sign anywhere. The energy in our home was peaceful, and everyone in our household was good. It was as if it never happened.

Later Amy called me back, and my teacher Paula Schermerhorn, who is a medium, came with me to clear her home. What we found made me understand what had happened to me the night before. Paula explained that someone who had owned the house prior to my friend had been playing with dark magic. By mistake, they had opened a portal that allowed a dark entity into the home, where it had trapped ghosts and other entities who were lost. It didn't want to leave or allow any of the lost souls to find their way home.

She then explained that I had threatened it when I told Amy that I could clear the house.

We went on to do a house clearing with the help of a few friends. It didn't take long to locate the opened portal and find the dark entity that was holding the ghosts hostage. We were then able to cross the entity and close the portal for good. After that we could release the ghosts into the light, and the angels came and took them home. I am happy to say my friend reported no more activity. It was over.

Cleansing and Purging Of The Soul

One of the things I have learned in my experiences is that, when merging into Spirit, I have to discard all of my old emotional baggage if I want to move into the higher realms. By letting go of all of my fears and doubts, I am no longer held down in the lower frequencies. I am always well aware of when my emotional baggage leaves my energy field because it feels like a dead weight releasing me. I describe it like sandbags dropping from a hot air balloon, allowing the balloon to fly to higher parts of the sky. It is such an exhilarating experience to let go of all of my troubles and worries with a new freedom, that it is hard to come back sometimes.

I am usually aware that it is my choice to let go or stay on the astral level that I am in when I first leave my body. There have been a few times, that I have talked about in other chapters, where the transition happened so fast that I was transported on an astral level to somewhere else, only to find myself there in an experience. My spirit guides have explained that this was able to happen because I had already been in some of those higher astral planes or energy patterns. In those moments the transportation happened because of a match in the frequency of my destination, which catapulted me there.

I discovered that after I was in a higher frequency or plane, I was able to come back without stepping into my old emotional baggage that I had left here in the three-dimensional world. The only catch was, if I didn't make a conscious effort to change my old habits in my day-to-day activities, then what I discarded would eventually return. This included placing myself back into situations that caused me worries or grief.

These old patterns brought me back to exactly where I was before the merging experience. Exasperated, I wondered what was the point, if I could discard my emotional baggage only to have it return. Then I remembered that soul sickness had taught me how important it is to be in the physical form as a whole. I came to see that I was learning that I could change on the spiritual level; however, I still had to work on the physical level, which included the way that I thought. One didn't work without the other in this third dimensional world. Once again I found that healing didn't occur without the alignment of the mind, body, and soul to make the full shift into the spirit.

If healing was what I wanted, I would have to work on all three levels at the same time. On a mental level, I had to go into a conscious process of letting go of my old emotions, which seemed to have a huge grip on my thinking. This meant really looking at my emotional triggers from all angles to see how they affected me. I started to examine where I was in that moment when I made the connection. I had a great deal of help from my teachers on both this side and in the spiritual realms. If I got stuck, I would just cry out for help, and soon my cries were answered. Often I ended up with some sort of struggle. Old patterns can sometimes be hard to break, even with the best intentions.

I found myself in life situations where I would get frustrated and had to question what I was experiencing in that exact moment. The goal was to see all aspects of an experience so I didn't get stuck on one side. I examined the mental and emotional levels from all directions. If it was a disagreement with someone else, I analyzed their emotional attachment as well as my own. Then I explored other sides and viewpoints, opening up new possibilities. I would try to see the bigger picture from a distance, without judgment. I learned that if I kept myself detached from an outcome, I could let it go and have a new experience, changing the way I thought about things. I started to let go of old frustrations and anger that held me down in the past. I started to blog and write in journals. This process was amazing in allowing me to release.

I worked with teachers who helped me do bodywork, moving energy within myself. I learned the art of Tai Chi and Qigong. I started to take walks around the block or through my neighborhood, which always helped me move stress. Then I shifted my focus to my eating habits, exploring different foods and their effects on my body. I even prayed or used Reiki on my food to change its vibration to match mine and burn more efficiently in my body.

On the spiritual realms, I continued my studies in letting go of my fears and judgments, so that I had more freedom to rediscover my spiritual gifts. I allowed myself to once more hear the other side and reconnect to my spirit guides. I could have a personal dialogue with them whenever I wanted, instead of waiting for signs or for them to show me something. I continued my journeys to the other side, either by astral projection or twilighting. I allowed myself to see and hear, while having a full spiritual experience in my body.

Each day was -- and is -- a personal challenge, even when making the conscious shift. I still come across old habits trying to slip back in. They are very familiar to my both my body and mind. The one thing that I noticed that really changed was the trigger points. They used to alarm me, throwing me off balance; but now they serve as signals for me that something in my life needs to be examined in more detail.

Again, I learned that the process of cleansing and purging is not a one-time fix. It is a life-long process that is important to do all the time, like taking a bath at the beginning or end of the day, because we are always bringing in or getting stuck in some kind of energy as we go along in our day-to-day activities. It is important to cleanse and purge our own stuff or other people's energy from our field that no longer serves a purpose in our lives. In the long run, it helps us to move into an alignment with our true selves.

The Firewalker - The Other Side of Fear

I knew the moment I met Daniel the firewalker teacher at the first meet up that I attended that I was going to be working with him but I avoided any contact at that time, since I was still feeling raw inside. A friend had invited me to one of his workshops on meditation right after I left my position at the church. I really felt no urge to go. (Again, meditation is not something I enjoy.) As the week went by, I was feeling more and more of a pull to take the class. Each day it got stronger until I woke up on the morning of his class screaming out loud, "Okay, I will go!"

I asked my very sleepy husband Steve to drive me. I was only going to poke my head in the door to see what they were doing and leave. As usual, it didn't quite go as planned. Daniel saw me and invited me in to join the class. I don't know when it actually happened, but somewhere in the class, I began to relax as we went through the meditations.

Afterward, I asked him if he taught any other classes.

"Yes, a few, and one you might like to try."

"Oh yeah?" I asked.

"Yes," he said, "the class deals with personal fears, and in the end you have the chance to walk on a hot bed of coals."

"Oh, not my thing!" I said.

A month later I was sitting in his firewalking class, wondering how it had happened. It was my good fortune that the place hosting the walk had not come through so we were not able to firewalk that day. We did, however, walk on broken glass barefoot, break an arrow with the tip at the soft part of our necks, and break a board with our hands.

I listened intently during the seminar, knowing full well I was going to bow out of the thrill-seekers part at the end. In my family I am the cautious one. I hold everyone's coat at Six Flags. I was there to just take the part of the class that dealt with fear.

He explained, "Fear is all about being a little uncomfortable. When we face a new experience that we have no data on we become fearful. Once we move through the experience, we look back and realize that it was a valuable lesson in our lives. Fear is what challenges us to grow in all aspects of our lives, and only we have the power to change it inside ourselves."

I remember him handing out the hard boards and me knocking on mine with my knuckles, feeling how solid it felt. I guess I made a face because he stopped the class and said, "Ana, What was that face you made? Tell me what you are thinking."

"Great!" I was thinking, "Now I can admit to everyone that I don't believe I can do this." All eyes were on me waiting for me to speak. I knew that my face betrayed my thoughts.

My answer went like this: "Well, I guess I am afraid. What if I fail?"

"Close your eyes," he said, "then, see yourself standing at the board. See your hand moving through the board and stopping at the other side." I am a visual learner, so this came up in a flash.

"I see it! But... But... I guess I doubt it?"

Then he shouted to the class. "Let's go out and break some boards!" He laid his hand on my shoulder with words of encouragement, "Ana, you can do this. You need to trust yourself."

Well, I love gentlemen. All the other women broke their boards first, and I was the last one standing. All eyes were on me, once again. I walked slowly up like I was facing the guillotine. I placed my board between the blocks, feeling very self-conscious. Time seemed go in slow motion as I went through the mechanics of this action. There was the count: one, two, three. My hand sliced through the board like a knife to butter. Utter disbelief ran through my head, then ventured out through the rest of me. How did that happen and my hand was fine? It made no sense to me at all. Yet, I did it!

Then we began the process of walking on broken glass and breaking an arrow on the soft part of our necks. The results were all the same. I was the last one, but each time a success. There were a few that were not able to do it, but I think my spirit guides must have felt like I needed the extra boost that day.

Now, when I am faced with fear in my heart, I have a sense that I can move through it instead of being frozen. I try to look at it as an adventure where a new experience can be a little uncomfortable. By doing this I know I will find success on the other side of fear.

The Wedding Pot

As I was getting ready for my friend Amy to come over for tea one day, I decided to pull out my grandmother's old tea cups to make the event a little special and honor her. When I looked in our old china cabinet for the cups, I found a gift from my wedding.

There it was, displayed in the case for show, but long forgotten. What really struck me as I picked it up, was that I was transported back in time. I was sitting in my friend Mary's living room, opening a box, pulling out the wedding pot and examining every inch.

One of the traditions Mary told me as I held it in my hands was that the Pueblo Native Americans where we lived give a wedding pot to newlyweds as a gift. It was a vessel with two separate openings at the top which flowed down into the belly representing the two becoming one joined together, holding life within.

"Beautiful story," I remember saying, but as I was holding it, I lost my grip and dropped it and it cracked. "Oh no," I said as an overwhelming sadness came over me. But Mary picked up the pot and said," Ana, it's okay. I am glad that happened because you need to understand that nothing is perfect. Life is certainly not perfect, and marriage is not perfect. There are cracks in everything, as there are many disappointments in life, but the real key is the love and the extra care that glues the vessel back together and becomes the strength of it."

Then time began to move again from the past to the present. My marriage flashed before me in a collage of pictures and emotions, some bitter and some sweet. Life is such a good teacher, and here in my hands was a small reminder of what life is all about.

As I placed the pot back in its spot, the doorbell rang. It was time for tea.

Chapter Six: The Art of Recovering

Stumbling In The Shadows "Is It Real?"

One of the many things that we all seem to deal with is doubt. I always tell my friends and students that I have been known for being a big doubter. I totally get the term "Doubting Thomas." I would have been one to have touched the robe of Christ after the resurrection, just to make sure it was all on the up-and-up. And yes, there are times that I have questioned, "Is this for real?" That is still very healthy, as there is a lot out there that is not real.

If these experiences had not happened to me personally, I would question them. I do know that they did happen. When I go into that place of doubt, I can bring up the memory, knowing full well it was a genuine experience. The memories are often left not only in my mind, but my body recognizes them also. I have talked to others, and they all have had some sense of doubt themselves at one time or another in their lives. "It is perfectly natural to question something when we are learning," I was told by one of my teachers. "This is all part of the natural process of exploring." Something else I discovered was that, because of my own experiences, when someone talks about their experience, I feel some sort of resonance of truth in my body or energy field when theirs is similar to mine.

There have been times when I was not sure and sometimes was confused when someone was telling me about an incident that happened to them. That is when I would go into twilight and ask a guide to help me understand what was happening and why I felt uncertain about what they were telling me. Sometimes the confusion comes from my own lack of trust, which causes me to hold off or block any feelings or connection to them. Other times it is the person I am talking to putting up a smokescreen. I have learned that I can trust my spirit guides when I don't trust myself.

Energy Exchange

We exchange energy as freely as we hand money to one another in the free world. The only difference is that we often don't see the energy exchange because it is not as tangible as a dollar bill.

As with money, we often find ourselves in great debt because we are not brought up to understand how to balance and handle our personal energy. I find it rather interesting that we don't teach our children how to handle energy in school, but we don't teach them how to handle money either. So where does that leave us? Often our personal relationships take up so much of our time and energy that we can be exhausted by the end or even the beginning of the day.

Personal freedom is discovering and understanding that we have this energy exchange going on all the time, anytime we are with someone. After we make this discovery, we learn about ourselves and our own personal power. Understanding the exchange rate in energy changes the dynamics of how we manage our lives and care for others. I remember when I first became aware of the energy exchange within relations. It had all become very apparent when I was working closely with different people in different situations.

At one time I made an acquaintance with a counselor to whom I mentioned that I could feel people's energy when I walked into a room. I had also discovered that I could physically move energy but was not really sure what that was all about. She asked, "What is your religion?" I was dumfounded. I realized there was nothing else to say. The energy I was experiencing had nothing to do with what faith I was.

Energy is very simple; it can be felt by everyone. The whole key is to understand how it works as we go about our daily activities with each other, giving and taking it without realizing what we are doing. You see it is how we are created. Energy exchange is the natural way we interact with each other.

Many of us are already pre-programmed about our thoughts on energy exchange. Some are programmed to interact in a healthy way, but others are not. A lot has to do with our emotional environment as we were growing up and our life experiences. Emotions are pure energy. There is nothing like having a reaction to someone or something to get the heart racing and the blood pumping, either in a positive or a negative way. Often what people ignore can be very real. Again, the energy exchange has nothing to do with your religious background but has everything to do with being human. We are exchanging our emotional energy with each other without taking the Energy Exchange Course 101.

The Teachers Of The Divine

One day I found myself feeling anxious from a confrontation. I was having a tough time maneuvering through it when I finally threw up my hands in frustration. In that moment I heard a very strong voice that I recognized speaking to me. It was one of the spirit guides that works with me saying, "Ana, let me show you what is going on from our perspective." Instantly I was transported like in a daydream, and I saw what looked like a computer image of two people standing, facing each other. They were drawn as outlines on a 3D grid, and I could see all the veins and organs inside each, through their transparent bodies.

My spirit guide asked me to watch: they wanted to show me what happened when someone was angry. As I watched, one of the person's liver lit up, and when it did the energy hit the other person's energy field and lit up their liver. Then the voice asked me to watch as they showed grief, and again one of the person's lungs lit up and then the other person's lungs lit up. This, all of a sudden, made sense. I began to understand that when one person was angry or sad, they carried that in one of their organs, but it also seemed to affect the other person in the same area of the body.

I heard the voice of another spirit guide say, "Ana, when someone is wounded and another wounded person comes in contact with them, the first person's energy lights up the organ that carries that emotion in each body. When this happens, one person may feel what the other person feels, or that person may become frustrated with the other person because he is being reminded of something that needs to heal within himself."

The voice got softer. "Ana, where in your body are you feeling this emotion that is upsetting you with someone else? They are not here to hurt you but to remind you that you have something within yourself that needs to be looked at so that you can work on releasing it. Remember that others reflect what you need to learn. They are teachers to help you learn how to heal. Step back and look at what you are not seeing."

That was all that was said. The image was gone as quickly as it came. I sat there thinking about what had just happened. I replayed the situation, taking a better look at the person who was frustrating me. This time I identified where the pain was within my own body. I was able to find and trace the emotion to something that happened to me in the past that made me feel powerless and that was being triggered by this other person.

With the help of a friend, I was able to express what had happened to me. Acknowledging it started the process of allowing me to heal so that I would not be triggered again with such an intensity of raw emotions.

I used to see a vision; of myself standing in the pit of hell with ice cubes in both hands, unaffected by anything happening there. To some this may be a horrifying experience, but to me the image is about learning how to stand in the flow and energy of the Holy Spirit -- to be a true vessel of unconditional love. It is about holding a space where one can't be hurt and can't contribute to the pain and suffering in that environment. That is what it is like to be able to stand in a true state of grace.

The Art Of Teaching

Something that has come to my attention over the years is the difference between teachers who are guided by the Spirit and those who are guided by the ego. I have discovered among my teachers a common thread. By watching their example, I am learning that out of meekness comes the strongest teacher of all.

What I see, rather than condemnation of their students, is a gentle way of guiding the students through an amazing amount of knowledge and experience with loving care. I see no ego or fear of losing their status of teacher. My teachers are excited for their students when they excel and are supportive when they fail, understanding that the students are hardest on themselves.

On the other side of the fence, I have friends who have gone to find someone to teach them and have been condemned and torn to shreds because of their beliefs and their gifts. I was taught a long time ago that a true teacher should never feel threatened or challenged when a student asks a question or has a different belief. The teacher knows that the student is growing and that, like children, this process is the student's way of moving into his own as the Creator intended. A good teacher shares their joy in the art of teaching that brings out a passion that can be contagious in inspiring their students.

If a teacher is in the place of ego, they will bring fear into the teaching, whereas a true teacher builds trust and is supportive of the student, teaching with love and nurturing. I have been truly blessed with the teachers in my life. I see that my own progress is due to their love and support.

Do You Believe in Angels?

As long as I can remember I have heard my grandmother and mother talk about guardian angels watching over us. In my own adventures in life, I have had my own experiences with angelic beings. On various occasions they have warned me to let me know something was coming up that I should be aware of.

The biggest encounter I have had with angels is when three of them showed up in person at my bedside as I was waking up one morning, because I had strayed off my life path. At the time I had truly forgotten what my soul contract was about, and what my purpose on this earth was. The angels finally had to come in person because they knew I was hard-headed and needed some form of intervention.

I used to tell my children the story of how the angels let me know when the time came for me to meet their father. I had just graduated from college and was looking for work. My mother suggested that I do temporary work until I found a job that fit me.

The day that I went for an interview for a part-time temporary receptionist job, I knew that I would meet my husband. As I walked out of the interview to the car, I heard very clearly, "You got it, and you will meet your future husband on this job." The angels had already warned me about the guy I was seeing at the time, a month before, when we were about to get serious. In a clear voice I had heard, "Stop! He is not the one! The next one." Needless to say, that relationship ended very soon after that.

I got the job at the semiconductor plant a month later. I had already forgotten what the angels had said. In the second week, I made friends with a co-worker who wanted me to meet this guy that she was seeing. She brought him by the reception desk while I was working and introduced us. He was an engineer working at the plant. As I was shaking his hand, I heard very clearly in a sing-song voice, "He is the one! He is the one! He is the one!" I brushed the voices aside, trying to concentrate on having a discussion with him, and to my surprise I found that we had a lot in common.

Driving home, I scoffed at hearing, "He is the one." I asked the angels why he was dating my friend. But my co-worker friend started dating someone else, and to make a long story short, we were married nine months later. A match made in heaven, some might say.

Then there was the time when I was sixteen and was out with my girlfriends on Camp Bowie Boulevard in Fort Worth, Texas. I was driving my mom's little blue Toyota station wagon with the windows cracked open to let the air in. A car drove up next to us as we were stopped at a red light and a person in the car asked my friend who was sitting in the back seat what school did we go to. I heard my friend say Southwest High School. At that moment I turned my head to look at my other friend in the front seat who shot me a glance just as I heard tires skidding on the pavement. Then the window exploded in what seemed to be slow motion as I watched shattered glass flying throughout the cabin of the car.

I drove home in shock with my friends. We were unhurt with only a few cuts but had lots of glass in our hair. When the police arrived to look at the car, they discovered buckshot from a shotgun. They let us know that it wasn't gravel that broke the glass. The policeman looked right at me, and said, "Were you driving?" I said yes. Then he shook his head and said, "You must have some big guardian angels." They had shot out my window on the driver's side.

Once, when I was in my late twenties, I was walking around an art gallery in Taos with my husband and two children, looking up at the paintings hanging on the wall, when I heard the voice of one of my angels clearly saying, "Stop! Look down!" It was so loud that I froze. Thank goodness I did, because when I glanced down at the floor, I realized that my next step was about to be on a steep staircase leading down to the next level of the building. Backing up, I felt an electrical shock pass up and down my whole body. I had to leave the gallery immediately, knowing I had come very close to having a serious accident.

Another time, when I was twelve, I was walking home from school when a white van drove up next to the curb and stopped. The sliding door opened and two teenage boys jumped out and started running towards me. All I heard in my head was, "Run!" Without questioning it, I ran as if my life depended on it, towards the entrance of a house. The boys saw that I was about to reach the door and ran back to the van, jumped in, then took off in a hurry. Later, when I had time to think about what had happened, I knew if I had paused for a second it would not have ended well.

Angels speak to us all the time. We choose whether we hear them or not. They are with us from birth throughout our whole lives, helping us even when we pass on to the next world. They help us when we ask for guidance, but it is up to us to listen. They don't tell us what to do or how to live our lives, as that is up to our own free will. They can let us know when we are off track, help us find our way, or warn us if we are in danger. They are not here to make decisions for us or take over our lives. They are here to help.

Soul Retrieval

One of the many things that shamans are known for is the ability to look for lost parts of someone's soul on the other side that have separated from their body. This process is called soul retrieval.

Many times when people go through a trauma or illness, parts of their soul will splinter off, leaving in search of a safe place outside of the physical body. In many cases, people say they felt like they were outside of themselves watching as something happened to them. Coma is another form of leaving the body where the soul goes somewhere else to find refuge. When a person is trying to cope with what has happened or is happening to them in their physical form, they escape by leaving their body. They can also be jolted or knocked out of the body by something. In many cases only part of the soul returns, leaving behind those parts that still feel very vulnerable. Those pieces can be returned to that person who lost them and this occurs during soul retrieval.

A shaman who performs soul retrieval will go on a spiritual journey for a person who needs to integrate parts of themselves that have splintered off. When a shaman goes on the soul retrieval they are always accompanied by an animal helper or a spirit guide who knows how to navigate and return from the other worlds and dimensions where those soul parts have gone. The animal helper or spirit guide's job is to protect the shaman from beings on the other side that may not be friendly. Remember, the shaman may be invading their space so some beings can get touchy. The animal helper or spirit guide will also explain or translate what is going on during the journey since they are familiar with the territory and the other spirits. The main job for the helper is to lead the shaman to the location where the missing soul part might be found, to determine if it is seeking refuge or is lost.

There are guidelines and rules to doing this work, as it requires high integrity and respect. Training and learning how to work with personal guides and animal helpers are very important, along with journeying to other planes and dimensional realms. There is also a learning process when making contact with your real spirit guides, angels, and animal helpers that have your highest good in mind. It is important to carefully choose who you work with on the other side. Some who volunteer may not have your best welfare at heart. They may not have good intentions. You have to trust and know who you are working with, as it can be dangerous work. If, for some reason, you are not in complete alignment with the "good of all," then boundaries may be crossed and you may lose your integrity, along with all the privileges of working with the spirit helpers. Something else that should be mentioned is that this work can also be done in other modalities, such as the Akashic Records.

Once, I was doing my own work in a class with my Akashic teacher Jodi and she wanted us to go into our soul's past history to retrieve a piece of ourselves that had been lost. I followed instructions and went into my heart, asking for help from the spirit animal I work with. It seemed I sat there for a long time, getting no response and no one coming to help me. Just as I was about to give up, I saw the tail of my animal helper moving back and forth. Then I saw her beautiful bright eyes as close to my face as she could get gazing directly into my eyes giving me the signal she was ready to go. I gave her a signal, then found myself in complete darkness, wondering why it was so dark. This seemed to go on for some time as I stood there in silence. I was starting to lose my cool when I realized that I was not alone. There were others there.

My first thought after that was "light," and as soon as I thought the word, a light started to come on slowly. As it did, I noticed I was in a cave, surrounded by people, either hunched over or crying. I could feel a heaviness of great loss and sorrow coursing through my whole being. Then I spotted my animal helper from across the room. As I made contact with her telepathically, she told me that I was in the Cave of Lost Souls. I noticed that she was sitting really close with her tail wrapped around a small child who was hunched over in the corner, cowering and crying.

Curious, I asked who that child was, and suddenly I found myself under a bed hiding and could feel pure terror in my heart. I knew in that second that my whole family was dead. I could see a pair of boots standing next to the bed with someone in them. I knew too in that instant that I was going to die, as they were searching the room for anyone alive. In my memory I knew it was World War II, and I was in Poland, and the boots belonged to a Nazi Storm Trooper. It would be seconds before they found me and shot me like the rest of my family, who had just been having breakfast at the kitchen table. I knew I was a child, a boy, and I was eight years old. I could feel the fear grip my heart and stick in my throat. Terror ripped through my whole body and sweat poured out my glands. The whole experience was so real I could feel myself gasping for breath and yet afraid to move or breathe.

Then I saw big golden eyes beaming unconditional love at me from under the bed where I was, as the tail of the large spirit animal curled around me. In that moment I was taken away, moving in mid-air with the strong muscular animal. We landed right in front of an adult woman. I recognized her to be me in this lifetime, the future. I also noticed the others from my class sitting in the room with their eyes closed, looking like they were asleep. I knew that I was the boy and also I was me, who I am now. Then I heard my angel spirit guide -- who was separate from my animal helper -- say, "This is a piece of you that was lost when you died, and now it is time to bring that part of you back." In that second I merged with this small boy in my heart chakra, accepting the piece of my soul that had been lost in another lifetime. The union was bittersweet, as the sorrow and fear came rushing back, running into the cells of my body, recording the past of the life before. Then I felt an enormous feeling of unconditional love for this beautiful child overriding that new information, which was embraced by my inner soul. It was a welcoming home and an acknowledgment of that small part of me that had been missing.

My animal helper rubbed my cheek with her face then left as I came back into the room into full awareness in my body. I was happy to include that part that had been lost. After my teacher asked us to go around the room and talk about our experiences, I found myself almost shattered as I described the terror that I felt as the small boy under the bed. I could still feel the incredible love that I experienced when I was brought back into union with myself, knowing I was home, safe and sound.

In The Heart Of Things

One morning I was talking with my husband, drinking my cup of hot tea and enjoying the morning. We sat on the bed and he began to work on his laptop. Since he was busy, I decided to watch a little television while enjoying the rest of my tea. I found a movie that I had been trying to finish that whole holiday season.

I started watching in the last ten minutes, which is where I had left off a few days before. I found the movie interesting: It was about a grief counsellor helping people, and it was ending with him discovering something in himself. What touched me were the relationships and the unspoken words as the actors played their parts. I noticed my eyes were wet. My heart opened up to the touching scene, and a warm energy shot through the core of my being with an amazing feeling of it moving out through my skin.

The emotion I experienced was so beautiful. I noticed a warm fuzzy feeling moving through my body and out into my outer energy field. It was all loving and healing at the same time. I took a moment to stop and be aware of what was happening to me. My husband, who was not really paying attention to me or the movie, however, looked up, feeling something shift in the room that got his attention. He looked over in my direction and immediately smiled when he saw I was touched. This is something we all experience in our own way, but most of the time we are unaware that our emotions can so powerful that they move outside of ourselves and affect others.

Smiling to myself, I felt good about how we become inspired when we hear music, watch a movie, or experience a work of art. This experience is powerful as it moves the energy around us and brings it alive. What if we were able to focus that powerful energy in a loving and healing way toward others to help bring healing into our physical world? This type of connection is what we experience through the heart of the sacred!

Fireballs!

I learned an incredible lesson one night, by chance, that changed the way I understood vivid dreams. But before I go into my memory, I have to mention that one of my teachers who is a shaman practitioner had warned in one of his classes that if someone ever pushes dark or bad energy your way and you throw it back at them, it is considered a form of black magic. The goal, when presented with dark energy, is to deflect it and push it into the earth, which has the power to convert negative energy into positive energy. The other option is to change the energy into a higher vibration so it won't hurt anyone. As an energy worker I try very hard to follow his advice.

In 2010 a curandera named Tonya came into my life, and for a while we were friends. After some time the energy in the room changed when the two of us got together, and very soon we decided to part and go our separate ways. I discovered later on, by chance, that she was an astral traveler. She was coming to visit me uninvited and making me uncomfortable. I ended up placing protection grids to keep her out of my energy fields.

One night, for whatever reason, I forgot to put up my protection grids. I guess I just fell asleep. Somewhere in the middle of the night I started dreaming that I was walking through a battlefield and was passing an old crumbling stone wall that was waist-high. As I walked by it, a fireball came out of nowhere and almost hit me on my head, missing me by an inch. I looked up just in time and ducked before another one almost hit me.

By then I had figured out that I was a target for someone or something. I crouched behind the wall, getting my nerve up to see what was hurling fireballs at me. When I did look, I saw Jan, who I used to hang out with, staring at me with anger in her eyes and a look like she wanted to hurt me. I immediately saw red. I had done nothing to cause this attack, but I picked up a fireball and lobbed it back at her. Thus began the fight of flinging fireballs in my dream.

What makes this dream unique is that as I was getting into the fight, a hand came out of nowhere and grabbed me from the back by my collar just as I got hit on the right side of the face, just below my nose. The sting was enough to arouse me from my dream. As I tried to calm myself from the emotions, I could still feel my face hurt from being burned. Finally I talked myself back to sleep.

I got up the next morning to wash my face. In the mirror was a quarter-sized stinging burn on my face exactly where I was hit in the dream. Embarrassed, I tried everything to cover it up.

I went to work at the acupuncture clinic and went straight to my friend Pam to tell her about the events of that night. She asked me right out, "What were you doing having a fireball fight when you know better?" I thought about it, and the only answer I could tell her was that I was mad! She burst out laughing: I had paid a price with the burn on my face.

As we talked in her office, another friend of mine Veronica who was volunteering at the clinic walked in and said, "Ana, what on earth were you doing last night?! I had to grab you out of your dream because you were in trouble and I got burned on my hand." She then showed us her right hand, and sure enough there was a burned place on it. Pam ended up having to treat both of us, but our burns took several months to really heal. I wore my mark on my face like a scarlet letter.

I learned several things that day. One of which was not to let my emotions take over my actions. I learned too that not all dreams are just dreams, sometimes we are astral traveling. Also, when we are in other dimensions, we can meet others and bring back physical evidence that we were there.

A good friend of mine asked me once, "If someone sends you bad intentions, why is it black magic if you send it back?" What came to me was that if someone is hurling snakes at you and you pick up snakes to throw them back, you are perpetuating dense energy. If someone throws snakes at you and you change them into flowers, you can change a negative energy pattern into a blessing. The other thing I learned to do is to deflect the negative energy into the earth. The whole objective is not to sink into the denser level. It was a good lesson for me and one I will never forget!

Healing Circles - The Change

In the early part of July 2009, I was visiting with two of my Reiki friends Caroline and Amy one evening after dinner. We had been together as a team for a few years, organizing and putting together healing circles. Our little circle was composed of seven ladies when we started out. We all were students and teachers sharing our own amazing experiences and knowledge with each other. Our circle lasted a year before we decided to let others join us.

The healing circle split off into two circles which again split, creating more circles. In time, I was sending out reminders and a newsletter so that people could plug into what was happening in the circles keeping up the network.

As we continued to grow, the circles helped people make connections to others that had the same spiritual gifts, allowing them the freedom to speak their truth without fear of judgement. Even though I looked forward to the circles and friends who came to participate, I found that running all of them out of my home was taking over my family life and our personal space.

The circles were envisioned to be offered as a free service to the community. People were finding out through word-of-mouth that we were meeting and inviting others to join. We were growing quickly and needed more space. Because of this, Caroline, Amy and I decided to meet to discuss what we were going to do for the next year. My friends were already being pulled in other directions but offered to support me in my efforts to continue the circles. I found myself wanting go deeper in learning more from the teachers who had come into my life.

As we discussed the future of the circles, we all agreed that it was best to move them out of my home to a more public place where they could accommodate a larger crowd. We also agreed that consolidating the circles into two would allow me to focus on the quality of the programs and finding teachers to support them. This would also free me up to take some personal time off to advance my studies and yet still be a part of the circles.

As I drove home from the meeting, I wondered if I was making a mistake with all the changes. "What was I thinking when we are doing so well?" I knew it was time for a change. I could feel my two Reiki friends wanting to step out of working with the circles altogether, but I was glad for their input.

For the first few months it seemed I was sitting on my hands as things were rolling into transition. A local store called The Power of the Rainbow, located in our hometown in Arlington, Texas, had graciously accepted to host our main healing circle. Someone else in our group had also stepped up to host one of the other circles in their home. Things were starting to happen, and people were helping to move the two circles to their new locations.

In early September, my life started to shift with all the changes. I was suddenly swept up in an amazing torrent of learning and studying. I found that I had no time for the newsletter, art, blogging, and teaching that I had done in the past year. I was mainly focused on spiritual learning. I decided that I needed to find a leader for the healing circle and step down. I was being pulled in another direction.

"The Spiritual Council"

In my early childhood I had heard my father Kelly talk about the "Spiritual Council," but I really had no concept of what he meant. Years later, I found a class at The Crossings soon after my first visit there and decided I needed to do some work on myself.

At this time in my life, I wanted to explore some of the spiritual teachings that I was familiar with from my early childhood. These were things that I had locked away at a great cost to myself. I knew that in order to rediscover what I had lost I had to go deep inside of myself and see what was calling to me. To my surprise, it was the path of the shaman that answered.

I remembered on one of my many trips to Taos that I had heard about a shaman practitioner who taught classes in Santa Fe. I started to search for her and found her on the internet, but her classes were not scheduled when I could go. I came across another class by Hank Wesselman, a shaman practitioner that I had not heard of, but I felt it was a good match. As I scanned the website I realized he was teaching at The Crossings. I made the decision to go, even though I was still not sure about signing up for the class. I did, however, notice that the tugging on my heart got stronger after reading the synopsis on the webpage. It reminded me of my father and some of the things he had taught me.

The class was almost a week long, and there were at least twenty students for the shamanic workshop. Some of the techniques were the same as I had learned from my father. However, there were other teachings that I had not had the privilege to explore. We were able to work with our medicine drums to help us access the spirit world through the rhythm of the drum, I brought mine to use in some of the activities. It felt great to be working with some familiar tools. After a few days, our teacher Hank announced that he was co-authoring a book with the shaman practitioner from Santa Fe. I knew then that I had made the right choice to come to the class.

One of the exercises that we did was recalling our dreams. I thought that was fitting, as I had been going through phases where I didn't dream or couldn't remember them. Hank, explained to us that if we asked ourselves to be conscious of our dreams just before falling asleep, we would be able to access them in the morning. He asked us to try it out that evening and we would talk about our dreams the next day. "Really?" I thought. I was thinking this was a silly way to remember our dreams, but I went along with it.

That night in my room after reading a chapter in a book and saying my prayers, I reminded myself to recall my dreams. Surprisingly, it worked! I dreamed I was in a beautiful office that had a large conference table with at least ten chairs around it. I saw all kinds of beings, angels, and people sitting at the table, with me at the head, in some deep discussion. I saw lots of papers, books, and charts on the table. When I started to pay attention to the discussion, I noticed it was about what I was doing in the physical world and things to come in my future.

After a while, I turned my attention to the room and I noticed large bookcases stretching from floor to ceiling against two of the walls. The room I saw was comfortably furnished and had art displayed on the walls and tables. I felt quite at ease in my surroundings. As I watched myself in the dream, I saw myself get up from the table and walk around the room to look at things in more detail.

There was a huge window on the left side of the office that started from midway on the wall and reached towards the ceiling. A medium-sized, tan couch sat in front of it with a small, dark table on either end. Each of the tables had lamps and magazines lying on them. One table had an old-fashioned magnifying glass, and the other had a bronze of an old sailing ship sitting on it. Curious, I looked out of the window to see a bright blue sky with white, fluffy clouds. On another wall at the back of the room was a large window, not as big as the other one. In front of it was a big wooden desk and a dark leather chair that faced the room. A small bookshelf full of books sat directly under that window. When I made my way back to the conference table in the middle of the room, I noticed a book lying there with my name on it. I remember nothing after that.

When I woke up, I could remember some of the details that were discussed in the conversations from the dream, but they were quickly fading. By the time our class started at nine in the morning, those details were gone. All I could remember was that we talked about me and were planning things. The image of the room stayed with me; I knew it was a business meeting about my life. The dream was nothing exciting, but I had some recollection of it!

A few years later, I met a teacher named Lonna Bartly who taught how to access Akashic Records through meditation. I had heard about the records from other teachers and was interested in them, so I signed up. I didn't want to go alone, so I talked my two Reiki buddies into joining me to take the class.

During our first guided meditation by our teacher, we were introduced to the Akashic Records, which are held in a great library located on an Astral Plane. Our teacher talked us through visuals, asking us to astral project and find the rooms in the Akashic library that held our personal information. Our instructions were to look at our room and then come back so that we could share with the class. Once we started, the room fell silent. I knew that everyone was off in the library looking for their rooms. I was beginning to feel a little silly, sitting there as nothing was happening, when all of a sudden I felt myself project to find myself in the Akashic library, facing a tall door.

What was so surprising to me was that when I opened the door, I immediately recognized the room from my dream of several years before, when I took the class with the shaman practitioner. Nothing had changed. The furniture, windows, and even the layout of the room were all the same. I was shocked! Lying there on the conference table was the same book I saw before with my name on it. "Oh, I get it!" Then there was a knock on the door, and as I opened it, my father, who had passed away a year before, came in and greeted me. He acted like nothing had happened and sat down to talk. Astonished, I sat down with him. I was still a little confused when I heard another knock on the door. I got up to open it, and a friend who had died by suicide, followed by a rather tall angel, greeted me by my name and came in, making themselves at home. They all seemed to think this was perfectly normal, but I wondered what was going on. Somewhere in my confusion I heard the voice of my teacher calling us back into our bodies. I quickly said my goodbyes and followed the sound of her voice back to the room where I could see my body sitting on a chair.

When I was grounded again in my body back in the physical world, I could hardly contain myself. I had forgotten about the dream that I had when I was at the shaman's workshop. All I could remember was that the dream was about a conference and it was boring compared to others.

Later, when I asked my spirit guides why we don't remember all of our dreams,they explained that sometimes it is because we are with a Spiritual Council that meets with us in the Akashic Records. That is when they review and discuss with us about our lessons here on this earth.

Part III
Recognizing The Journey

"A journey is a person in itself; no two are alike. And all plans, safeguards, policies, and coercions are fruitless. We find after years of struggle that we do not take a trip; a trip takes us."

John Steinbeck

Chapter Seven: Embracing the Gift

Energy Follows Thought

The statement, "Energy follows thought," helped me understand a lot about mystical experiences. When I was first learning, I used to wonder, what did it all really mean? Was it the mind or a consciousness beyond the physical body that controlled where energy went?

I began to look at my own experiences of merging with my higher self when I shot out of my body when astral traveling. At the time, I never knew when I would have an out of body adventure. They happened spontaneously; I could be washing dishes, taking a bath, driving a car, singing, or shopping at the mall. I didn't eat anything different, deprive myself of sleep, chant, meditate, or take any drugs to make this happen. I do want to note that this occurrence is quite different from twilighting, vivid dreaming, or reading the Akashic Records.

In those moments astral traveling, I knew without question that everything is created out of tiny particles which vibrate with unconditional love of our Creator. I also knew that we and everything in the universe are all connected. Nothing in the universe is separated from each other or from anything that exists. I learned that once we are able to merge into the higher frequencies, separation between ourselves and God no longer exists. Everything in the entire universe vibrates as one expansive thought and is alive.

During one particular merge I knew I had the choice to expand, fully conscious, into unconditional love with the Creator. On the other hand, I could just be a part of it and stay on the sidelines of the whole experience, sampling it. The choice was all mine. I was completely conscious and in control of my decisions. I had full freedom of my own thoughts.

When I wanted to make the merge back into myself as an individual, I discovered that the physical body is on a much lower frequency. Sometimes this merge came as a choice or as a fear that plunged me back into my body without question. My senses that were highly acute during the whole occurrence would begin to tone down as I completed the merge. I had no feeling of light-headedness, only a knowing that I had been somewhere and sampled something amazing.

After each experience I discovered that something was different and soon began to take notice of a pattern. The events not only changed the way that I processed things, but some kind of physical transformation seemed to happen within the cells of my body. I say this because my body seemed different and responded differently. It was not anything drastic, but the bursitis in my hip was gone. Even the arthritis that was beginning to develop in my hands from knitting was gone. Now I could knit without pain, and I caught myself forgetting that I had it. Other things changed, like my thought patterns and the way I looked at things. I felt different inside and could go inside myself to assess what was going on. My physical brain also had full comprehension that I, or anything that existed, was ever separated from Source. My whole being rang with this knowledge. I understood without a doubt that this is not a question of faith but a full knowing, without a doubt, that God exists.

Later on I discovered, when I was with others, that I knew when someone was in their truth, speaking from their heart. In those cases, if they were in their integrity, I would feel my whole body resonate like a tuning fork. On the other side, I knew when someone was not in their truth. It was, and is, a very strange experience. Eventually the sensations would wear off through time as I integrated back into my own life and into my own habits. Then it would happen again.

The Essence Of Energy

I was taking a class on using tuning forks to work on the body when I started to understand how connected we are, even in the physical form. It's incredible. Everything we need is built within us. Sometime at the beginning of the first day of our Acutonics class while our teacher Pam Durham was lecturing, my spirit guide interceded to help me understand what I was learning. I heard very clearly that I should remember that the physical tools that I held in my hands were toys, because we had the ability to be co-creators linking with the thoughts of our Creator granting us the capacity to move or experience energy with our own bodies and our own minds. In other words, we have the capacity to heal without the physical tools. I caught myself raising my hand, interrupting the lecture, to report to the teacher what I had just heard.

Pam smiled, stopping mid-lecture, and allowed me to make this announcement to the class. Then she said that it was correct but to remember that most people in our physical world do not know or understand this, so it is important to have the physical tools to help with healing. She went on to explain, "Most illness comes from the energy fields outside the body and then after some time moves into the physical form. Once an illness is experienced in the physical body, it is important to help the client move through a process of healing, which may include using tools. If the client does not have the physical experience, the healing may not happen, as the client will continue to hold on to a block that stops the natural flow of energy in the body."

I finished the class that weekend, but somewhere in the back of my mind I mulled over what I had heard from my guide. A few months later, I got a phone call from my daughter Cameron, who was in college. She explained that she had had some soreness in her joints that was really severe. As it happened, she was at some event at the school when the pain came on, and she didn't have any access to medicine. She decided she could move the pain out of her body by using her thoughts. She told me that she worked through her body with her mind, cleaning out the places where she was hurting and releasing the pain out through her hands and feet. It was exciting to her that it worked!

After hanging up, I thought about Reiki, and how it worked just by channeling healing energy from Source through the hands. I then began to wonder about acupuncture points on the body. If we could do the same with the acupuncture points, using the thoughts instead of needles, how would that change the way we heal? I then saw something that you might describe like a daydream. In it, I saw someone lying on a table and could see the energy running through all of the person's meridians, or energy pathways. Energy was being channeled without the use of any physical tools, using pure thoughts and imaging from the mind. I could also see the body light up as it accepted the energy, accelerating the healing the process. It was incredible to see the human body becoming the tuning fork!

Objects Of Obession

If you are like me, you may have things in your home that you have collected over the years from different places. In some of those cases, you might have brought something home with you that you were unaware of. An attachment, such as a ghost, being, or an entity, may be connected to the item that you brought home with you. That happens more than we realize, as these beings are a lot like people in the physical world, and often they will become attached to objects, not wanting to release them. Of course, this can cause problems for the living.

We hear about haunted houses and people having attachments all the time. We forget that when we fall in love with an item, someone else may have fallen in love with it also. The object may have even attracted the attention of a being, or in some situations it may serve as an open portal. In any case, if you are experiencing supernatural phenomena, it doesn't hurt to check to see if there is an item that was brought into your home or business around the time the disturbance started to happen.

As it happened for me, an innocent day of shopping started a whole chain of events relating to this topic. It all started when a friend of my daughter's didn't have the extra money to buy a dress for prom. My daughter Cameron and I were driving by a yard sale one day in the late afternoon and caught sight of a sign advertising prom dresses. The dresses looked a lot like what we had seen in the stores, so we decided to stop and take a look. As it turned out, a few of the dresses were the same size as my daughter's friend. We decided to take a gamble, and we picked up a few, hoping she might like one.

Cameron took the dresses and hung them on the back of her door in her room for storage until we could take them to the cleaners and show them to her friend. What we didn't expect was that we had brought something home with us that was attached to the dresses. That night, Cameron had a bad night. Her spirit guide kept waking her up to let her know that there was something in the corner of her room that she needed to be aware of. She was on alert all night, and by the time morning came, she was exhausted.

Later in the morning, Cameron finally made her way into my bedroom to tell me about the strange experience that she had the night before. She shared that she was awakened by her spirit guide wanting to get her attention. Once she was awake, she had a strong sense that someone was staring at her with an intense hatred. She described a lizard-like being that stood upright like a human, giving me a very detailed description of its body and head.

Around this time I was helping with some classes in the evening during the week and had just heard about reptilians from a few people. Even after talking to these people, I was not entirely convinced of their true existence because I was in a place that I had to learn by my own experiences.

It wasn't until the day that Cameron told me what she saw in detail that I started to believe that reptilians might exist. I had not shared with her any of the conversations I had had with other people about them, so she couldn't have gotten that information from me. I pulled up a picture from the Internet of a reptilian, and she confirmed that was what she saw.

I called my teacher Paula and told her what had happened, giving her a description of what Cameron had seen. It wasn't even a question for my teacher of what we were dealing with. She came directly over to help clear the being and immediately discovered a portal that was open. She used the whole experience to teach me how to release the attachment and find the portal, which was attached to one of the dresses. Together we closed the portal and blessed the room. We also cleansed the dresses, making sure there were no other attachments. I was counting my blessings that she came; she was glad it turned out to be a teaching experience.

Portals can be opened many ways if the timing or situation is right. The one most people hear of is when people are messing around with magic or playing with Ouija boards and don't know what they are doing. When portals are opened, other beings can come into our world of existence. In this case it was not a ghost attachment but a being from somewhere else, who was very angry. One of the prom dresses was serving as a portal, which was still open when we brought it to our home. Once we were able to locate the portal, we were able to send the reptilian back through it and seal it so it couldn't be opened again.

After clearing and cleansing the dresses, I donated them to a church sale. I didn't want the reminder of the ordeal that had happened. I knew they were safe. My daughter's friend found a dress at a store somewhere else for a good price, and we were excited for her. We never shared with her what happened.

Teaching Reiki

I struggled for a long time with charging clients for Reiki, even after I got all my attunements. I felt that if something was given to you by Spirit, it was meant for all and therefore should be free to all. My Reiki Master Teacher Holli and I went over and over with this. I had a lot of issues around charging for something that belonged to everyone, even though I was happy to pay for the attunements myself. Reiki was something in my life that I really felt called to learn.

Holli explained to me that most people don't see value in a spiritual gift if they don't pay or trade something of equal value. I have to admit that I struggled with this idea for several more years. I had met people who could give some form of healing with their hands that resembled Reiki without any attunements. So my question was: Why was it important for people to have to pay to go through the attunements and learn how to give Reiki?

It wasn't until my spirit guide stepped in and gave me a lesson, that I learned why it was important to charge for such a beautiful gift. I was transported back to the very first day I had my attunement, and was shown how blocked I was at the time because of my conflicts of stepping into my spirituality. I again felt the pain, frustration, and anger because I couldn't find my connection with our Creator, even while I had melded myself in the church. I truly needed help in finding my joy and love for life again.

Then I was shown my heart. From the very beginning of my first class, there was no question of why I was there, as I felt called to learn Reiki. I could see and feel once again when my teacher Holli placed her hands on me. The whole process of the attunement allowed me to finally step aside. I got out of my own way and allowed the pathways in my body and spirit to open up letting the energy flow naturally through me again. I remembered the connection immediately and saw myself crying. What my teacher did for me was something that I couldn't do for myself because of where I was at the time. I needed help. Of course, I went back and took more classes and became a Reiki Master Teacher myself. I saw again that with each attunement, the energy and the connection got stronger. Attunements opened me up and allowed me to be able to let go of more and more of my own dense energy that kept me stuck.

Reiki is not a religion. Reiki is about learning how to let the life force that comes from the Source our Creator to clear out blockages that we put in place for whatever reasons in ourselves. The Reiki Master Teacher is a vessel; he or she allows the energy to flow through them to the student or client to help them heal by freeing blockages. Teachers do not put their own energy into the student or client. The energy that flows from the Reiki attunement is an interactive hands-on prayer that merges God's love and energy to flow through the teacher into the student.

When this happens, the student's physical body and energy bodies come back into balance, which brings the chakras into alignment so that they can spin, opening the energy pathways. Once they are opened up, they allow the body to heal, which leads to better health and connection. This in turn brings peace and harmony back into balance of the mind, body, and soul.

The other thing that was brought to my attention in this lesson from my spirit guides was that the attunement helps the practitioner to carry this gift in their energy field without any worries of not receiving the Reiki energy, as the teacher hands it down to the students directly. The practitioner, once attuned, can open the connection any time they want and allow it to flow as an energy prayer of healing. Also, I was shown why it was stronger when it was passed on from Master to student using the attunement. For those who did it naturally, it would enhance their energy flow, making it stronger when they were attuned.

As a teacher I was reminded of all the knowledge, preparation, time, and effort which goes along with teaching a class. After contemplating on all that I was shown, there was no doubt that it was okay to teach without feeling guilty in asking for payment.

India

In February of 2010, my husband and I were invited to go to India as guests of some dear friends who were getting married. My husband and I were both thrilled to be invited to the wedding. All we had to do was pay for our plane ticket and our friend's family would take care of the rest. I couldn't believe they would invite us in such a busy time of their lives and take care of us on top of that. They insisted that we come and not to worry, so we decided to go. We would be gone for two weeks, and we spent a good deal of our time prior to leaving fussing over our packing.

I remember going to our little library in my husband's office, looking for a book to take on the plane to read. As I was looking at all the books on the shelf, I heard very clearly to take a certain book which I had already read. "No," I thought to myself. I had already read that one and was working on Volume Two, which was already packed. There was no need for me to have to carry that on the plane and lug it through customs, having already read it, so I left it where it sat. As I scanned the titles, I found another book that caught my interest – a novel that would be fun to read and take my mind off the long flight.

We had a wonderful flight. Another one of our closest friends named Robin was also going with us on the trip, and we talked the whole time. When we got to India, we were welcomed with open arms and unbelievable hospitality. If you don't know very much about Indian weddings, in the very least, they are incredible. Our host and hostess who were our friend's parents treated us like we were family. It was beyond any of my wildest expectations. We felt like we belonged. People were so sweet, and we were even given our own private apartment.

What did surprise me, though, was that there were a few people who knew about me being able to see auras and being a Reiki Master Teacher. I was also at the time working with an Akashic teacher in the meditation form named Carla and was learning how to access the records. I had no thought, prior to the trip, that I would be approached by some of the wedding guests, who were dear friends of the bride, to talk to them about spiritual gifts. People seemed to be curious about me and what I was learning. I must admit that I was delighted to share with them and talk about healing. It came as a breath of fresh air for me, and I felt the freedom to talk about my own experiences.

What I was not prepared for was that a few wedding guests really wanted me to do some sessions with them in between the celebration ceremonies and parties, which lasted a week.

In the beginning of that year I had been learning how to work with clients, but I was still under the supervision of my teacher when it came to the Akashic records. I had been teaching Reiki for a while on my own, but the records were a whole different ballgame. When I was approached in India, I felt my fear that I was there without my books and without any of my teachers' supervision. I knew that someday I needed to feel confident in working with clients by myself. "Great," I remember thinking. "Permission from the heavens, but no one to turn to on the physical realm if I need help."

I ended up doing a few sessions and working with some of the guests. It was very gratifying for all of us. My spirit guides from the other side came in loud and clear. I soon discovered that I had no need for any books or my teachers' support, as it was all supported by the higher guidance. Trust is what I learned from the whole experience. Complete trust.

There was one young man who was asking questions, and I knew at the time he needed more information. As I looked at him, I heard laughing and then very clearly, "He is the one that the book on the shelf was for." I knew in that instant that the information in that book that I decided I didn't want was important for him to have. Oh, I felt very small. Then I realized that I had Volume Two in my possession as one of the two books I had taken with me for the trip. I spent a little more time catching him up on Volume One, giving examples from my own experiences. Then I gave him Volume Two. It would have been so much easier if I had just listened in the first place.

Later, on the flight home, as I snuggled up close to my husband, I knew that not only was I blessed with family and friends, but I also recognized that I had discovered how to trust my spirit guides. I learned that I was given the "thumbs up" by my spirit guides to teach on my own. Without a doubt, they would be there to support me anywhere, even as far away as India.

Psycho-pump - Tribute To A Friend

During our first week in India, I felt a great loss inside my heart, like I had lost someone who was very dear to me. I couldn't get away from the feeling. I talked to my kids and family, so I knew they were fine. I shooed the feeling away, not knowing what had happened, but I still felt a loss and emptiness inside myself. With all the events I just ignored it thinking I would find out sooner or later what was going on.

All in all, our whole trip was a wonderful experience. It never occurred to me that a few days later my joy would turn into grief. As I stepped off the plane from our trip to India, I didn't realize how really exhausted I was from the flight and layovers. My husband, who is an engineer, calculated that our trip home was about 27 hours including lines, flying, and delays, plus all the security checks and customs we waited for.

We returned on a Monday, and I began once again to feel this great loss and hole in my life. By Wednesday morning, I was hiding in my bathtub, sobbing as if my heart had pieces missing. I know from my teachers that when the body grieves, it is all right to allow the tears to flow and to feel the emotional pain that comes with the physical experience. Why was this happening? I felt so sad that someone had left me.

As I sat there in my tub crying, I went over all the things that we had done when we returned. I even called a friend whose husband was in the hospital, to find out how he was doing. He was fine and in good spirits. "This must be a part of the jet lag," I remember thinking to myself. I had called and emailed my friends and family to let them know that I was back. So many of the emails and phone calls were returned with happy greetings that we had returned safely. It didn't make sense that I was in a state of grief like someone died.

After a few days of resting, I went to visit everyone I could think of who live in the area. There was one person on my list that I really wanted to get in touch with. My Reiki buddy Caroline was not answering the phone. She was one of my closest friends that I ran around with, and I hadn't heard from her. That was not unusual as she didn't like phones, but when her emails bounced, I made a special trip to see her.

As I drove up to the house, I saw her van parked in the driveway. A wave of energy went through my brain with the thought, "It is like she is dead." Silence and stillness engulfed me as I got out of the car. Quickly I brushed it away. "What a terrible thought!" Why would something like that sweep through my mind? Then I caught myself uttering, "That is not true! Quit thinking like that!" I walked up and knocked on her door and waited for her to open with her warm greeting. No one came, so I thought, "Okay, she must be running around with a friend on an errand." All I could do was leave a note on the door to email or call me as soon as she could. I missed her!

Later that evening I got a phone call from her sister, letting me know that she had been in a coma for a few weeks and hadn't regained consciousness. She had passed away that day, and her sister just wanted me to know. As she spoke, a numbness took over my body as my brain tried desperately to process what I was hearing. Shock had taken over. I sat there not knowing what to do. The grief hit me in waves moving through my body, even though I knew that death was not the end. My physical body was going to go through the process with or without me involved, so instead of fighting it, I allowed myself to have the experience.

One of the things I remember after the call is that I could hear my friend's voice in my head laughing. Later that evening, as I climbed into bed, I felt like I couldn't stand it anymore. I decided I was going to find out where my friend was. I asked my husband not to let anything bother me while I did an astral projection into the other worlds. He agreed to keep my cat off of me and anything else that would disturb me. I laid down beside him and willed myself into an immediate trance, homing in on the vibration of her voice that I could hear in my head. My whole focus was poured into the intention of finding her, wherever she might be. I just had to know if she was Ok, and I wanted to say goodbye.

Quickly I shot out of my body and immediately found myself in a large living room with lots of furniture. I was doing a self-check to make sure I was all right when I noticed there were people walking around and sitting in chairs and sofas in the room as if they were at a cocktail party and were enjoying visiting. I scanned the room and rested my eyes on my friend sitting on a couch, drinking out of a large cup. I watched her with amusement as she placed it on the coffee table in front of her. She liked Dr. Pepper, and for as long as I can remember she was always drinking one. She was sitting alone looking somewhat out of place.

Happy to see my friend again, I made my way across the room and seated myself right next to her. Words came out of my mouth, expressing my grief of missing her. I told her, "I cannot see you," meaning in the physical world.

She replied, "I am here."

I then said, "I could not find you when I returned."

She said again, "I am here."

Once again, I said, "I could not see you."

She said again, "I am here."

As we talked, people were chatting and moving around the room. Someone noticed me and politely offered some food from a tray they were carrying. This confused me, as I was very aware I was in the spirit world and I didn't think you could eat on that side. Then I remembered from my training that before a person makes the crossing, that person still continues the motions of old habits like eating until he or she realizes that food is no longer necessary. So it makes the sensation of eating like eating in a dream.

While I was processing this information, I was suddenly ejected out of that world back into my body. I felt myself coming into the full realization that I was beginning to wake up in the physical plane. As I came back into full consciousness in my body, I realized that my husband was sitting next to me working on his computer not paying any attention to the cat that had pounced on my solar plexus. Immediately I told him, "I found her and I am going back to talk to her! Guard my body and don't let anything disturb it while I'm gone!" Once again, I closed my eyes and homed in on her voice. A memory of the room flashed in my mind and that was all I needed to eject myself out of my physical form. I made my way back in seconds and found myself sitting next to her on the couch as though I had never left.

While we sat there for a moment, I was able to regain my bearings. I noticed that some people were leaving the room through a doorway. Whenever anyone opened the door, an amazing bright golden light came through the room, lighting up it up. There was this deep feeling of compassion and unconditional love that vibrated through the light, as though it was talking to me. It was magnetic, making it hard to ignore. Then I wondered why my friend hadn't moved when the door was opening. I finally asked her if she was going into the light. She looked at me as if she was a little confused and asked me, "Are you going?" I had a brief thought about it, but a gentle voice somewhere in the room told me I was not to go into the light. I told her that the light was not for me but assured her that I would go someday when it was my time. Another group of people got up to leave the room. I took my friend's hands and helped her off the couch. I said goodbye and let her know that I would see her soon.

This is where the experience seemed to get a little strange. After I watched her enter into the light, I astral projected from where I was into the dream world. This was a lot different from the world I was in with my friend. During this experience, I was still aware that I was no longer in the same plane of existence as where I had been. It was that clear. I could even tell the difference between the dream world which we go to in our dreams at night and this world of transition. In my dream, I found myself trapped. I ended up having to go through the motions of the dream to get back to the physical world. It was like a play with a written script that had to be followed. I finally woke up at 3 a.m., when I was able to break free and be fully planted back inside my body.

As I recounted my journey into the other world to my Reiki friends, one of them asked, "How did you know you were not dreaming?" It was a good question. I answered that I was conscious in both dimensions like I am conscious in the physical world. The big difference is that in the transitional world I can think, reason, and interact with the environment. The whole experience is much like our life here in the physical plane of existence, with only a few differences, for instance the food. In the dream world, even though I had the ability to think and reason, the dream seemed to have a full expectation of what it would play out to be. It was kind of like being caught in a recording. My experience with this particular dream was that it was like being stuck in one of my favorite sitcoms on television where I had lines and a role to play.

It was very obvious that I had become caught up in something quite different in the dream world, as opposed to the experience I had when I was out of my body in the transitional world, talking to my friend. It might help to think of the difference between sitting in a hot tub and sitting in a bathtub. They are the same kind of experience but unique and different, each in their own way.

After the experience I discovered that the grief still had to process through my physical body. It didn't instantly go away. It lingered for a full week. It was not as strong as it had been those first few days, but even so I could still feel the emotions of loss move through me as I missed my friend. Once I was able to physically process the grief, I could feel myself move back together, leaving the emotions of feeling left behind. Soon I found that I was able to live again with peace while still sending love to my friend where she is now.

Weeks later I began to realize that my body had picked up the fact that my friend Caroline was in transition of leaving this world. Even though my brain was not aware of this, my physical form was fully aware. I was already in the mourning stage when I was in India, but I didn't know or comprehend it. I also realized that the day that I went to her home, part of me already knew she was leaving, as the thought had passed through my head. Still I had pushed my thoughts and feelings aside, thinking I was just being dramatic or imagining things. Yet, here again was another example that we can pick up energy and can read between the spaces. I learned again that our bodies are connected to our souls and all the energy fields around us.

Akashic Records

I would like to step back a little to talk about how the communication opened up for me to converse back and forth with the spirit guides and record keepers. It was the summer of 2010 when I found myself restless. I couldn't find anything that I could do to satisfy myself. I could feel deep down within my own core that I needed to do something.

One of the things that I could latch on to that summer to help ease my restlessness was a passion to write an adult children's book about energy and Source, as the story had been given to me in my past experience and visions. I spent most of the summer writing. The illustrations in my head would not leave until they were down on paper. I became excited as the words came to my mind almost automatically when I placed my hand on the pen. I became a little obsessed with the project. I didn't want to do anything else.

After the book was completed, I had this overwhelming feeling that took over me like a hunger craving which I couldn't satisfy. It had nothing to do with food. It was a feeling that I had to experience something in my life, and I was not doing it. I didn't know exactly how to pinpoint it or find what I wanted to do.

This desire pushed me out of my nest. I went to find an end to the gnawing at my soul and to bring some relief from this craving. As I spread out my search, questioning what was really going on, I soon discovered that I had a strong desire to communicate with the angels and guides who I knew were around me on a more auditory level. There had always been some communication with them, but often I was blocked. I wanted to have full communication with them, like having a conversation with someone in the physical world. I wanted to hear their voices when I asked a question instead of only getting bits and pieces of hearing things. I knew deep down that full communication was possible. Somewhere along my life journey I had blocked out my hearing. Now I felt very strongly it was time for me to open up the communication with them on a whole different level.

Later in the summer, I was in my Qigong class, and someone said that they knew a teacher named Jodi Lovoi who taught an Akashic Records class. I was unimpressed; I had already taken a meditation class to access the records with another teacher. I had become somewhat frustrated as everything was in pictures or symbols when I tried to access information. As I listened about the way this teacher taught, I decided I might try to contact her and see if I connected.

I called Jodi the next day, leaving a message. She soon called me back while I was waiting for a movie to start. I went outside to the lobby to take the call thinking that I was wasting my time; however there was an energy in her voice that gave me pause. As I listened to her speak about the class, I knew by the tones in her voice that she was meant to be my teacher. I signed up.

Driving to Jodi's class a few weeks later, I had a lot of fears that I would not be able to connect and it wouldn't help me in my own journey of remembering. I moved past the fears and was happy when I arrived at her door with other students. I was surprised at how comfortable I felt in the class. I discovered that the little prayer that we used helped me move past the blocks that I had put up. The prayer seemed to give me permission to hear the spirit guides and other angels. My guides and record keepers came in so clearly that I could hear all of them as if they were in stereo. It was amazing! I quickly signed up for the next class, wondering what else I could learn.

In Jodi's second class, I watched her do a soul retrieval in the records, which was astonishing. I couldn't help noticing the heavy amount of grief and suffering that surrounded the woman who had volunteered that day for the demonstration. Before we got started, the energy that hung in the air was so thick I almost couldn't breathe. I tried to calm my own emotions as she reminded us to use one of the techniques that she taught us to protect ourselves. She then opened the woman's records, moving on to demonstrate the techniques, as she walked the woman through a soul retrieval.

The woman was not hypnotized. She was fully aware of the process in the records. What was powerful was seeing her suddenly grasp the concept, as it dawned on her that the only one holding her back was herself. There, somewhere in her own records, she stepped into her personal power and gave herself permission to let go. Once she did this, she was able to follow our teacher, with the help of the record keepers, who led her through a process to work through her own fears of release. The whole demonstration was amazing to watch and be a part of, as it unfolded in front of us.

When it was over, the woman said, "I was in counseling for ten years and could never seem to release the pain that was stuck in those old wounds." She told us that for the first time she could understand why she had had those past experiences in this lifetime, which helped her to move on, so that she could heal by letting go.

The Akashic Records are a wonderful tool to learn. They can be complementary to other healing modalities. The lessons that I have learned while working in the records have been extremely valuable. In the beginning I found that the biggest part of learning how to use them was trusting the guidance of the record keepers so that I could maneuver around in the records.

I did go back later on to examine if the restlessness and craving for something was still there. To my own surprise, it had left. I knew then I was where I was supposed to be. I went on to take other classes and learned how to read other people's records in the Akashic Records.

The Toolbox

When I hear the term "toolbox," I always envision a doctor's black bag that carries all of his tools and medicines when making house calls. When I use the term in a spiritual context, I am referring to the toolbox or medicine bag that is unique to each individual energy and spiritual practitioner. Their toolboxes help them to practice different healing methods and modalities. They also include their knowledge and expertise on how they work with the astral or physical tools that they choose to use with their clients.

An example of an astral tool would be Reiki. As you already know, people are attuned to it, and Reiki energy just comes naturally out of the Reiki practitioner's hands whenever it is needed. Some practitioners use other things to enhance the experience, such as crystals or oils. Intuitive healing, clairvoyance, channeling, Akashic records, or recognizing energy patterns are most often in the astral form, but there are physical tools that complement these modalities also, when needed. Just remember that you may encounter someone using physical tools with an astral modality to enhance the experience, but whether to use those tools is up to each practitioner.

Some of the physical tools that you might come into contact with are: singing bowls, tuning forks, needles, drums, and rattles, just to name a few. They may be used in clinic settings or private practices. There are a lot more tools out there than can be listed, but I will stop there. The important thing to note is whether the practitioner is comfortable working with the tools that they use. They should be knowledgeable about them.

Some teachers and practitioners will only use one healing method or one type of tool. Then there are others that have many different kinds of healing modalities and use a variety of tools. Just know: As long as the client is comfortable with the healing method, it can be a match for both the client and the practitioner.

In the past I was taught that the only tool that was ever needed was built within us, meaning that we don't have to look outside of ourselves to find tools to help us in our healing. My own spirit guides have said that the physical tools can be labeled as toys. I used to argue this reasoning with one of my Acutonics friends. My friend always told me that most people are not ready to only work in the astral realms but need to have something physical to know that they are being helped. Personally, I enjoy working with the physical tools when I want to add to the healing experience, but I do realize that healing starts on a different plane before it reaches the physical. My point is not to judge. Remember that energy is energy.

Singing bowls are amazing. They can tune into the right sound, resonating to help bring the physical body energy back into balance. The same goes for the tuning forks. Remember that the physical body is also a form of vibrational movement. The same goes for the tuning forks. That is why it feels good to hear and to feel that physical vibration on the body as it moves the energy. Another way of working with these frequencies is to tune into the astral planes, bringing the vibration back to the physical plane by using vocal tones, intention, or the laying of hands on someone. It all works the same way. However, a tool's effectiveness will depend on the client.

One of my clients was very insistent on seeing or feeling something on the physical realm; otherwise she didn't believe that it was working. A couple of times I tried to use the same process without physical tools, but she was afraid that she wasn't getting the same benefit without them. Her fears kept her from giving herself permission to heal. Because of this belief, we ran into energy blocks.

I had another client who could move through the same process without using any tools. In her case, she could be anywhere doing anything and would call me up on the phone to work on her. She achieved the same benefit of healing in a few minutes that the other client had using the physical tools. She was also perfectly capable of doing this process herself, but she wanted the guidance and reassurance. In the end, both clients were able to experience the same exact healing process. The shift to healing in their bodies depended on their belief in the actual method.

Toolboxes are wonderful, and the knowledge that goes with them is unique to each practitioner. I always enjoy speaking to other practitioners about their different tools. Some are happy to share, and others like to keep that private. In essence the toolbox is the energetic working relationship that the practitioner has with his or her own spiritual gifts, on the physical or astral level.

Communicating With The Other Side

Someone asked me what it is like when I hear the other side speak. I told them that sometimes I get a full knowing of things or I hear a voice in my mind that is different from my own chatter or thoughts. Angels, record keepers, spirits and guides communicate on a whole other level, using telepathy, energy, impressions, and more. Ghosts can imprint their memories into your mind that can become as real as if you had the experience yourself.

In most cases, I can feel the spirit guides and ghosts around me if I can't see them. Often, when I hear more than one voice speak, I feel a shift of energy in my energetic field as they step up one by one to talk, like speakers at a podium waiting for their turn to use the microphone. There is always a deep respect for me and a respect for the others who come to speak. The spirit guides come in when there is a teaching or if I ask them about something. I find that I am only told things for the highest good. If something is not for me to know, I will only hear silence.

Another way that the other side communicates is by visions. Sometimes I will see in my mind something like a daydream. Other times it is like the physical world changes and I am actually there watching and participating in an event. A good example of this was when I was having a talk with someone about an incident that had happened a week before in the room that we were sitting in. My spirit guides were with me, and as the person I was interviewing was telling me what their part was, all of a sudden the whole room changed, and I was transported into the time when the incident took place. I found myself sitting there with the people who participated as I watched the events unfold all around me. The person I was talking to did not seem to realize that I was in both realities at the same time, but my focus was on the other side. The energy in the room had been imprinted into my mind's eye, and what I experienced was like replaying a 3D movie. What I witnessed and heard in the room during the time of the incident didn't match at all to what I was being told. When I came back into the physical reality I thanked the person and left knowing that he had not been truthful.

Sometimes I get a craving deep within me for knowledge about something. This leads me down a path to try to learn about whatever I have to know, until I feel satisfied. If I ignore it, then it only gets stronger until I begin my search. For example, when I was learning about particle waves, for about a week that is all I thought about, and yet had no idea what they were. Any books or television programs that week that I touched or just randomly picked up somehow had something to do with particle waves. Articles jumped off of pages, capturing my attention. I met people all week who talked about particle waves. My whole inner radar seemed focused on learning about them. Then one day I didn't want to hear about or have anything to do with them anymore. I was done, and all the information about particle waves stopped making itself known.

When I get a feeling like the gut feeling or a sensation in my body, I acknowledge it and ask my spirit guides what that is all about. Most often I will get a clear verbal explanation or see a daydream of what it is in my mind's eye. The trick here is to recognize when something is going on in the body and ask about it. This could be getting a feeling in a specific chakra, part of the brain, or even an organ in the physical body. For example, for several years my arms used to let me know when something was amiss. I always got a sticky sensation that ran up and down them. Then, when someone was being openly honest, they would tingle. The thing to know is that each individual's body picks up subtle energies differently.

Another thing that happens is that I get information out of the blue, like a full-knowing. Other times, I am in a class-like situation in my dreams where things are explained. Sometimes I buy a book or read something and find that what I had learned from the astral lecture was reinforced by someone writing a book about it. I asked one time why I needed to have the books, and I received the answer that it is important to see what I learn in another form so that I fully acknowledge it.

Since the other side doesn't recognize time the same way we do, I have had to ask for some of the teachings to be moved to when I am not in the middle of something. Once I was having a full vision and download right in the middle of the movie Spiderman at the movie theater with my family. I was enjoying the time with my family, and it wasn't the time for me to give the spirit guides my full attention. It was, however, the time that the they chose to teach me. In that case, I learned that all I had to do was to just ask the spirit guides to not do teachings when I am having family time, or at the movies. They honor this still.

Communication with spirit guides varies from person to person. Something very important to watch for is being told what to do or being bossed around by beings from the other side. If this is happening, revisit who is guiding you and who you are getting your information from. This is a huge red flag that you are not communicating with your personal spirit guide for your highest good. Your true guidance will only have the utmost respect for you and keep your boundaries sacred.

I had a friend who was just learning how to hear and was getting a lot of information at one time. But the ones that were claiming to be her spirit guides were telling her what to do. There was no respect for her boundaries or personal will. This is a sure sign of a disembodied being with an ego of power and control. In that case, tell them to go away or send them on to the light.

I can't stress enough, as a word of caution in communicating with the other side, how important it is to know who you are really talking to. Since there is a high level of trust, you have to be able to know how to find the spirit guides that were assigned to you and not the impostors who need an ego fix by communicating with you on this side. There are guidelines and teachers who can lead you through a safe process of learning how to develop a relationship with those who are there to guide you in this lifetime. You desire help, not hurt, for yourself or others.

Water Under The House

One day I was talking to one of my spirit guides and made the comment that I had always wanted to live on water. This made my guide start to pace up and down the room throwing his hands up while shaking his head. I thought it was almost funny; I wasn't sure why it had made my spirit guide react this way. I heard him saying, while pacing, that he didn't understand. Then he made the comment, "You said you wanted to live on water, and you live on water!"

I was not sure why my spirit guide was saying that I lived on water, since I didn't even own a swimming pool and there was no water around that I could see where we lived. Suddenly, I got a flash of the street signs around our neighborhood. They all ended in "Springs." Hmmm... I remembered that I knew there was also a creek across the field behind our home. "Wait a minute!" I thought. We do live on water, but it is under the house in a natural spring. "No," I said to my spirit guide, "I didn't mean I wanted to live on water. I wanted to see the water from my window! I meant that I wanted to live by the water."

My spirit guide immediately stopped pacing and looked at me and said, "Then why didn't you say so!" That started me laughing, as I understood how easily things can get confused. My Akashic teacher always said to make sure I am clear when I ask questions and not to be afraid to ask the questions in more than one way.

The Crystal Ball

A few years ago I was watching a program on the History Channel about Nostradamus. They were talking about how he used water to see some of his predictions. I started to wonder about crystal balls and how they worked, since I didn't have any experience with them. I had only seen them on Saturday morning cartoons, so I thought that I might see what it was all about. I went to a rock shop and was surprised at how expensive a crystal ball was. On my budget, I could only afford a ball that was about an inch-and-a-half in diameter. So I purchased one. I took my prize home and placed it on my desk, wondering what on earth to do with it.

For days I walked by the ball, wondering about it. Then I remembered a television sitcom where all you had to do was gaze into it. I guessed that was when you were supposed to see something. Finally I got the nerve to sit down and stare into my ball, having no idea what was really going to happen.

What I saw was kind of strange. I saw the reflection of three people standing behind my chair leaning over my shoulder and looking into the ball with me. Surprised, I immediately shot my head up and looked around the room for the three people, but I didn't see anyone. Thinking that I was seeing things, I looked back into the ball and saw the same three people. Again I shot my head up, looked behind me, and saw nothing. I knew ghosts were in the room, but they were not showing themselves. In a loud voice, I told whoever was looking into the ball to please step outside the room. Then I was aware of the energy shift, so I knew they had gone. Taking my time, I gazed back into the ball, only to see the reflection of three ghosts standing outside my doorway, leaning into the room, trying to get a look at what I was seeing in the ball. "This is silly," I thought. I picked up the ball and placed it back on a shelf, where it sits today, collecting dust.

Out Of Body Flight

When I was in my early thirties, I realized that something strange used to happen to me when I drove out to see my grandmother. I had travelled the road at least a thousand times, but every once in a while, I got disoriented. The feeling of panic would spread across my body, making me feel as though I was lost.

The road, that I had made the journey on over and over a few times a week, would change. The landmarks wouldn't look the same, and I would have to pull over with my two children in the back seat and try to gather my thoughts so I could figure out where I was. Once I got myself together, the road and the landmarks would begin to change again, and I would know where I was.

After a few episodes of this, I started to get worried that I might have some kind of brain tumor or my blood sugars were off, making me see things. All tests were fine, and I continued to have the same thing happen randomly as I went to visit my grandparents. Finally, I decided to really focus as I drove. I discovered that somewhere in the drive between my house in Arlington and their house in Fort Worth – a twenty-minute trip – I would leave my body. This didn't happen all the time, but it occurred enough for me to catch myself.

I learned quickly that my thoughts would trigger me, and I would astral travel to other places in the world in a blink of an eye. I explored different roads, saw different landmarks, and came back somewhere between our two houses. As I became aware of what was happening, I soon discovered that I was bringing back the full experience as I merged into my body. The information from these experiences was so strong that it told my brain that I was not where I really was. And thus, when I came back, I wouldn't recognize my own surroundings that were familiar to me. I believed I was somewhere else.

I quickly learned that I could control my thoughts and keep myself grounded in my body during the drive so I didn't freak myself out as much. I was safe driving, as I was in alpha-mode driving, on automatic pilot with all the responses, but the memories were being altered. By understanding how this worked, I learned that if I went into the past or into the possibility of a future event, I could bring back either a negative or positive energy thought form which would alter my body chemistry. This turned out to be very useful as I began to learn more about how the astral planes work.

Chapter Eight: The Courage to Move On

The Clinic

The very first time I set foot in the acupuncture clinic was after I met my friend Robin in Fort Worth for lunch. The sun was shining and we had finished our meal, so we decided to walk down the beautiful, old Magnolia Avenue to see what was going on. I was enchanted with all the different kinds of businesses and thrilled to see what people were doing on this side of town.

As Robin and I walked down the street, we saw the acupuncture clinic. Wondering what it was all about, we decided to stop in and take a look around. We were greeted by Pam Durham, the owner, who took us on a little tour of the place and told us that she also ran the clinic. I didn't know then that I was going to become very close to her and eventually would be working with her, doing energy work.

I knew I was drawn to her, feeling thirsty for the company of another with the working knowledge of energy healing. I was delighted to find that I could speak in the healing language of energy with her without fear. To be able to have an intelligent conversation about our spiritual journeys was refreshing. At the time I still had not met a lot of people outside of my little circle of friends and teachers who understood the vocabulary and language. Robin and I took some brochures and promised to keep in touch. I followed up a few weeks later and asked if she was interested in renting out a room to me to practice Reiki and to teach a few classes. She seemed happy that I asked, and soon I was doing contract work at the clinic. Later, when I had learned how to read the Akashic records, I started to do readings there with clients. I was so excited about the energy at the clinic that I wanted to hold my circle meetings there. It soon proved to be a lovely arrangement, and we began a fast and steady friendship right after.

We worked closely in our energy work for a few years. What I learned from the whole experience is that we grow at a faster rate when we are immersed in working with healing energy every day.

The time did come when my path was leading me towards another direction, and I had to say goodbye to Pam and move on. Looking back, I am truly grateful for all the wonderful experiences and the amazing people that came in and out of the clinic.

Tuning Forks & Acupuncture

I had always wanted to know more about tuning forks, and right after I started working at the clinic, I got to see what they really could do. I had the chance to witness how they were used, as my new friend Pam, the acupuncturist, used them on her clients at her clinic. It was fascinating. By combining the vibrations from the tuning forks with the energy points on the body used in acupuncture, a tuning fork has a tremendous result in helping the body to heal.

One day I got to experience this first hand. It all started when I got up one morning and my throat was swollen. I don't have any tonsils; however I became concerned when my throat felt like it was about to close up. Still sleepy from the night, I decided to take some allergy medicine, but as soon as I took it, I started to become very drowsy. All my thoughts clouded over.

I got back into bed, deciding to take a little nap before going over to the clinic to see clients that afternoon. All I could do was lie there and watch the room spin. I ended up being knocked out all morning and waking up just before noon, an hour before I needed to be at the clinic. I was still very drowsy, and my throat was even more swollen. I couldn't swallow. I called Pam to let her know I wasn't going to make it. She did an energy check on me over the phone and asked me what I took. I told her and said that I was having some kind of reaction to the medicine. She asked why I took the medicine instead of doing energy work. I told her I was tired and wanted a quick fix to get on with my day. Instead I only made it worse, and now all I wanted to do was to go back to sleep. Pam then asked if I could get myself to the clinic somehow so she could work on me. I told her I just wanted to go to bed, but she was insistent. I finally agreed, too tired to argue. By the time I reached the clinic, I was miserable, not to mention exhausted. Mucus clogged up all the passages in my head and went down into my lungs, making it hard to breath.

I wasn't very coherent, but I was grateful that the secretary had cleared my schedule. I crawled up on the table in one of the rooms. I curled up into a ball, just wanting to be left alone in my misery. Pam got out her tuning forks and had me lie on my back. That was a feat all in itself. She began to work on me, hitting the forks with her striker and placing them on the different acupuncture points on my body. The whole session took less than ten minutes. When Pam finished, she announced she was done and told me to stay on the table to rest. She assured me I was safe, then stepped out of the room. I lay there wishing I was home in my own bed, feeling sorry for myself for a few minutes, when I noticed I could breathe out of my nose again. As I lay there in wonder about my nose opening up, I realized that my throat had stopped hurting. I swallowed and started to feel it opening up. Within five minutes, my thoughts were much clearer. I continued to lie there on the table in wonder, when I discovered I wasn't drowsy anymore.

It was like magic. I started to feel like myself again. I sat up on the table, taking it easy in case dizziness hit me again, but it never did. It was amazing! In ten minutes I was ready for the day. I'd been watching her work on people who exclaimed how the tuning forks had helped them. At the time I knew something was going on, but now I was a true believer. Since my schedule was cleared, I went to lunch with Pam and another friend. Later, I went home and enjoyed the rest of my day.

I signed up soon after that to take a tuning fork class from Pam. On the second morning of the class at four a.m., I woke up with this humming in my ears that wouldn't go away. This had happened before and often went away on its own, so I was not too worried, but it kept me up most of the night. I learned later that a lot of my friends also have heard this humming noise.

During the class I complained of being tired. As I told my story to the class about the night, others chimed in that they, too, had heard humming that kept them awake as well. I was not the only one. Pam, our teacher, asked us if it sounded "like this," as she struck the chimes and forks, which were calibrated to the planets. We went through a series of sounds until one particular fork was hit, and in unison, the class said, "Yes, that one."

Our teacher then said, "That one makes the same sound as the vibration of the planet Venus." While she was speaking, it dawned on me that I had watched a program on the Mayan calendar on television a few days before. It talked about how the Mayans used the planet Venus to make all their astrological charts because it was the planet that they could see the best. This resonated with me because we were fast approaching 2012. Pam reminded us that the energy that had recently come upon our planet Earth was the heart energy that is ruled by Venus. This energy raised the vibrations of the earth at this time to the next dimension. It is all about connection and clearing the energy of the heart Chakra.

It wasn't until I was driving back home after class that I got a flash... It was the planet Venus, Mayan, heart attacks, strokes, and lots of clearing relationships that need to be let go of. Anything that is related to this type of energy that is stuck in the heart chakra is going to be moving out whether we are ready or not as Venus moves closer to the Earth.

This is also the time that we would be reminded that any stuck negative energy can manifest in the body as an illness. This energy was driving people to clear out old patterns that were no longer useful in this lifetime. By doing this, they can move on to a higher consciousness that will bring about growth on a spiritual level.

Resistance to this energy can cause not only major illness but also death. This means that we are all clearing out our closets to move on to acclimating to the next level of energy consciousness that is penetrating the earth and moving everything to the next dimension.

What was 2012 all about? It was about learning how to let go of the negative things in our lives that hold us captive and how to bring in more positive things in our lives for that growth to occur. Think about it: When we make the change, we open up to a life that opens our hearts to unconditional love. This is very powerful; it is the unconditional love that is the building blocks of all and everything.

Pearls Of Wisdom

One of the things my spirit guides have shown me about relationships is how we relate to each other on a vibrational level. Everything in the universe vibrates, and so do we. We all find others that we resonate with, and we move away from those whom we don't, unconnected.

When two people start out in a relationship, they start out on the same vibrational frequency, which is why they are attracted to each other. Once the relationship starts, things change on many levels. If the people in that relationship are in agreement and can work things out with all the changes, their lives will continue in harmony. In most cases, since we are all unique, learning our lessons in life at different levels, one person may end up growing, and the other may end up getting stuck. This case affects the balance of that relationship, whether it is a love, friendship, work, or other type.

What I am saying to you is nothing new. You see this all the time. The part you want to be aware of is knowing when to make the compromises to continue, or deciding when the whole relationship needs to be terminated for the good of all.

When someone changes to a higher vibrational level, you will notice it in the person's energy fields as they begin to make changes in their lives. The person will start to learn, grow, and prosper at a much quicker rate than before. When this happens, doors open and new opportunities come up as things start to shift in a different direction. Watching a person blossom can be exciting as they make new friends, change jobs, and find new relationships that are more suited to that individual's life style.

The person who is stuck is caught in the same vibrational frequency field that they started out with, and they continue attracting the same type of relationships and experiences that vibrate on that frequency. For example, a person who goes out with the same type of person over and over again is stuck on the same level as the people they are attracting in their lives.

In a relationship, if one individual is growing and the other is stuck, it causes a wedge between the two as life lessons are achieved and mastered. It doesn't mean that someone is less than someone else. We are here on this earth to learn, not to judge. We all learn at different times and change our frequencies depending on our own life lessons. While this is true, some people have a hard time being around people who are not on the same vibrational level. They may seem to be a bit uncomfortable or out of place when they are with people who are on a lower or higher level of frequency from where they are.

I do want to point out that just because a personal relationship doesn't work does not mean that those people will no longer continue to be in the others' lives. Each relationship is different. In some cases, the one who is stuck may catch up or even pass the other. There is still the chance that one will digress to a lower vibrational field and then will have to relearn the same lessons again until mastered.

In any case, we do find where we are all supposed to be, and as long as we don't judge or compare ourselves, we can concentrate on the life lesson ahead. One thing is for sure: We are multi-dimensional beings, as we always have one foot in the physical world and the other in the spiritual world. We have the best of both worlds. What an amazing experience we all get to enjoy as we learn from our own actions and from one another.

Judgment

Judgment. How many times do we run into this, not only with others but within ourselves? Judgment can be something that we become aware of when our lives become unbalanced. Often it will come with a fear that we are carrying inside. (If there is only love in our hearts, there is no room for what we fear.)

Sometimes we think that others are very judgmental; however if you really get down to the nitty-gritty of listening to your own inner being, you will find that judgment of self is strong. As I have this amazing opportunity in my own life to interact and visit with people, I am able to reflect on what is going on within myself. I find that we as human beings beat ourselves up for not being perfect. If it is not about perfection, then there is always something else we can find fault with. We hurt ourselves for: not being smart, our weight, our appearance, power, money, age, relationships, jobs, sex, control. The list goes on. And we judge others by our own standards, which we can't attain in our own lives.

The first step in healing our emotions inside is to be aware of what is going on. Find the fear, the prejudice, or the lie that we accept as truth. There, in that awareness, we can free ourselves from our own inner bondage and grant mercy to ourselves and others, allowing ourselves to live in the grace.

Lyndon B. Johnson once said, "Peace is a journey of a thousand miles, and it must be taken one step at a time." It is a long path that we will walk. Think of the freedom you will have in your soul when you get to the end.

Healing & Clearing

My spirit guides explained healing and clearing to me in very simple terms one day while I was on my way to visit a friend. It seemed to make a lot of sense. Take for example a refrigerator. Most people have one, and it is important to keep adding fresh food to it for us to eat in our day-to-day lives. But it is equally important to make sure we clear out and clean the refrigerator so that we are not growing "science projects," as my children put it.

That same process is a lot like the energy in our energy fields. We are constantly being bombarded by other people's fields, along with radio, television, and other kinds of waves. There are things that are happening around us in the universe that affect us, not to mention our own energy and emotions that no longer serve us. As we clean out our fields, we may notice that we need to let go of old attachments or patterns that cause us to be stuck in the same lesson over and over again. It is important to be aware of all that we are holding on to that needs to be let go of, like the "science projects" in our refrigerators that no longer will be good for us.

The optimal choice is to learn how to do this for yourself so you can do your own self-maintenance. If you get stuck or need help clearing, it is important to ask for help from someone who knows how to do this type of energy work. By doing work on clearing your own energy, you can move into higher states of healing and connection. It is only when we have the power to release the old energy patterns that we free ourselves from being held down.

Spirit Guides and Spirit Animals

I am still amazed when I check in and I hear my spirit guides. Most of the time I ask them for help or state my intention before I work on something when I need their assistance. Other times they come in with lessons when I am still or teach me in my dreams while I sleep. On a few occasions they have come for me to do some work when I am doing Reiki, but is always my choice to go with them.

On one occasion, my friend Jan asked me to do Reiki on her back pains. I was happy to help and invited her over to the house to lie on my Reiki table. As we were getting close to finishing the session, I noticed my animal helper sitting a few feet away on the other side of the table. She was swinging her tail back and forth patiently, waiting for me to acknowledge her. Smiling at her, I asked her why she was there. She responded with a look that looked right through me into my soul. I knew in that moment she was asking me to go with her. "Yes," I said. "Yes, I will go with you!" I thought.

In a flash, I shot out of my body and landed in a place that looked like an old building. My spirit animal was right there by my side, taking me through a doorway that led into a room. The room had gray walls with only an old church pew sitting off to the back of it. On the pew I saw my friend, hunched over crying as an overwhelming feeling of fear emanated from her energy field. I was grateful that my spirit animal had brought me to this long-forgotten place where a piece of Jan's soul was stuck. I knew when I saw her that our job was to take this soul piece and reunite it with her on the physical plane. I sat down and started to explain what we were going to do, asking her to come back with us. She agreed and stood up to go.

I thought that was it, but then my spirit animal took us both to another place that was quite different from where we were before. Now we were on a planet with nothing on it except a tree with roots that were visible on the top of the ground. There we found another soul piece of my friend crouched under the tree. Once again I found myself explaining what my intentions were, and when that soul part agreed to go with us, we were whisked away to another place.

This time Jan's lost soul fragment was stuck on a path of rocks leading across a stream. Fear of falling overwhelmed me as I felt the energy from her move across the water. I could see that she was too afraid to move. Quickly I began to convince the lost soul part to go with us, so that we could bring all three parts of her back. Finally, with coaxing from the other two soul fragments, she agreed to cross the stream with the help of the animal helper. She climbed on the back of my spirit animal, and they crossed without incident. Then we were off. We all shot back into this three-dimensional plane of existence and landed inside of my heart chakra's energy field.

I stood there holding the pieces but had forgotten what to do with them. I heard very clearly to ask Jan if she wanted the pieces back. I explained to my friend that I had just gone on a shamanic journey with my animal helper while we were doing Reiki and had retrieved three fragments of her soul. These pieces had detached sometime during some trauma she had suffered in this lifetime. I asked if she wanted them back. "Of course," Jan said. I knew then to blow them into her heart chakra. In that instant she started to cry, and I could feel her body relax with relief as we talked about the journey. Jan went on to share the different times in her life when trauma had happened to her that she remembered leaving her body feeling as though something had disconnected. Then she hugged me and thanked me, happy to have those other parts of herself back. I was truly grateful to my spirit animal for knowing that she needed these pieces back.

When working with the spirit guides and spirit animal, often you might feel their presence or see them when they step into your aura field. Sometimes you may even hear them as they come to assist. Other times they will help while you are dreaming or coming out of a dream. In these instances you can ask questions, which they will answer if it is time for you to know the answer for the greater good. They won't answer if for some reason the person they are working with is stepping out of their integrity. There is a code of ethics on the other side, and they are careful not to cross the line when it comes to a person's free will. They don't tell you to what to do. They only answer your questions and help you when it is for the highest good, when you ask to grow spiritually and to remember your connection to others and to God.

Another time, when I was at the clinic, a woman came to me for Reiki. While I was working on her, I got a message from her spirit guides. I asked her if it was all right for me to give it to her. She was happy to receive it, but what made this different from other messages that I received was that her spirit guides said the message was not for me or my knowing. I remember laughing, not understanding how they could relay a message to me to give to her without me knowing what it was. I didn't believe they could.

I explained what they said and told her I didn't know how they would give her the message. With that, the spirit guides gave me some kind of phrase that made absolutely no sense to me, and I related it to my client. She laughed and said that she knew perfectly well what they meant. She thanked me and said that she needed that information. Shocked, I went over the phrase but had no clue what it meant. Then I heard her spirit guides laughing at me. The other side has a great sense of humor.

In my personal life, I will find myself looking around or asking if the guides are there if I don't see them or feel them around me. Often I see them when I ask or hear the answer, "Yes." I know that we are not alone in this world and that we are always being watched over. They are always here to guide us if we ask for help. They all understand that our lives are our own and that it is our free will to make the choices that we need to learn in this life. All we have to do is ask in integrity, and they will help us when we do.

Encounters

A friend asked me one night at one of the healing circles, how long have I been working on my spiritual path? I had to answer, "All my life, but I resisted it until it came looking for me." If you would have asked me earlier in my life what I wanted to do in my life I would have given you a hundred different answers and never touched the subject of spiritual teaching. That was for "those" people. It turned out I was one of "those" people.

I thought about her question knowing it was something I had to do in this lifetime. I have no regrets now when I see all the amazing things that I have been able to be a part of and to experience. My life feels full when I see where I started, and where I am now. I see too that I have only good things to look forward to.

I have enjoyed learning about ghosts and how to live with a great respect and compassion for them. My ghost encounters can happen anytime. To answer the age old question, "Do ghosts see you in the shower?" The answer is, "Yes," and if you are aware of them then you can set limits as to where and when they can come and go. I used to have ghosts contact me in my tub. No, they don't seem to care if you are naked as they are occupied with their own issues. I finally had to tell them to stop, as it was my own down time.

When I began to allow my spiritual gifts to emerge without blocking them I discovered that I could see these incredible beings around people, that were not ghosts. These beings are "light beings," as they are just pure light surrounded with more light in the outline of a human form. The feeling I get from them is peaceful and they seem to be there for the person they are around. I learned from one of my teachers that most people call them guardian angels or guides. I use the term spirit guides when I see them now.

Once, when I was doing Reiki on my friend Leslie, I was in her home and she was laying down on my massage table. I was working on her when I looked up in the mirror and saw two tall beautiful light beings on both sides of me, with their heads bent down toward me. I could see them place their hands on top of mine and when I did, I felt my hands go down with a slight pressure from their touch. Peace and unconditional love flowed out of them during the whole session.

When we finished my friend was excited about how the heat from the Reiki went into her lower back as she could feel it working. Then she told me that she opened her eyes and I was nowhere near that spot on her back. She said that is when she saw that I was standing at the foot of the table working on her feet. She didn't understand how that could have happened. So we got to talking about the two angels that came to work on her during her healing session.

A few days later I found a book called "Hands of Light," by Barbara Ann Brennan [5] that talked about energy healing. What caught my attention was that there was a picture of two light beings helping with an energy healing session. Since the healing energy of Reiki comes from the Creator I now understand that our guardian angels are also there to help.

I do see the shadow people and to tell you the truth they look just like a shadow of a live person. What I pick up when I have encounters with them is an unhappiness or fear. I have learned that those who don't move into the light get stuck somewhere between this world and the other side, which makes them ghosts. You could call it a purgatory. For whatever reason, they are afraid to cross, maybe lost, or perhaps missed the beautiful light that takes them on to work out their own evolution.

Other Beings

I have talked to a few people who are afraid of the other side and the beings that you might come in contact with. Those beings are no different from the people that you meet here in the material world. I want to also point out that human beings are capable of being as loving as they are of being destructive. It is up to you to discern which is which when it comes to whom you want to come in contact with. The same works on the other side.

I want to be very clear about this. It is important for you to know who and what you are dealing with on the other side as much as it is important to know who and what you are dealing with when it comes to other human beings in the physical world. You can use your common sense if someone is trying to lead you astray. You begin to learn quickly who and what might not be the best contact or healthy relationship for you. Just think about how many people are in jail because of not following their integrity or following the wrong person. Again, this works on both sides of the spectrum. If you are not in a good place to know which is which, you could get into a lot of trouble, just as you would in the physical world.

If you want to make contact with the other side, there are some ground rules, just like there are on this side. Like we tell our children, just don't make friends with any stranger. Take the proper precautions as you normally would. It is best not to jump in with both feet if you have no idea how to make friends on the other side. There are some beings who don't like human beings at all, as well as beings who would help in a heartbeat if you needed them.

Know that angels, spirit animals, and the record keepers are wonderful to work with. They are the safest. But again, there is a process of learning who is there to work with you and who is just curious. I have been on journeys and have come across spirit animals when I was searching for my own. I met some animals who just wanted to know what I was up to. The only reason they came was to see what I was doing. In those cases I made sure I was very clear in my purpose and my intention of who I was looking for. They then made their way on to do something else, leaving me to my task.

Angels are there to help you stay on your path by warning or protecting you if danger in your life will take you off your path in following your soul contract. They don't give advice but are only there to guard and watch over you.

The angels will also intercede by delivering messages from the Holy Spirit if you are not able to hear or block them.

The record keepers can be found in the Akashic Records. They are the keepers of the Book of Life and of knowledge. They also take care of the Akashic library and keep all the notes on everything that has ever been thought, mentioned, or acted upon since the beginning of time. If you consciously access the Akashic Records, you will have the honor to be working with these beautiful beings.

Spirit beings, which term covers a broad range of the spectrum as they are all over, not just on the other side, tend to want to see what we are doing. I see them everywhere. When I do a journey to the other side, I am always in the company of my spirit guides or my spirit animal, whom I trust. On a few occasions, I have ventured off by myself when I was in a real hurry, but that doesn't happen a lot. The spirit team that I work with know the ins and outs of the different dimensions, so that I don't get lost in my travels. They also know – and can identify a lot quicker than I can – who to trust.

When I started to meet my team, I learned how to identify them with the help and the loving guidance of my teachers. I was reacquainted with my spirit guides that have been in my life since I can remember. I must say that it was quite a reunion!

The Visit

In a past chapter, I talked about body jumping. I would like to share what it is like when someone else decides to visit you in your body. It happened to me a few years ago when I was on my way to have lunch with Jan I was running late, so I used my cell to call and let her know I was running behind. Lucky for me, she was also running late, so there was no need to rush. Right after I hung up and backed out of the driveway, I suddenly began to have a familiar feeling that someone I used to know and work with was there in the car with me. Immediately, without question, a clear image of him popped into my head. I knew one thing for sure: This person was still alive on this earth.

The strong, old, familiar feeling of being in their presence began to overwhelm me. The essence of that certain person from my past was so strong I could feel him seeping into my energy field. I started to feel a little confused when I realized that I couldn't shake off the feeling of being invaded.

His energy moved inside my physical body, somewhere right around my solar plexus. By then the connection was so strong that there was no doubt I had a visitor. As I assessed the situation, I realized I still had my own thoughts around me. I felt like he was not there for just a friendly visit but was searching for something in my thoughts or memory process. It felt like he was trying to experience my energy so he could read what I knew.

I know this sounds so strange. If it had not happened to me, I would have thought it was crazy.

Very quickly, I received a clear inner guidance to send unconditional love towards this person's essence that was invading me, to block him from searching my energy. As I did this, I realized that it not only stopped him from reading me but also started to change my field of energy. It healed the tear in my field that allowed him to enter, causing disharmony, which threatened whatever his mission was. With this one action, I could feel myself relax, sending him love and acceptance, and felt him lose his grip inside my chakra.

I mustered up all the energy I had, I started to send out as much unconditional love and goodwill towards this person as I could. I let love open up, and it flooded my physical body and energy field in massive waves. I felt him starting to pull out of my chakras and energy fields, completely letting go. And as quickly as he came, he was gone. I was left with a feeling like someone had walked out of the room and left me there all alone. I took a moment to catch my breath and assess myself again. My personal privacy had been invaded without my permission; however I was still feeling all the love that was in my energy field, so I wasn't mad.

I was still driving to meet Jan for lunch, so I blew off the whole experience. I had no way of explaining it to my friend.

The next week, I learned from another friend who still had close ties with the person who visited me about a dramatic experience that happened to him around the time of the "visit." From what I gathered, my visitor thought I was somehow involved.

I told Jan what had happened to me because she knew about me and my work. She understood but hadn't had that happen to her, so she didn't know how to comfort me. It took me five months to have the courage to bring it up to one of my teachers, who told me that he knew how I felt being invaded. That meant a lot to me, having that validation that someone else had felt what it was like to have someone merge into your body. I was grateful. We had an interesting talk about cracks in the aura and how they can make one vulnerable.

Out of the experience, I learned that energy can be used for many things. Furthermore, there is a rule that the Masters and the Teachers go by: Watch your integrity and always ask permission when working with someone else. Use your gifts and talents wisely for healing and for good. For those who do body jumps, do not use them for personal gain by violating someone else's boundaries to find out information. That act is considered to be without integrity and is frowned upon in the healing community. I also learned that if someone is working without integrity, others who work with energy will know by seeing, sensing, or dreaming about what that person is doing.

Haunted By The Living

One of the things that I have to keep reminding myself is that the living can haunt people just as much as the dead. One of my experiences that helped me to remember that fact happened when a dear friend of mine, whom we will call Sally, broke off a long relationship and had to sever all ties with the other person to save her sanity. Not only was she dealing with a broken heart, but she was having some strange experiences, as if the person never left. As friends and outsiders in their relationship tried to help her move through the transition into a new life, Sally was still feeling very connected to the other person. She kept telling us that she was feeling as if she were under some sort of spell and felt that the other person was still holding onto her somehow.

One day Sally asked if I could spend the night and hang out with her to keep her company. I agreed and went over to listen and talk with her while she grieved the lost relationship. Throughout the evening I had this strange urge to ask if I could sleep in the master bedroom, but I did not mention it, as it sounded weird even to me. As we were getting ready to go to bed, Sally asked where I would like to sleep. When I wasn't sure where to sleep, she offered the master bedroom, since she had been sleeping in the guest room. I immediately said yes and went off to get ready for bed.

Just before I got into bed, Sally came in to say good night. As we were talking, I felt a strong presence in the room that I recognized immediately without any question as the person she had broken up with, whom I knew. I felt the person walk through me, looking for her. There was no denying it; it took my breath away. The sensation was as strong as if the person was standing in the room with us. Then it was gone.

I looked directly at Sally and said, "Did you feel that?" \

"Yes, I did" she said. Both of us seemed relieved to be validated and yet uneasy at the same time. We talked about it and finally, as it was getting late, we said goodnight and went off to sleep.

Sometime in the middle of the night, I awoke. Every muscle in my body was tense, and I felt as if someone were in the room with me, watching me sleep. I was wide awake and on high alert. My brain immediately identified the presence in the room with me as the same person who walked through me earlier that evening. I could feel them looking for her, and just as I was understanding this, they left the room. I went back to sleep, not feeling threatened. I was again awakened in the night with the feeling that someone was in the room with me. This time my body recognized the presence and I was able to relax back into a sound sleep. Again I made a note that it was not me they were looking for.

Morning finally came, and I related my story about my experience in the middle of the night to Sally. She was not surprised. She broke down and said that was what she had been experiencing all along. Sally was being haunted by the living. I was able to confirm what she was feeling. I knew that her connection with this person was not going to be easy to break.

The Power Of Words

My father used to remind me every time I visited him in West Texas that words have power not only when written but also when spoken. I don't think that many people are aware of just how much their spoken words affect their relationships and reveal who they are behind the layers. Words are powerful in creating things here in the physical world, and they can bring about change, both good and bad. They can start and stop wars. They can heal or bring someone to their knees. They can entice you to try a new product or change the way you feel about yourself.

But the really wonderful thing about how words is how they reveal what makes each person unique. You can learn so much about a person if you dare to take the time to actually listen to their words and the way that person puts their sentences together. You may find that you have a key to a secret garden. If you listen without projecting your own experiences and really hear what is being said, you find that you can communicate on a whole new level.

If you were to look closer, you would find that we all get careless and sling words around without realizing how powerful they are. Things that come out of the mouth could disempower someone without their knowledge of the damage that was done. I guess that is why spiritual teachers warn us to stay in the moment when speaking, as you have the choice to be mindful of what you say.

We often speak our fears and concerns without the intention of speaking our truth. The words just slip out of our mouths. Often the speaker is unaware that they have shared something intimate about themselves that reveals the true depth of their relationship and a tear within their being.

It is truly amazing what words can do, and I have only touched a tiny part of what they create in our lives. As you look into words, you may find that they can empower, tear, impose, build, heal, and encourage ourselves, others, and the world around us. What do you do with your words?

Validation Of The Spirit

As I share some of my experiences in life, I would like to mention how I investigated experiences that happened to me a lot, which led me down the path of making the conscious decision to learn about the spirit world. It also helped to push me back on my path in communication with Spirit.

As I have mentioned before, I was having experiences that were happening throughout different times in my life. A lot of my experiences were spontaneous and could happen anywhere or at any time – while I was driving, sitting at my desk, or just living life. One of the things that happened through the years is that I would get a tingling sensation in my body, and a feeling of warmth, compassion, and love would drape over me like a nice, fuzzy, tingly blanket coming up from the center of my back. Then an all-encompassing feeling of unconditional love and acceptance would shoot through my spine like fire, and it would explode out of my body though my heart. A feeling of pure bliss and ecstasy would follow, as love felt like it was beaming light from every cell in my whole body.

Instead of fighting it, I would just surrender and allow myself to move into the experience. I would then feel a connection of being a part of everyone and everything. A feeling of love for all those around me would sweep over me and through me, moving out of my skin and merging into the energy all around me. The feeling would last a few minutes, in complete connection, then wear off during the rest of the day. This was a little different from the knitting experience, which was more of a conscious recognition of being out of my body. In this experience, I felt the true bliss of being in my body, connected in spirit, and a part of all creation.

I decided to try to find out what this was and why it was happening to me. This was before I had discovered the Akashic records. I needed some answers, so I began to talk to very close friends, who suggested that I start learning meditation. This is not what I wanted to hear, but I needed to know why this was happening, so I decided to go ahead and try meditating once again.

As it always happens, once I put the intention out there, the universe answered. A continuing education catalog arrived at our house within a few days of this decision, and as I was looking through it, a meditation class stood out. That was almost too easy. I called and enrolled.

The first day of class seemed to be a little uncomfortable for all of us who attended. We all sat as far away as possible from each other with eyes cast down, not daring to look around the room. When our teacher Dr. Sarai Stuart ND arrived she quickly moved us into a circle since it was a really small class. That is when I noticed a calming presence around her which flooded the room as we all moved closer together. After taking roll she announced that we were to go around the circle saying our name and why we were there.

When it was my turn, I was somewhere in the middle of why I was there when Dr. Sarai stopped me mid-sentence and said, "So much will change in your life the next nine months that you will not know yourself as you know yourself now. Oh honey, you didn't volunteer to come here; you were dragged here." Then as quickly as that she moved on to the next person, and my sentence was never completed. I sat there stunned by what she said as I knew deep within my heart I was meant to be there. I also felt validated that the whole experience in her class was another step in my journey of self-discovery and spiritual awakening.

She kept us busy for the rest of our class sessions teaching us about meditation. We learned about the kundalini and how to find colors in the mind's eye. We learned how to quiet the chatter in ourselves so that we could experience a peace in connecting with our higher selves. Through it all I found that I felt that something amazing was happening to me. For me, by being in the class I had a freedom to share and explore experiences that happened to me without any fear of being different.

I might not have the answers you are looking for, but if you are reading this, you are somewhere close to the same path. As we share our experiences and stories, we come together in a unity of understanding. We discover that we are not alone in our journey of finding our path in this life. This process is the way we all grow, the way to find peace, and the door that opens up the journey into the sacred heart.

Chapter Nine: Stepping Into Power

Personal Power

Personal power is a lot like owning a set of keys and finding that you end up having to search for it again and again. Many of us lose our personal power in our early childhood or forget that we have it. Often if we do find it, we wind up giving it away. We give it to someone who doesn't deserve it or even have a clue what to do with it, because it really belongs to us. We compromise ourselves and put ourselves in powerless positions, where we can't move, because of fear. This only perpetuates the monotony deep down inside of ourselves, where we are prisoners of our own loss of power.

Finding our personal power is taking back our lives and forgiving ourselves so that we can begin to heal. I say "Begin" because this doesn't happen overnight. There is much to overcome, and the hardest part is being gentle with ourselves so that we can listen to our own hearts. The true lesson here is to be comfortable with your own power and not to be afraid of it.

Losing one's power is splitting oneself in two and sometimes into many fragments of oneself. The journey begins by waking up and becoming self aware of the losses. Then the process of finding out who we are and where all the pieces that we have lost are hidden. The pilgrimage becomes an amazing puzzle as we piece together our lives. As we start on this private odyssey from within, the healing process begins.

Twilighting

I have mentioned the term "twilight" in other chapters, and I wanted to give a better description of what it is all about. As I have said before, twilight is the time just before you fall asleep or just before you wake up. It happens to all of us. It is when we have one foot in the spirit world and the other foot in the physical world. Some people call it a trance, but we all experience it, whether we know it or not.

Some people can go into twilight without having to lie down to fall into that state. They just have the ability or have practiced enough to be able to reach twilight when they want to. There are also the Shamans who use the drum to create a rhythm that stimulates the brain and allows it to relax enough, merging into the theta state that creates the twilight to journey.

In my own case, I use it when I feel I am not in clear communication with my spirit guides or record keepers, when I can't get myself out of my own way to communicate with them. Sometimes the inner ego will want to take over. That is when twilighting becomes essential as it helps to eliminate the distractions that block the connection.

Lifetime Lessons

As I began to heal, I started to grow, and I eventually moved on to learn other modalities that were taught in my dreams by Spirit and Master teachers on both sides of the physical and spiritual realms. I have learned in my own experiences how to help guide others to discover themselves and step into their own personal power, as they explore the healing modalities and expand their quests for self-healing.

In many cases I find that there are a number of people who are afraid to talk about past lives. It scares them, or they don't believe past lives exist. The truth is, past lives affect a great part of our souls' evolution and our spiritual development. When you step into the spirit realm, you soon discover that there are no longer limitations to God or the whole universe. Looking at past lives helps to bring old patterns of behavior to the surface that are held onto by the soul and affect the body and the world we interact with. There is a massive amount of information about ourselves and the universe that is beyond our comprehension, even in this lifetime. By examining past lives, we discover that we can see how we have made choices in the past and in this lifetime that influence the way we learn and grow. Often we as human beings limit ourselves, thus creating a sense of wanting to control others by what we know from our own perspective and understanding of limited resources and fears.

In my own experiences, I found that by learning to move in the spirit world, I soon discovered modalities and tools that helped me learn more about myself and my connection to Source, which was liberating. These experiences allowed me to find that connection to Spirit and my own soul on a whole different level.

It is important to know that by taking the time to learn and contemplate on our own experiences, we often discover that we all have that ability to become closer to that connection in the higher levels. This allows us all to have a stronger understanding of how things work. Just the simple step of letting go of our own dirty laundry allows us to move into those realms where we are able to find the love that we were originally created from. The truth is, you have all the spiritual support that you need right by your side, every step of the way.

I would like to make clear that working in the records or any of the healing modalities does not infringe on free will or the sacred contracts that were signed by you and the Creator. You still have a life mission with lessons to learn in the physical world which includes carrying out the life in which you chose to learn them. What it does change is how quickly you learn from your life lessons and are able to heal and move on to the next. It is more of an acceleration of the learning process.

When you examine your life from the outside and from the soul's perspective, you lose some fear and anxiety, knowing that you are one half physical body and the other half spirit. This is when many of us make the discovery that we have a life in both worlds, living in a simultaneous connection that links each to the other, coming together as one.

When I first became aware of this, I was glad to have learned from an experience. I had learned how to avoid a situation when I saw the same pattern. I was proud that I had mastered the pattern in my life that brought me so much grief. As I was celebrating my success, I heard my spirit guides laughing. They were happy for me, but told me to get ready, as there was another life lesson to learn. I realized then that it was an endless sea concerning life lessons, as we human beings look at things. It is so different in the spirit world, where time does not exist as we know it. The whole process of our mission is filled with experiences that are a conglomerate of lessons that are to be learned as we discover ourselves and become whole.

Trusting & Letting Go

One day I made a discovery when a song kept playing on my radio called, "Bulletproof Romance" by Lady GaGa [6], as I drove around doing errands. No matter what station I put the dial on, it was there. Even after I got out of the car and was grocery shopping the song kept playing in my mind. The main lyrics with the words "bullet proof" is what stuck.

Finally, I stopped at a little rock shop called The Power of the Rainbow in Arlington, Texas, and the owner, Trey, who is a shamanic practitioner, asked why he could see a bullet proof vest on me. I shrugged my shoulders and told him about the song that was making me crazy. He then smiled and said that I was picking up energy around me that was not good for me. The song was a gentle reminder to watch myself. I was in a state of being more vulnerable to lower vibrations because of my fears at that time. My job was to be aware. This meant checking in with myself and clearing my fears. This also included being mindful of anything else that would bring me down into a lower vibration.

Being human, we don't always live in the higher vibration. You may have had the training and the tools to handle conflict, but something may push a button for whatever reason that brings out a part of you that is angry, sad, humiliated, or upset. In that instance, you end up moving into a lower vibration. Often we will dip into the lower realms, opening ourselves up to be attacked or pick up a hitchhiker from the spirit realm. What I mean by "dipping" is that since we are all human, we can be thrown off-guard by our fears, which triggers us to fall. This will open you energetically to the lower-level entities that had not seen you before, when you were in higher realms. Once they see you and taste your fears, they may become interested in you because of what you are experiencing. This reminds them of their own Earth life and entices them to want to re-live it, through you.

One thing you need to know is that by being in this lower energy, you can create a hole or tear in the energy field that keeps you safe from these lower entities. The more fear you experience, the more you feed the entities on those lower vibrations. You begin to lose your personal power and become a victim of this lower plane. The only way to stop this is to remember your personal power and move back out into the higher frequencies.

A good example of this is when I got up once in the middle of the night to get a drink of water. I saw a woman hanging out in the corner of my bedroom. (Just to clear things up: she was a ghost.) I noticed that when I passed her the hairs on my skin stood up. When I came back and still saw her there, I knew we were destined to have some sort of contact. Since I was tired and just wanted to go back to bed, I ignored her. Somewhere within me I still had anxiety and fear that she wanted something from me.

When I started to get settled, I felt her fling herself on top of me. I didn't even have a moment to respond; she held me down. I knew I was still awake, but I couldn't move or speak. All I could do was feel her weight on top of me.

As I lay on my back, I could see her as she put her face in mine, screaming at me and shaking her head in anger. In that moment I felt fear surge through me like an electrical current as I helplessly lay there in complete terror. Then, out of the blue, I heard, "She needed my help, and I didn't help her. She is really mad! You know how to handle this." I remembered then to release my fears. As soon as I let go of my fear, she let go of me and I could move again.

I called in the angels and saw the golden light hit our dark bedroom like a blast from a bomb. I knew then that my call was answered. I felt them take over, bringing a sense of inner peace that now flooded the room. Knowing that I was safe and she was going to be cared for, I turned over and went back to sleep.

This dance of the ups and downs in higher and lower levels of vibrations is normal for humans. Being aware is key, and learning how to change keeps us in balance.

The trick is to stay longer on higher ground so that it becomes your everyday experience, rather than falling into the lower realms. Once we go back into that higher ground, there is no need for protection. However, we are often thrown off balance during our everyday experiences, so it is important to recognize when we get off course. True, protection is not needed when we exist in that higher level, yet staying in the higher frequencies is an art that we all work to master. As a precaution, it doesn't hurt to add a little protection, when you think of it, just to be safe.

Energy, as a big picture, is really something that I don't think a lot of people consider, and yet we send out signals all the time. The other day I was driving when something triggered my emotions that made me angry. I sat at a red light, getting mad, until I realized what I was doing. I could feel the heat of the emotional energy moving through my body and out past my skin into the air.

Then I heard very clearly, "Pull it back and send it out of your feet into the earth." I decided to take the wise advice, and I felt the anger release. Then I had an overwhelming feeling to send an enormous amount of love out from my heart center instead. Amazingly, I could do this without hesitation, and again I experienced the energy moving through my body and out of my skin. This time, though, it was a beautiful feeling. The whole experience took the time for the light to turn green.

Wow, if I could change my feelings in a moment and send love instead of anger out to the world, how powerful is that? Then a thought came that when we live in anger and fear, those emotions are sent out, becoming part of the air and energy that is around people, animals, plants, and the earth. This is real pollution. No wonder we can get so angry. But the truth is that we have the power to change it all. As I drove on down the road, I realized that I was in my own personal power, and it felt great!

The God Spark

When I was seeing clients at the acupuncture clinic in Fort Worth, a young man named Kirby Cory came in for an Akashic reading, and I began my adventure of learning about and understanding the God Spark. It happened quite by surprise; Kirby had brought a few of his drawings of geometric shapes for me to look at. When I opened up his records, the drawings started to pop out as three dimensional shapes. They all lifted off of the paper and moved so that I could see them from different angles. It was much like looking at a computer screensaver, where you can look at all the sides of an image, only there was no screen. To my surprise, the shapes took form in mid-air in front of me.

While I was watching the geometric shapes, I heard my guides say, "These shapes are a part of a set of five that come together and are used for healing." My client passed me another drawing, which raised off of the page just like the others. Again I heard very clearly, "This one is a vehicle that is used with the mind to access information from all dimensions with no limitations." As I watched, I was shown how the vehicle was used and how to access knowledge. Surprised as I was, I explained to my client what I was witnessing.

As Kirby passed me another drawing I recognized it from deep within my own soul as what everything is created of. I knew without question that this geometric shape was a drawing of the molecular structure of something smaller than an atom. In that moment I understood it was a building block of the consciousness of the entire universe, which was created out of it. It was a tiny part of an unlimited mass of God Sparks put together, holding everything in place. I can't describe the pure joy of seeing and recognizing this shape as it moved in its 3-D form in front of me. It had no limits in and of itself. All I heard was, "Yes, it is," from the spirit guides, giving me confirmation that what I was experiencing was real.

After the reading I was both excited and numb. I didn't really know what to do with the information that I had just experienced. All I knew was that Kirby was very special: he had the ability to bring this information into this dimension, and I was getting to be a witness.

A few weeks later I was watching the science channel while I waited for my family to get home from all their activities of the day. I listened, half-interested, while focusing on reading a book, when I heard that scientists were trying to build machines to find this particle that was smaller than an atom that they believed existed. I jumped up from where I was sitting and turned up the volume. I was amazed at what I was hearing and became very excited. I knew they were looking for the God Spark! I wanted to reach into the television to tell them that it was real and all that I knew about it. Of course that was silly; it was a television program, and without scientific credentials, I didn't dare think they would want to hear about my own personal experience. They would figure it out on their own.

Days later I showed it to Veronica, just to see her reaction. She said without hesitation, "The God Spark." Almost like, "Silly!" I had never shown her the drawing before, and we had never talked about the God Spark, as it hadn't come up.

The next morning as I was coming out of twilight, I asked my angels and guides about the God Spark. I heard very clearly, "This is the energy that is being revealed, not only on the earth, but throughout the entire universe. Everything is connected, and everything is becoming aware of itself and how it was created. It is, as you might call it because of your background on this planet, the 'Christ Consciousness' in your own terms, but others would call it something else."

A year later, it was announced that the scientists had discovered proof that the God Particle really existed. Also during that same time, I had lunch with my friend Ruby and I asked about her son, my godson. She was telling me that he had gone to a Bible camp where he had learned about the God Particle. He had learned that it was the building block of all things. She described what it looked like because he had shown her a crude drawing of it. I was amazed how very close it resembled what I had witnessed in Kirby's Akashic Records that one day.

The Voice

I was once given a beautiful opportunity, as a gift from the angels, to make peace with myself. It started with a gentle pulling on my heart and soul to go back to the church that I had been part of, which I had fled with open wounds. I was called to sing once again and to step into something much bigger than myself. Despite my personal fears and frustrations, I followed the call and was greeted by people who knew me, who seemed to understand that I was healing that part of myself that separated while I was there the last time. The people who had served on the church staff were long gone and had scattered elsewhere, so I was starting over with just the remaining members of the congregation.

I soon discovered that the choir director was of the understanding that if you wanted to sing and make joyful noise to the Lord, then you should be allowed to express yourself. I must admit, I am most grateful that they let me sing, as singing is one of my biggest passions, but not one of my greatest talents. Every Thursday and Sunday, I drove up to the church to express myself, and I sang with great joy and love for anyone who wanted to listen. I always prayed before I stepped up to sing, inviting the angels to join in. Once as we had just finished singing for Sunday morning service, our director said, "It sounded like there were a hundred voices singing and there are only four of you." I laughed. If he could only see what I see! Angels love to sing.

One particular Sunday morning, we were singing the "Revelation Song," by Jennie Lee Riddle [7] and I remember hitting and holding a note. I lost myself in the harmony of the tones created by the voices and the music. It all came together at that moment in unison making an incredible chord that echoed through the sanctuary, resonating in my soul. A burst of pure joy exploded out of my heart. I felt myself being shot out of my body like a rocket, merging with the All. I found myself connected to the physical world, and yet I wasn't. I was somewhere inside the music, surrounded by a blinding light encompassed by unconditional love that was a part of my whole being.

While I was enjoying the space I was in, I heard a very loving, but strong voice clearly whispering, "Ana, they are still there." An awareness swept over me. I realized then that I had left my body. "Oh yeah," I remembered thinking as I began to bring myself back, realizing that I was still holding the note. I was very aware of myself returning, trying to stuff myself into my body. I found it to be very dark when I tried to look out at the congregation with my eyes. It took several seconds for my eyes to adjust, so that I could see, after being in such a brilliant light.

As I made the adjustment, I noticed that not only was the congregation still there, but some were listening with their eyes wide open, as though captivated by the music. I also noticed that many of them were engulfed by a beautiful glow of golden white light that surrounding their bodies and extending out a few feet all around them. Those people appeared intent and very focused on watching us as we sang. Others I saw were looking down, digging in their purses or searching for things on the pew. Darkness surrounded these people who seemed to be very nervous and uncomfortable. As I watched, a huge wave of energy rolled over the entire congregation. It started from the right, rippling through the whole room to the left side. It all happened so fast I didn't have time to analyze the situation. We were at the end of the song and had a still few more songs left to complete the service. Quickly, I asked my spirit guides what was going on, but I heard no answer. They were silent. All I could do was continue singing with the band, keeping up with the music as we moved into the beat, while still working to integrate myself fully back into my body. When we finished the song, everyone sat in silence for a moment, until finally the pastor got up to do the blessing. It took him a few seconds to get his thoughts together. The music had touched his heart.

Later, on my drive home, I had time to ask the spirit guides once again, "What happened?" I heard very clearly in a loving voice: "The resonance of the note created a vibration that moved you into ascension. You were catapulted into that space of pure love. As you did this along with others, many remembered from where they came, and moved into that same vibration. You all created light and brought out that sense of unity in unconditional love. The others you saw with darkness surrounding them were afraid, holding onto the dense energy. They were uncomfortable moving into that space of light and unconditional love, for whatever reason." Then my own thoughts went to a form of judgment, as I could see where people were in that moment. When I did so, I heard the voice speak very lovingly again, "Ana, you must remember not to judge those who are afraid. They are where they are supposed to be. They will move into that space of light and unconditional love when they are ready to let go of the denser energy, in their own time."

"Oh my," I thought, "is that really how it works? Free will?" When we remember where we came from and finally "let go and let God," then we remind others from where they came. We attract others, drawing them with us, as we move into that space of light and unconditional love. If God created us in his image, then we all have that light within us. How amazing it is to remember that we are a part of All that is.

Remind me, Dear One, when I forget from where I came, and try to hold on to my stuff...

A Gift Of Love

Once when I was on my way to see a friend, I started to sing in the car, which can be a little awkward when you stop at a light and people look in your direction. No one could hear me as I was singing at the top of my lungs, when something beautiful hit me square in my third eye and heart center.

All I know is that I was perfectly normal with my everyday concerns and the next thing I knew, my heart was opening up and tears rolled down my cheek as joy welled throughout my whole body. My brain felt dizzy, like I was somewhere in between space and where I was sitting at the stop light. The thought that went through my head was a child holding their breath until they turned blue. I have known at least one child in my life who did that, which was an odd event.

Next, I saw my daughter playing the piano as I walked through the house, listening to her emotions as her fingers struck the keys. It was not the force of hitting the keys that betrayed her, but rather the vibration of the notes that hung in the air that blended to create the sound.

I realized that love is like the notes in the air which are all around us in everything, every being, even in what we don't see. But like the child, we are holding our breath until our bodies turn blue. We hold it until we are starved and deprived of the oxygen that carries life through us. So I guess the question is: Are we really living when we are in this state?

The light turned green, and as I drove on I started to assess my own life.

The Lesson From The Curandera

One evening my husband Steve and I went to the movies on a date. At the time, I was so excited about just the two of us getting away for a few hours and enjoying ourselves. As we waited for the movie to start, I felt like my bones were starting to ache. I pushed the feeling away and continued to visit with Steve, determined that it was not going to spoil our evening. The movie soon started, and somewhere through the first half of the movie, I began to feel like my nose was stopping up. Then my ears started to ring. Soon after, I began to feel like I had a fever, not to mention wanting to toss my cookies on the floor. I felt like I was coming down with the flu. The thought that went through my mind was to tell Steve I needed to go home, so I could curl up on the bed to sleep it off with some medicine.

I don't remember why this thought hit me at the time, but I remembered that my records were open, as I hadn't closed them from the afternoon when I was doing some personal work in them. I decided to ask the record keepers what was going on and why I was hit with the flu so fast. I asked them if I was getting sick. The answer I got surprised me: "No."

"No?" I thought. They must not have understood my question. So I asked again and got the same answer: "No."

"Oh, then why do I feel like I have the flu?" I asked.

They answered, "Someone is in your energy field, and the energy does not match yours."

"Who is it?" I quickly started naming people that I knew and asked if it was one of them. I went through a quick list of names that popped up, but when I came to the name of the curandera, whom I had just made an acquaintance with, I heard very clearly, "Yes." In that instant I felt my body respond to the name, feeling nauseous. The name and the energy were a match.

Then I asked my records keepers why this person was in my energy field, and they answered that she was looking for me. Her different energy made my energy body feel like it was being invaded or attacked, which also affected my physical body, making me feel like I had the flu. The record keepers showed me a drawing of triangles, which represented her energy, and circles, which represented mine. Neither was wrong or right, but when the two mixed, it felt different.

With this information, I was able to ask my guides and my record keepers to please escort the curandera out of my energy fields. Then I asked them to seal them off so that this energy would no longer be able to get into my fields, track me, or find me without my permission. After that, I asked for all residue to be removed from my energy fields and to release all symptoms from the encounter. In less than ten minutes, which included working with the record keepers, all the flu-like symptoms were gone from my body. I felt well and at peace once again.

I was amazed how quickly my body felt free of all symptoms after working in my records. I was also able to enjoy the rest of the movie and have a wonderful evening with my husband. I never forgotten what I learned from that experience from working in my records and energy fields with the record keepers. I also thanked the curandera for teaching me a valuable lesson about energy.

Protection vs. Not, "Higher Ground"

Something I want to point out in greater detail is that, in a perfect world, we don't need protection when we are in an extremely high vibrational frequency. The problem is, as human beings, our fears and emotional baggage can be the culprit in leading us to open doors that let other-worldly things from different dimensions enter our energy fields. Dark energies are very attracted to the lower emotional vibrations. That means that our lower emotions emit dense energy and set off something like a perfume to the lower energies. Think of it like leaving a trail of bread crumbs for dark entities to follow. Once our fields are open to lower vibrational frequencies, the dense energies and dark entities are able to come into our them. We unknowingly invite them in to join us in our own misery.

So this is what you need to know. We as human beings have the ability to program our energy fields to keep out lower vibrations by using different techniques. There are quite a few books out on the market that talk about doing this. You have to find the techniques that work best for you. By being aware of your energy field and where you are on the scale of love and forgiveness, you have the ability to build up protection grids that will strengthen your field. Just by being aware of your emotions and where you are will give you an idea of whether you are in a vulnerable spot. Once your fields are on a higher vibration, you are no longer visible to the lower entities and will be off their radar. This is the only time you don't need to worry about protection.

I would like to point out that your energy can change with the emotional body. An emotion that catches you off-guard may drop you into a lower vibration if you are not careful. I know that we as human beings are perfectly capable of reaching those higher states of vibration when we are in the presence of our higher selves and of the Holy Spirit. We are also human.

Again, if you plan to work in the spirit world or you are just interested in it, take the extra time and do research on some techniques for your own protection. I would like to mention that prayer is very powerful. For example, you can imagine surrounding your energy fields and physical body in the color blue, that looks like a blue egg, to keep from picking up other people's energy. Sometimes you will find people surrounding themselves with white light for protection.

However, even with this information, these methods may not work for everyone. We are all so different in our energies. Our beliefs play a huge part in picking out something that matches our own frequencies. I can't stress enough to take the extra time to read and try out the different methods that you feel drawn to. Trust your inner guidance on what works best for you and what feels right. You will know.

Also remember that there are times when we are just out there with all of our energy fields open. In this case, people, without really knowing it, may get into our energy fields because they are curious or just thinking about us. They may mean you no harm, but it may feel really weird to you on an emotional, energetic, or physical level. If this is the case and you become aware of it, just ask them to leave. Then ask for assistance from your spirit guides to remove them from your energy field. After a while you will be more in tune when this happens and quickly change the circumstances when something does not feel right in your energy field or body. There is no reason for you not to step into your own personal power.

Integrity - Practitioner

Integrity plays a big part in working with energy. What is in the energy worker's heart affects which way the energy can go. When looking for a practitioner, it is most important to find someone that you resonate with. You will know, if you get a funny feeling in your gut, whether that person is compatible with you or not. It is crucial that you go with how you feel and that you trust your inner guidance. Believe it or not, your physical body and energy bodies already know what will work best for you, even if your brain can't come up with a reason. So many times we push that feeling of being nervous or uneasy aside, only to regret it all later. Then there are times we wish we would have taken the time to work with a practitioner, as we felt a connection to them but talked ourselves out of working with them.

Most of the time, finding someone that works and fits in with our energy fields relates directly to where we are in our lessons in life. They may be just what we need at that time, and later on, we may decide that we need to find a different practitioner, as we have graduated from that point in the journey. In either case, it is not our responsibility to judge but to use our discernment to find the right practitioner.

Dream Time

One of the biggest gifts of the spirit that some miss is dreaming. Many know that dreams are important, but with the distractions of the physical day, dreams are often only remembered if they cause fear, like nightmares. Remember that we are fifty percent spirit and soul, while the other half is our physical body. Sometimes it is good to take a little extra time to investigate to see what is going on in our dream life. It is important to know that there are several aspects of meanings when it comes to dreams, which can be noted under different categories.

Dreams can be a warning or communication from your higher self that something is coming up in the future. In my own experience, once when I was stuck and needed help to move on, I had a dream that someone was coming into my life that would create a lot of change to help me move. I even had the name on my lips the next morning but couldn't remember it when I was fully awake. Sure enough, that person showed up a few months later and allowed me to grow more spiritually in my life. Looking back, I see now that that difficult experience in my physical life was only for my greatest good and highest potential.

Dreams can also be a connection to people that we know, who have passed on to the other side. They can open up the veil that separates us from the spirit world, with messages that can be brought through to this side. How many of you have heard or seen someone in your own dreams, who has passed, wanting to say hello or give you friendly advice?

One of my most favorite aspects of dreaming is that it serves as a classroom, which is more like an interactive movie that we get to participate in. Master teachers or spirit guides explain or demonstrate things in dreams that teach life lessons. Often these tend to be the dreams that most people forget and remember later. You may also have a memory when coming out of a dream, knowing there was something important that you can't remember. These dreams are the work of the spirit, which is integrating the memory into your soul and subconscious mind. Later on, when you have achieved the lesson, you begin to remember the dream. Sometimes, when the time comes up for you to use the knowledge, it will surface.

Conscious dreaming is a wonderful way to work on remembering dreams. By doing exercises to help you remain conscious when dreaming, you can bring back parts of the teachings to help with life lessons on this side. Some of the teachings in the dreams are so advanced that they don't make sense and can be confusing when you try to bring them back to this world, even though you remember them making sense when you were there. That is why most people don't remember their dreams. In the spirit world there are different ways of communicating that may be unfamiliar to you in our physical world.

Dreams can also be an opening into a portal to the astral world. There are so very many dimensions where our physical bodies can't go, but we can when we move into our energy bodies. We can navigate with ease, and often we can be accompanied by others that we know in those other worlds. Sometimes those experiences can be so incredible that we don't want to wake from our dreams. Another part of traveling in our dreams is that we have the ability to visit others that are in the physical world. The people we visit may or may not see us when that happens.

The last aspect of dreaming that I wanted to bring up is about healing. Dreams are powerful when we have gone through a traumatic experience in this life. Dreams can help us with our own healing when we have lost parts of ourselves. As we move through the astral worlds, taking the time to investigate what is going on with our bodies, we may find that parts of us are lost in other dimensions. Sometimes it may be that part of us that just doesn't want to come back. This type of dreaming is associated with Soul Retrieval, which is best done with the help of the master teachers, spirit guides, spirit animals, or record keepers on the other side.

Dreams are amazing, and there is so much more to them than what we realize. They even help us in resting and rejuvenating our physical body. If we only knew that we have the same power to create like we do in our dreams, our whole world would change.

Classes During Dreams

I don't think people realize how important our dreams are. Most of us think that we can only analyze dreams by the symbols. I agree this can be most beneficial when we do this. There are, however, other layers to dreams.

When we are deeply caught up in a vivid dream and we are learning from our higher selves or teachers from the other side, we see, hear, and participate. We feel as though we are awake. When we are learning in a dream state, a single thought can transform an experience into a reality on the other side. My spirit teachers will come in and narrate what I don't seem to understand, explaining what I am seeing and helping me get the whole picture. Most of the time, my teachers know my questions before I can even assimilate them in my thoughts.

Later, in my waking state, I might find that I have a question, and I can ask for something to be made clearer. In that case, I see images or hear an explanation of what I am asking about, as I am coming in and out of my twilight state. In some cases, they may not explain or answer until I work through a process that needs to be finished, before we go on to the next lesson where that question may be addressed.

As I have talked to other people, they have the same experience, but one of the complaints that I have heard a lot is that the person does not get a lot of rest when they are going through a class in their dream state, and they feel intruded upon. I have learned from my own experience that it is important that we do go through the classes because it was contracted with our spirit guides before we were born. Those who are in spirit don't view time as we do, so it is essential for us to communicate with our spirit guides that we want to learn. However, it is better if we learn these lessons on certain nights or at a certain time, so that we get our rest in this world. It is really up to us, as we have free will and can stop the lessons all together if we want to.

The Dream

I dreamed one night that I was really sick, and everyone in the world was sick. I saw myself talking to my friend and telling her when I remembered getting sick and how it started. We all suffered from the same illness. Next, I saw a screen on the wall telling everyone how sick we were and how bad the symptoms were and how bad the pain would be that we would all experience.

As I looked around the house, I realized that there were screens on all over the house, so I decided to go for a walk.

I noticed on my walk there were screens everywhere, all saying the same thing. I saw this man who stood out from the rest of us, and I asked about him. Someone told me that the man was crazy and to stay away from him. I noticed too that he didn't seem to be sick or suffering in any way, shape, or form. "He is not like us?" I asked. That was when I woke up.

On my drive to work the next day, I turned the radio on to listen to some music. I liked the song that was playing, so I turned up the volume and started to sing along. That was when I realized what was coming out of my mouth: "I am a victim!" What? What did I just say? I listened to more of the words, which I did not like, so I turned the dial. Another song came on. This one talked about a co-dependent relationship. The next song was about hating someone. What?

Later, when I got home, I turned the television on and was surfing through the channels. Again I became aware of what I was hearing and seeing, only to recognize that a lot of it was about fear, loss of power, or taking someone else's power away from them. The dream made me more conscious of the subliminal messages being broadcast around me, giving me the choice to participate in them, or not.

Chapter Ten: Healing

Reading The Akashic Records

When working in the records, people often want to see what is ahead for them. They want to know their future. I let people know how it was explained to me by the spirit guides who have been teaching me. The very first time they showed me how the future works, they showed me a big tree. I remember seeing it, thinking, "And? It is a big tree." I could hear them laughing. They think that we humans take things way too seriously.

Then I heard my name as they began to explain, "Ana, the branches on the tree represent how energy works when you are following it. It changes and grows from different angles as you maneuver your way to the top. The energy flow will change as you follow the different branches. It is the freedom of choice that changes the energy flow from one branch to another. This all makes life much more interesting as you progress in your lessons. In the end we all reach the same destination."

When I look at someone's records, I can see the energy in the records by the choices they are making and how they will move as they continue to follow that energy pattern. I always recognize that the way it all unfolds is really up to that person: which patterns they choose to continue and which to stop, if they want to work on something. A person is in charge of what they want to accomplish learning in this lifetime. Soul contracts that we have made with others allow different patterns that will help us accomplish what we need to learn. There are also different degrees of lessons and choices that one can choose from to reach our goals. Learning one's own life lesson is all about free will.

Now this works backwards too. You can follow the energy back to the past, moving into genetics to find the energy patterns that no longer serve. If a person wants to change an old pattern, there are tools that can break it and bring the life experience into balance. Again: Understand that everything is made out of energy, which can be changed into different energy patterns that can replace the old patterns, releasing the unhealthy cycle and its triggers.

A change in pattern can be something as simple as forgiveness of others or self. True forgiveness allows us to release our fears and anger so that our soul can heal by aligning the emotional bodies back into harmony with the higher energies of the spiritual bodies. This one act of release changes the brain waves in the physical body that send signals to the cellular body, creating a new chemical balance within the physical tissue. When this happens, a trigger no longer has an effect on a person as it would have in the past. Now a past trauma can be seen as outside of the person, rather than experienced as happening in that moment.

I find in the records that there are no limitations as to what you can do or learn about, but you have to be willing to dig in deep and ask the questions to make the changes. Something that I learned in the Akashic Records is that, since we are physical and spirit energies, we have two very different experiences that come together to create our human experience in the physical world. On the physical level, we have DNA and other information programmed into our cells and body. This allows you to change your genetic makeup by breaking patterns that have been passed down from generation to generation. The spirit, on the other hand, is the higher self linked to the soul. It brings in experiences that were attained from other lifetimes.

Now, as a bonus, we add in a third aspect to the equation, the mind, which tries to assimilate all the information that is gathered by bringing the soul and body together. So now, to obtain optimum healing, we are working with the soul, body, and mind. The body on a physical and genetic level, the soul level with past life experiences that we bring into this world with us, and last the physical mind that is integrating the others, trying to make sense of it all as we move through our life lessons on this planet. Exciting work, don't you think?

The Akashic Records are not about finding your fortune or winning the lottery. The records are about healing and working on improving yourself as you learn more about you. They are a way to go deeper into your life lessons to understand how things work or why they are as they are. Having this information also allows you make peace with some of your choices and work on bringing healing and balance into your life journey.

Teaching Of The Divine

There have been times when I have questioned others when they have said that we are God. It is also said that we are made in God's own image. In my mind I could not really wrap my head around those statements. I knew our limitations as human beings, so how could that be?

Then one day, while I was thinking about that, I was lifted out of my body and landed on a beach. My first thought was "So?". Then I heard, "Ana, think of yourself as a single grain of sand on this beach. You are an individual, but you are also a part of the collective. Now think of God as the whole beach of sand. You are only a tiny part of it."

"Wow," I thought, "How amazing is it to be that connected to the Creator?"

Then I heard, "With that understanding, think in terms of the whole universe as one consciousness and you as only one very tiny part of it. Think of all the others who are a collective, along with everything in the universe, which are also a part of the One, the Creator." This thought reminded me of the knitting experience,   when I merged into consciousness that was created out of an amazing amount of unconditional love, which was a part of everything. Nothing, even the air or what I would have considered non-living, was left out. Everything is connected. When I made this connection, I heard the voice again, saying "She got it!"

After many years searching for the meaning of that, and upon this discovery, I learned that what my father used to say – "Treat everything with respect, as it is alive," – is the truth.

Quantum physics is now starting to explain this phenomenon using atoms and molecular structures to help others see this. They explain how sound and light come together to create a hologram in what we now know as the Matrix.

From this discovery I have learned that we human beings are quite capable of being a part of miracles and our own healing when we tap into the Source. We are never left out of the circle, and yet our fears keep us from progressing. Often they destroy us. I understand also that reminders from the Holy Spirit, spirit guides, and the Creator link us back to the origins of our own beginning, allowing us to grow in the process of our own evolution.

Teachers

I like to go back to the old saying by Lao Tzu, "When the student is ready, the teacher will appear. When the student is truly ready... the teacher will Disappear. " After becoming a Reiki Master, I wanted to truly connect with a spiritual teacher on the physical plane and just learn. At that point I felt I was driven to find a teacher. I spent hours on the Internet researching and trying to sign up for classes. Every time I signed up for a class and paid for it, the classes didn't fill up and were canceled. I had one teacher, who had been teaching for seven years, tell me that she had never canceled a class and thought the pattern was strange.

After about six months of failing to get into a class or find a teacher, I signed up for a Reiki session with another Reiki Master. I felt as if I was somehow out of alignment with the universe and wasn't finding where I needed to fit in. I thought if I got help with aligning my chakras again, I might be in a better position to find a teacher. What happened next was not at all what I expected.

As soon as I walked in the door, the Reiki Master started laughing and said that I was not following my path, that I still had things to learn in the spirit world. When I got those lessons down, a teacher in the physical form would appear. She went on to say that until then, nothing on the physical world with a spiritual teacher would manifest. I decided to test her for the next six months. I continued to sign up for classes and meetings. Nothing happened. The meet-ups were canceled and the classes didn't make. Finally I threw up my hands in defeat.

Soon after that I started to have dreams that I was in a classroom, learning about my life in the spirit world. For a while I didn't realize that I couldn't bring all the information back to this world when I woke up the next morning. Eventually the dreams started to spill over into my waking world, and vivid memories of me agreeing and understanding what was being said in the dreams started flooding back. The dam had broken, and I was remembering all of the things I had learned, which were important in my physical journey. It was an incredible experience. Afterward, I woke up every day for several weeks with a kind of memory from my dreams. And then, as quickly as the dreams started, they stopped, and I was able to meet and work with teachers on the physical plane. The teachers came in and out of my life as I moved through my experiences. Every once in a while I still have dreams of meeting with the Teachers and guides about things that I need to know or understand.

Trading

Trading is something that you see a lot in the healing community. Healers exchange services to experience what other healers in the community have to offer. It helps educate other healers so that they understand more about what services are being offered by experiencing it themselves. It is also a great way to advertise what is available in the community.

By exchanging services, healers can make recommendations from their own experiences to those they believe will see a real benefit, as they know how the modality will work. Certain healers don't want to trade, and that is okay, as it is their path. What I have experienced in the healing community is that there is a 50-50 ratio of those who are willing to exchange or trade to those who are not. I like when someone makes a recommendation from their own experience rather than just hearing about it.

Journaling & Blogging

When I first started to work on myself in my own healing journey, I was encouraged by my counselor at Golden Willow to keep a journal. So much was happening in my life it was hard to keep up with all of it.

When I started to journal, I discovered I was able to see patterns. For example, I started to write down when I saw ghosts. As I did so, it become apparent that it happened more than I realized. I was seeing them day and night, at restaurants, movie theaters, schools, people's houses, churches, on the street... You name it. They were there doing their own thing or just hanging out with the living. To me it was an everyday experience, like seeing trees. They are there and you notice them but don't really think much about them unless they catch your attention.

As I journaled, I could see how often I was actually having the experiences. When friends met me to go do something, they found me starting to take real notice of whomever I saw hanging out with us in the same room. After a while, I went back to not noticing them, and now I only notice if someone asks me about them or if the ghost or entity does something out of the ordinary.

Once I was visiting with a lady I had just met, and two ghosts were being ridiculously funny behind her back. It was like kids making bunny ears behind someone who is getting their picture taken. I had trouble pretending they were not there. The two jokesters were enjoying themselves, making me laugh and causing her to give me strange looks. Finally I just confessed that they were behind her, and she smiled, letting me know that she was aware of them. She even knew who they were. At that time I had not developed my hearing so I was only seeing.

By writing down my dreams and the interactions with people in my life, I soon discovered patterns in the dreams. This experience is different from what I have talked about in the classroom dreams. These dreams were more about symbols in my waking life that meant something to me personally. These symbols would stand out in my dreams and help me to learn more about myself and relationship patterns that were healthy or not. This allowed me to be more aware of what to look for in my waking life. I would then work on patterns that returned again and again that needed to be changed by looking up symbols and words. These symbols were very vivid. They popped up in my conversations and in my dreams again, letting me know that I needed to focus on the choices in my life. Guidance and love from the other side is always there when we are in line with healing ourselves. By writing this down, I could see it more clearly and could go into it on a much deeper level.

In 2008, I decided to go ahead and bite the bullet and start my own blog. I was not sure what I would write; however, each week I wrote from my heart or from an experience. Some of those blog posts are in this book and some are not. I ended up writing three blogs, as I realized there was a great deal going on in my life. As I started to work with more clients at the clinic, I stopped writing on the blogs due to lack of time. In the summer of 2011, I knew I was going to write this book. I had no idea how. My only question to my spirit guides was, since I am dyslexic and only wrote short blogs, how could I write a book? I was told by my spirit guides to just write what had happened. That was all I had to do.

Tai Chi & Qigong

As I have mentioned before, I was taking classes in both Tai Chi and Qi Gong during the time I was working at the church. It was recommended to me by one of my spiritual teachers to help me relieve some of the stress and tension that I was feeling. During that time I learned about a wonderful Master Teacher Martha Fiddes who was holding Tai Chi and Qigong classes just across the street from the church. How could I go wrong when something landed right at my feet? I signed up without hesitation, as it was just too easy to go across the street and try a month of lessons.

I was so excited. I had taken Tai Chi when I was sixteen when my father was trying to keep me out from under his feet and signed me up for a class, one summer in Taos. It all seemed quite natural. I started to learn the basics, again enjoying myself as we worked on form and postures. I stayed with the class for a year and changed over to the Qigong class. I was really drawn to the energy and moved up into the advanced level. I loved my time away from everything when I went, just being in that calm moment gave me a chance to take a pause from life.

During that time, one of my friends Kolton was in town visiting and asked if I would like to meet up. I said sure; I didn't have a lot planned that day. I did have my Qigong class that evening, but I thought I would have plenty of time. We had so much fun catching up though that we lost track of the time, and I realized that my class was coming up quickly. I invited Kolton to come join me, as our teacher always encouraged people to try the class out to see if it was a fit. I, of course, called to ask permission out of respect for my teacher, and she said it would be fine.

I had forgotten that I was in an advanced level, but my friend seemed to be right at home with the movements and poses we were working on. Somewhere in the middle of class, I heard an exclamation of wonder come out of my his mouth as he shot me a look of excitement. Later on I asked him what happened, and he asked me if I saw it. "No," I said, I was really working on my own energy and form. With much excitement he told me that his hands were engulfed in a blue flame right before his eyes as he was moving energy with them. "It was amazing," he said. He went on to tell me how he felt the energy between his hands and what he experienced. I was excited for him, as this occurrence is something you can tell people about but to actually experience it is beyond words.

After class my friend and I parted ways. He had to leave town the next morning, and I was busy with my family. Later on, we did get to talk more about energy, and it was so much easier to talk to him about it, since he understood what words sometimes can't say.

Feet - The Souls Of The Feet

I was having tea with my friend Amy and she was telling me about how sensitive the soles of the feet are. Knowing that she had spent time in New Mexico learning about herbs I decided to focus in on what she was saying with an open mind.

"No, really," she said! "Try this sometime. Take fresh garlic that you cut up then rub it on the bottom of your feet. In a few hours you will be able to taste it with your tongue." Anything that that we put on the bottoms of our feet is absorbed immediately, running through our bodies very quickly. Something that might give you pause when taking care of your feet.

Of course it wasn't until I woke up the next morning at four am that the thought came to me how many times I had read in the Bible that not only did they wash their feet, but they also used oils or different kinds of herbs on the bottoms of their feet.

Is this only a way to care for and cleanse the feet? Or could it be a way of caring for the body as a whole? I have heard stories of people in the past putting Vicks on their children's feet when they had a cold to help them breathe better.

If our feet are that sensitive, then by not caring for them properly, what kind of an effect does it have on the whole body? What is in the inside of our shoes? What about foot powders and sprays? How does that affect us?

Good Vibrations

We and everything around us are made up of some kind of molecular structure. There is no hocus pocus in this term. We have atoms that are always moving in and all around us, as we learned in science class at school. Everything, whether we see it or not, is moving.

Energy can affect the way that these atoms move. Energy can come in the form of sound, emotions, heat, and many others. Now think about this: Radio waves and television signals move through the air. We cannot see them, yet we know they are there.

Emotions and thoughts are the same way. Your thoughts have more power than you realize. They can change your molecular structure to create someone who is positive, whom people are excited to be around, or to create someone negative, whom others try to avoid.

The human body is amazing in the way that it picks up these energies. Think about the last time you walked into a place and the hair on the back of your neck stood up. When was the last time you were around someone who was stressing you out and your stomach was hurting? Or when was the last time you couldn't wait to be around another person? Your body was picking up the energy from that person that resonated (or didn't resonate) with you.

Now let's put this into perspective. If you are sending off negative signals, your atoms begin to vibrate in that way, and people who are in the same state will be attracted to you, as will anything in that state that is not seen with the naked eye. If you send off positive signals, then the body vibrates in a higher form, and people with that vibrational frequency will feel comfortable and will be more attracted to your vibration. That is why we attract the same type of person over and over in our lives. The choice is really up to you.

Sometimes we leave this energy with things around us. For example, if a person was depressed and sat in a particular chair all the time, then finally decided to sell it in a garage sale, where you bought it, you may get it home and learn that this chair gives you a funny feeling. If you feel emotionally uncomfortable when you sit in it, you are picking up the energy of the chair from the other person. This is when you need to decide to get rid of it or change the vibration. This is called cleansing. It can be done by praying over the chair or asking someone to help who knows how to cleanse it, thus changing its vibrational frequency.

Sound Vibrational Healing

I have often wondered if people are aware that the resonance of our voices can not only bring us in union with our mind, soul, and body, but also with everything else, through its vibration. It seems to be a gift that all of us take for granted. Most of us are not even aware that the connection exists. Sure, we use our words to express our opinions or ideas. We forget that the true vibration of sounds plays a big part in connecting us to everyone and everything else around us.

I first became aware of this when I was nineteen and was visiting a convent while on a mission trip with a friend who was Catholic. I had always loved to sing and had been in choirs and taken voice lessons while growing up. But it wasn't until this one experience that I truly realized that there was something else to it.

I recall that we were awakened early to go to a morning Mass. The nuns sat on one side of the sanctuary, while the priests sat on the other. It was so early, yet there we were sitting in the cold of the chapel. When the nuns opened their mouths to sing, there was something that words can't describe in their passion to praise God.

I remember my heart swelling up and not being able to see as the tears fell on my hymnal. A flow of energy burst though my body as love came crashing in through every pore. My head became light as my breath was caught in my throat, making me choke on the words that tried to escape from my mouth. Then as I pulled myself back together, my voice blended in unison as the notes vibrated though my whole being. It was something I will never forget.

Years later, I was learning how to chant with my meditation teacher. She taught us about the organs in our body that respond to the vibration in our voice. These included: The brain, heart, lungs, spleen, liver, kidneys, and stomach. With our focus on those areas, we could connect to opening up places that were blocked with stress. This made sense to me because I was already learning Qigong and we did a similar exercise, using our voices to bring the vibration of the body back into balance. We would use different tones that matched with the sounds that our organs made within our bodies.

Our Qigong teacher gave us one sound to match each organ within the body. We were to focus on each organ while we chanted its sound until she cued us to the next one. Then she led us into the chant. At first, it was awkward. I was just trying to match her tone and get the chants right as I tried to focus on the area of the body she asked us to start with. As we repeated the chant, however, it finally started to flow. As it did, I noticed a warm rush of energy moving through my body, spinning in the area that I was focusing on. It felt warm and soothing, and I started to lose myself in the moment.

She switched to the next chant, and the sound's vibration moved up my body to each center. When we reached the very last one at the top of the head, I felt an explosion of energy and release, and I began to cry like a baby. The tears flowed out of my eyes like a fountain. Embarrassed, I tried to recover what dignity I had left, but my body had other plans, and it released all the tension that I had been holding in.

The whole experience was powerful. I went home limp. I recovered in the next few days with a renewed sense of passion for life. At that time I was singing with my daughter in a little band at our church. I noticed that when we were singing I began to open up as we performed. I was not only more conscious of what was happening inside of me, but also felt a connection to something much bigger than myself. I felt connected again with the great Creator and all that was created, as the air pushed out from my lungs and moved through to my heart chakra. Through my experience, I had learned to open up and allow the breath of God to pour into my whole being as I raised my voice.

Just before the Christmas holidays, I met a new friend for lunch, and she shared almost the exact same experience. For me it was another confirmation that life has so much more to offer than what we see.

The Space Suit

Once, when I was working with a client with Reiki, I was suddenly taken out of my body. My consciousness was somewhere in outer space, where I heard my name being called. I saw an astronaut floating around in his space suit. "So, what is the big deal?" I asked and then I heard my name again. "Ana, remember that you are fifty percent human body -- that is, flesh and bone. The other fifty percent of you is soul, who is connected to your spirit. You are living in a space suit that you call your physical body while you are on earth, but you are still very much the spirit within the suit. Never forget this."

Dyslexia

During a Reiki session my spirit guides came asking me to go with them. I was taken out of my body and shown the image of my cat scratching at a mirror. I laughed. I always think it is funny that my cat thinks there is another room in the mirror. Then I heard one of my spirit guides say, "Ana, people who have dyslexia are really gifted. They remember what it is like to be on the other side. They still see the reflection. These people have the ability to see the other side a little easier than most. They have not forgotten what it was like when looking from the other direction." Then I was shown a child with ADD and again my spirit guide spoke... "Ana, the people on earth think there is something wrong with these beautiful beings and label them as special needs. People on the earth plane try to change the nature of these beings because they do not seem to fit in your world. The truth is that they are gifted and have never forgotten what it is like to be spirit. They have not forgotten what it is like to be free, moving about with the least effort, and yet, they are forced to fit in. Remember this."

I know now that there are a lot more programs that work with helping people who are dyslexic since I heard this message. The world is discovering that instead of changing people who are dyslexic it can change how it works with and accommodates them.

There was another time, when I was in the middle of working with a client during a Reiki session, when all of a sudden I could feel myself drift into what I know now as theta waves. The next thing I knew, it was like watching a movie. My guide came into the picture and a sense of knowing came over me. In that moment I understood that my dyslexia was really a gift of the spirit. I could see the way it worked from a different perspective from what I believed to be true about it on this dimensional plane. As this was happening I had a thought that it was funny because I had always felt that I never really "got" the rhythm of life, as it seemed so many around me did.

What was shown to me was that we here in the physical realm have it backwards. Many believe that we are our bodies, that our lives on this earth plane only revolve around our physical lives. The truth is that we are spirits who came to earth to incarnate in a body. We are so much more than what we even realize. We have forgotten who we really are. Once we remember we are spirit, inside the form of the body in the third dimensional world, we can expand not only our thinking but how we live our lives.

I understood that the reason there are dyslexic and ADD personalities is that these are the spirits who still have that connection. They still see things in tune with Spirit, rather than the physical mind within the physical body. Everything is separated, trying to make sense of it all. When you are in the spirit, you can move around and do many things at once with only a single thought. This ability does not emanate from the mind but from the pure consciousness of the soul. In this third dimension that we live in on the earth, a person with ADD has trouble fitting in with others' ability to focus. This is because the unconsciousness of the soul that is connected to the spirit, which has no limits or boundaries, has been thrust into a physical body with many limitations. That can be confusing to a person who still remembers, somewhere within themselves, what it was like to be on the other side, without any constraints.

A Visit From The Angels

One day in the late afternoon, sometime during December of 2010, I was waking up from a nap, coming out of my dream state. I opened my eyes and saw a beautiful light-being standing in front of my bed, watching me wake up. I remember taking my time, closing my eyes again, and opening them back up to see if what I was seeing would go away. Every time I opened my eyes, the being was still standing there. It seemed to be waiting patiently on me, so after deciding it was not going to go away I asked with my thoughts, "Why are you here?"

I heard an immediate response, "Ana, would you like to see what it is all about?" The last time when I was asked this question, I was afraid to see the answer. Since then, I had spent a few years mulling over whether I wanted to know or not.

I answered, "Yes, please!"

Instantly I was given an image in my mind which was a bit like watching a movie. I could see it all play out inside my thoughts in high definition with surround sound. I saw people sleeping and waking up from their sleep, afraid of what was happening to them. They were seeing, hearing, and feeling things that they didn't understand. People were seeing ghosts, angels, and loved ones that had passed. Others were feeling vibrations and hearing things that they had not heard before. Still others were able to heal, tapping into the feelings that were happening inside of people, the earth, and other beings. There was so much fear. It was all happening so fast. I could see that many didn't understand what was going on.

Then I was shown what looked like candles, shining a light in the darkness around the world, touching others with their lights. I could see the candle lights spread, like in a candle light service where all the candles were being lit. I was then given the understanding that it was about learning and teaching others not to be afraid of the beautiful gifts that were given to them. People were waking up without their masks and finding their true selves. Then a feeling of inner peace flooded the whole vision, and the world grew very bright. I had these words imprinted in my mind: "Heaven on Earth!" All I could say was, "Ooooooooo, Aaaaaaaa, Wow!" I could feel warm tears rolling down my cheeks as I watched in awe the light illuminating the world.

The beautiful light being said, "There is much work to be done," and faded from my sight.

Clearing Chakras

When I was first starting to learn about energy, I didn't really understand just how important it was to clear the chakras. The first book I read on chakras, recommended by a healer from Taos, was called "The Wheels of Life." [8] It is considered the bible of chakras. The information in this book helped me to connect the dots in understanding how the energy fields affect not only our emotions but the physical body as well. Since I had studied Qigong and Reiki, the book brought it all home.

What I learned is that often we forget that not only do our bodies consist of the physical cells and tissue, there is also a great deal going on with energy fields. All matter, and the things that we even consider solid, are still created out of tiny atoms and even smaller particles, what some are calling the God Spark. If this is so, then why is it silly or "hocus pocus," that working on the micro part of the way we were constructed is strange? If the universe and the vibration that keeps us intact are in balance within our own cells and tissues, then it is easy to see how the chakra system can affect our bodies and our health.

I want to briefly mention the chakras, to expand a little more on how they work. As I was learning about them I came across another wonderful book called "The Book of Chakra Healing," by Liz Simpson. [9] This book is valuable because it goes into detail about how the emotions are affected when the chakras are too open, too blocked, or when they are balanced. It explains that the chakras, when balanced, spin clockwise. The higher chakras, which are above the heart, spin faster than the lower chakras. If, for some reason, the chakras become slow or blocked, the whole system will be thrown out of balance. Chakras can spin counter clockwise, too fast, or become too open, again changing the natural flow of energy within the body. This all has a great effect on the way we feel or move as we go about our daily lives.

A good example of this is a broken heart. Pinpointing this emotion is easy, as it seems to hit us in the heart area, the fourth chakra. The heart chakra rules over relationships, so when we are out of balance in that area, we feel it right in the heart. When this chakra is too open, we can become obsessive, even overdramatic, with loved ones. If the heart chakra is spinning too slowly, we tend to have difficulty with relationships, making others feel smothered with our affections. This slow spinning is due to being clogged – not being directly connected to the Source – so we use others as surrogates to fulfill our needs for love and connection. If the heart center is blocked, we tend to draw inward, rejecting others, feeling undeserving of love. When the heart chakra is spinning counterclockwise, we can be confused about the way we feel in our relationships. If our heart chakras are in balance, we can step into our personal power, feeling connected as the energy from Source allows us the freedom to love unconditionally. We can then express ourselves in a healthy way.

Often when I work with a client, I like to ask them to sit quietly and go within themselves to pinpoint where the emotion that we are working on is located within the physical body. Since emotional energy can be felt in the physical form, most people can tell where they feel they are being affected in the body. Once we find the location where the emotion has resided, we can open up the chakra that is being influenced and start the process of clearing it out. Then we work on bringing the chakra back into harmony with the body. If, for some reason, the person I am working with can't find the location of the emotion, then, with their permission, I will go into their energy field to locate it.

It is important for me, when I am working with a client, to teach them a few basic techniques to clear the chakras themselves. This allows each person to be in charge of their own healing. They do not need to be reliant on me or someone else. If the client requests for me to remove the block, I am also very happy to do this for them. I still want them to learn how to step into their own personal power of clearing their chakras themselves.

Once, a dear friend of mine was going through a difficult time in her relationship when we were working together. My spirit guides made it very clear that, no matter how much I wanted to "carry her up the mountain" to help her with this experience, I would not be doing her or myself any favors. They said we wouldn't make it very far up the mountain. The best way for her to heal was for her to learn how to take responsibility for her own healing and for me to accompany her but not do all the work for her. I could do what was the best for the both of us which was to share with her what I knew and hold her hand as she learned how to take the steps up the mountain on her own two feet. When I told my friend, she understood. Together we began to climb, both of us learning simultaneously, as we shared the journey just by being there for each other. I have to say that both my friend and I learned a great deal from going on the journey, supporting each other. We are still very good friends today, years after the experience.

Learning the basics of the way energy works in our body through the chakra system, while practicing clearing these energy fields, is a wonderful way to keep yourself healthy and in harmony with the world around you. There are many books and information on the Internet about the chakras, if you are interested in learning more about them.

Other Healers

As I examine my life now, years later, I am so very honored to be counted among my friends who are out there teaching others how to heal and find their connection. I have learned a great deal by watching, while also being a part of the different healing communities as I continue to work on myself and to grow.

I have learned from many who are healers and teachers how to work with people on both the spiritual and physical planes. As I watch other healers interact with people I am always surprised what they see and how quickly they pick up on patterns of energy that even they are working on within themselves. When these patterns are recognized it is not something that is judged but it is seen as something that needs to be shifted. It is considered to be a beautiful thing to grow and understand that we are all here to learn.

Don't get me wrong, there are healing communities that are on a different level of vibration. I have been in a few communities where they wouldn't lift someone else up unless it helped them. This may happen if the community is based around fear. I have also been with others that are all about lifting each other up in love. The success of one person is a success for all. Again, it is not about judging what is good or bad. It is all about where we are at that time in our lives to bring forth what we need to learn about ourselves. By not judging others and ourselves we are not as distracted in recognizing what is being mirrored back that needs attention to heal.

A Lesson From The Other Side

One of the most common questions asked of me is, "How does your husband feel about what you do?" I always tell people how much he supports me. He is an engineer and thinks with his left brain, so I am always grateful for his perspective when we talk. My husband is sensitive, but he doesn't mind telling people what he thinks. Often I have heard him tell others that he hasn't had experiences like me, however he believes me. That all changed when he had his own experiences.

One evening I was having trouble sleeping while he was working on his computer in our bedroom. Usually that is not a problem, but that night I was tired. For some reason I couldn't settle down. I asked him if he wouldn't mind moving to the next room so that I could go to sleep with the lights off. He agreed to move to the living room to finish his work, and after that I quickly fell asleep. I awoke around two in the morning and realized he was not there, so I got up to look for him. I found him on the couch, where he was sound asleep. He looked uncomfortable, so I decided to wake him up and help him move to the bed.

The next morning when we awoke, he told me about his experience on the couch. He said that he was just starting to drift off to sleep when he became aware that someone was standing next to him in the living room. When he tried to open his eyes or move, he found that he couldn't move or talk. Then, he said, he saw electrical currents of light that looked like lightning bolts flashing in his head. His heart started beating really fast. He felt that he was going to have a heart attack as an energy seized his body. Somewhere within himself he knew that it wasn't a real heart attack that took over his body, but he couldn't do anything about it. Then, as fast the energy settled over him, it let go, allowing him to move. He said the whole time he knew he wasn't asleep, but he couldn't explain why he knew someone was in the room with him. Exhausted from the experience, he finally slept.

I told him that the day before, I was taking some trash out to the garage, when I noticed two ghosts standing there. I felt sorry for them and invited them into the house, letting them know they were welcome as long as they didn't make any trouble. I was busy that day writing, but I did notice a smoky energy darting past me a couple of times while I was getting up and down from my desk. Once the family came home for the evening, I quickly forgot my strangers and didn't think about them until my husband told me what had happened to him.

Feeling like a bad hostess, I quickly opened the energy grids and asked the angels for help in crossing the men who had found their way to our garage and were now in our house. It didn't take long; the angels found them in the living room standing behind the coffee table. I watched as they surrounded the ghosts with unconditional love, and I saw another person, who seemed to know them, step in from the other side, and help them cross so that they wouldn't be afraid. It was all so beautiful to watch, and when it was over, a peace flooded the room. Soon after, I apologized to my husband for not letting him know we had guests of the ghostly kind.

Collage Of Life!

Once, in a class, I was given a project to make a vision board, a collage depicting what you want out of life and what you see yourself doing that makes you happy and successful. If you are a spiritual person, your vision board will reflect that. If you are a material person, it reflects that too.

The task is simple: Come up with what you dream about by cutting out magazine photos that represent your dream. You can also draw your own pictures on a board to see your goals. This is an ingenious idea, as your subconscious mind sees most things in picture images. You can connect to your super-subconscious mind, which is connected to everyone and the energy of everything that is what you want out of life.

This project lines you and your subconscious up with what you want. It is like plugging into a computer to use spell check. It tries to match up your dream with the right action. "Ask, and you shall receive," or manifest.

My husband and I decided we would sit down one morning to do a vision board together, since we were in transition in our own lives. We were really excited; there was a lot of room for major changes. We sat down with our coffee, magazines, and materials to create a family vision board, smiling at each other. As we got into the project, we discovered that we both had very different ideas of what we wished to do and create. We could not come together on a dream. If we couldn't decide on what we wanted together as a couple then what kind of message were we sending out?

After the third cup of coffee, with lots of stressing out over what the other one wanted in life, we stopped. We realized that the reason we couldn't pull our resources together was that both of our energies were being funneled in two very different directions.

Then what I call "magic" took place. We each understood that the other person is quite different from ourselves. I began to listen to what he wanted, and he listened to hear what I wanted. Wow! What we discovered was that communication, compromise, and respect for the other person's needs and wants helped us to really see each other. Suddenly we were discovering what each of us was trying to live out in our own lives. It was all clear and all on a collage of visual images cut out of paper.

We had just completed Couples Therapy 101, without going to a seminar. To end the story I would like to say that we got it together, completing our collage on one poster board but we didn't. We decided to create two separate vision boards. We each have our own collages, which we hung up side-by-side in our bathroom so we could see them each day. We agreed that the combination of the two different ideas is not a bad thing, as they work hand-in hand-to create the same dream.

Part IV
Teaching

"The possession of knowledge does not kill the sense of wonder, and mystery. There is always more mystery."

Anais Nin

Chapter Eleven: Teaching Others

Spirit Teachers and Animal Helpers

Many of us have heard of having a guardian angel that watches over us throughout our entire lifetime on this earth. This is true. We also have spirit animals watching over us as we go about our daily lives. I always find it amazing how much love, support, and help we have from the other side, even when we feel we are completely alone. The truth is we are never alone. We are always looked after, even in our darkest hours.

Did you know that angels, spirit guides, spirit animals, and loved ones make themselves known to us as we all go through the different stages of our lives? By learning how to communicate and interact with them, we can change the way we view life. We can learn how to shift our thoughts and energy so that we can have that relationship with them. Most of us as adults have been taught to shut these amazing beings out of our lives, often forgetting what it feels like to be in contact with them. We lose our own connection as we get lost in the third dimensional world. Through the eyes of a child, we can see the world we have forgotten. Children remember their lives before they were born.

Spirit animals have been tremendous in teaching us not only about ourselves but also how to travel in the different dimensions to find those lost parts of us that have been scattered throughout the universe. Through these adventures we are able to experience in our sleep or in twilight, the true discovery of who we really are. Angels also accompany our souls as they guide, watching over us, only helping when we ask. We give them permission so as not to interfere with our own free will.

Our angels and spirit guides come in as teachers, in dreams, thoughts, or visions, connecting us and reminding us why we came to this earth. I always have a sense of ease in relationships with my spiritual teachers on the other side. I can feel their strong presence when they enter my energy field. I feel the sense of comfort, knowing that they are with me when I ask for assistance. Each of us has this ability to work with these beautiful and helpful beings. We just have to ask.

The Silent Language Of Trees

My friend Amy has the natural gift of communicating with the plant world. The information she receives from the plants helps her tremendously when she works with herbs to make healing tinctures. I do not have the privilege of this gift myself. Rather, I watch her in amazement as she gets information directly from the plants. It reminds me of the ancients finding cures for those in their community.

One day, I met her in her home for tea. She was telling me about her efforts to communicate with a tree in her backyard. She was worried because it wouldn't communicate with her at all. She knew, in her own way, that the tree was grieving. She pointed out to me that it had poison ivy growing on one side, the side that was facing her yard. She wanted to ask the tree about it. No amount of coaxing could convince it to say a thing to her. She said that it seemed strange that the poison ivy was only on that one side of the tree.

She told me that a few days before, she had decided to take a walk around the grounds outside an art museum in Fort Worth, after seeing the exhibits, when a certain tree caught her attention. She focused in on it, and it began to tell her about the tree in her backyard. It told her that her tree was afraid of the negative energy that was emanating from a space in the backyard. It also told her that poison ivy was a helping plant to trees and grew around them to protect them from other danger.

Of course I had to question, how could the tree on the museum grounds know about the other tree where she lived? That made no sense to me at all. She explained that the roots of all the trees in the world are tied into the earth, and the vibration of the roots within the earth makes a wonderful communication system. They have their own language that moves through the vibrations of the roots. This means that they are connected to all the trees on the earth, each knowing when another is in distress. They also are connected by their leaves, picking up vibrational energy through the molecules in the air. Thus they are in touch with life and the goings on of the planet.

We discovered later that what the tree in Fort Worth had said was true. We found a huge portal open in the backyard, causing a great amount of stress on her plants. Once the portal was closed, she found that she could grow things in that area of the yard, where before she could not. The plants now live and continue to flourish. The tree finally trusted my friend, and they began to communicate with each other.

This experience made me think about all those people who tell you to go hug a tree when you are down in the dumps. When I realized how connected plants are to the earth, it made me wonder how I missed all of this. As a small child, I used to love to lie in the grass while listening to the wind blow the leaves in the trees. I used to pretend they were talking to each other. Who knew that this was all real? How unconnected and out of touch have we become from the earth? How did we lose our understanding of the way nature works? What caused us to be so out of balance, disconnected from nature, the world, and ourselves?

Once again I was reminded that life is a learning process. We are here to have experiences as we learn to open our eyes and ears. It is about discovering while exploring our connection to each other, Source, and everything around us.

Soul Contracts

I hear a lot of people ask why things happen to them. Most people feel like they are a victim of someone or circumstances. Based on what they are experiencing, it may very well seem that way. When you view things from a much higher or larger perspective, you find that situations in our own lives affect more than just ourselves. An event in a person's life is like a ripple in the waves that change the flow of the water. I was surprised about what I discovered when I first learned about soul contracts, especially when I started to observe how things were working on a deeper level.

Before I go on I would like to mention something. What is chaos to us may not be chaos to our creator. What we see as order may be out of order from the higher perspective. As the spirit guides like to remind me, life is an experience to learn on a much higher level.

When you go into the soul contract, you can see things that you can't see when you are in the middle of the storm. From our own perspective on the earth plane, it is by having hindsight that we understand things. The gift of the soul contract is to be able to look at it all from a deeper level and to understand the process of the lesson, while going through it.

A soul contract is when a group of souls get together on the other side before they are born and incarnated on the physical plane, to have a life experience. As a group, they decide when and where they will meet up with each other in their lifetime on earth and help each other grow on a soul level. This means who will be the parents, siblings, family, friends, co-workers, or spouses in the lifetime. Just like a play in a theater, each soul takes a role in the human drama that will unfold in each of their lifetimes together, including the roles of the protagonists and the antagonists. As a group, they will come to create a learning experience for each soul on the highest level.

What is forgotten is that we are all created out of the same vibrational frequency of unconditional love, we must remember that we grow the most when we find others in our lives who cause concern and frustration, when we are aware of what blocks us from our soul connection to Source and ourselves. We are often limited in our abilities to see our way out when we are in the middle of an experience, but angels and spirit guides can help us see a much larger picture when we ask for help. We must learn that we are all guided by our own souls to honor our contract as created by ourselves and others. We have agreed to come to this earth to help each other learn who we really are and how we are connected to God, our Source.

One afternoon, I was having lunch with two dear friends of mine. One of them was going through the process of a divorce. Her husband was abusive, and she had to leave the relationship or lose herself. She asked me what I picked up intuitively, and I told her the whole experience was an agreement between her and her soon-to-be ex in a soul contract. My dear friend looked at me. I could see pain in her eyes as she said, "What am I supposed to be learning from all this pain and suffering?" My heart ached for her, and I didn't know what to tell her. I kept quiet and wondered why she had to go through what she did. It wasn't until later that she told us a most amazing story.

She explained to me and my other friend what she had learned about a processing system in another country that was set up to care for abused women. She had been learning how the legal system worked. She told us about her own abuse and how she was starting a website to educate and answer questions for women in her country who were abused. She was bringing aboard professionals and legal counsel to answer questions. She talked about women being able to tell their own stories on her site, to reach out to others who needed to know they were not the only ones going through abuse. As I sat there listening to this incredible woman, I watched her transform in front of me, from a victim to a woman who was taking back her own power. She was already talking to people who could help her put it all together. My other friend and I were both in awe, watching the transformation happen right in front of us. The whole visit was an enormous inspiration to the both of us. We felt honored and blessed to be in our friend's presence as we listened to her story and learned what she was doing.

As we sat there, tears welled up in my eyes, and I felt my heart being touched on so many levels. When she saw my tears, then also noticed my other friend tearing up as well, she paused. I saw her envision all the pieces of the puzzle fitting neatly together. Recognition registered in her eyes. She had remembered her soul contract. A smile spread across her face and pure light shone out of her whole being. It was a sight to behold.

Human Teachers

When you first awaken, you become very aware of those around you. You begin to see those who my father used to call "still asleep."

A fair majority who have recently become conscious of what is happening around them begin to search for a human teacher who can explain these new experiences to them. Keep in mind that a student-teacher relationship is very important to keep in balance. It is vital that the student not surrender their personal power or follow blindly under a teacher. This alone can cause a great deal of pain, confusion, and codependency in the relationship.

Though there has to be trust, it is okay to use your own common sense when it comes to following someone's leadership. There are going to be times that a teacher fulfills the learning experience, and then the time comes to move on. The most important part of having a human teacher is learning how to trust yourself to recognize when that relationship is growing or withering. Take responsibility for your own actions and know that it is okay to move on when the time comes.

Once, I went to a workshop in Austin, Texas, with one of my good friends Lilly who loved going to work with this particular teacher. At the time I did think it was kind of strange that it was her third time going to the basic level workshop, but I thought maybe she was just going to give me support.

It was a big class and I was sitting with my friend when the teacher started scanning the room with his eyes. He stopped abruptly and looked directly at Lilly in the audience. The teacher said that he thought he had seen her before. She admitted how many times she had taken his basic course. I guess what surprised me the most was his response. He seemed a little agitated and asked directly why she kept attending the first level workshop. My friend responded that she enjoyed the workshop and getting away from the rest of the world. He then said that it was important for her to grow. He was concerned that she was not growing if she did not move on to the next level or find other teachers that could help her expand. He was glad to see her but wanted to make sure that she was not blocking herself or afraid to move forward in her own spiritual growth.

The impression that was left with me from witnessing this was that this teacher was focused on his students learning how to continue on with their evolution in their own spiritual development and not being hindered by fear or even by him as a teacher. He was interested in the highest good for each of his students. I witnessed through his interaction with his students the rest of the weekend that teaching, for him, was not about money, ego, or power. As he worked with us, I noticed that he would walk around the room and engage with all the students. That alone was a feat in itself, as there were so many of us. When I left, I knew that this teacher was someone to watch as a model for when I was working with other teachers.

In my own experience, my dad played a big part in my own spiritual path. Most of the time I had experiences, I would ask him what they were about. He explained what he could from his own experiences or from the lessons from his teachers. As a child I was very curious, wanting to know how all things worked. I always had lots of questions for both him and my mom. Sometimes he would ask me if I could observe some silence. To his disappointment, it would last for about 30 seconds. Then, when I thought I couldn't take it anymore, I would blurt out what I was thinking. Finally he would assign things for me to do to keep me busy on the physical realm, with some sort of spiritual lesson attached to satisfy me, allowing him some peace.

Much later in life, I started to listen to that tiny voice within myself. As I allowed myself to grow, I began to explore following my instincts. That was when I found my first few teachers, who guided me as far as they could until the next one showed up. My Master Reiki teacher showed up in my life. Then I found a teacher who understood meditation and color energy. Later on, my mentor introduced me to another amazing teacher who helped me bring back my gift of sight and hearing the other side. When I was under a heavy amount of stress, the Qigong Master teacher appeared. Then another teacher came into my life, letting me know it was okay to move energy and light again. I was reunited with a medicine man and the shaman practitioner, who reminded me of the Spirit teachers that surround us. My Akashic Records teachers showed up in my life, along with a vibrational healing teacher. Through it all, I learned that I was being gently guided in finding my footing by trusting Spirit and myself again.

The main role for human teachers is to help us as we learn how to trust ourselves again. They teach us how to get out of our own way so that we can expand. They stand beside us and are there to hold our hand as we gain confidence in what we are learning. They celebrate with us when we finally take flight and are delighted with our discoveries. In the end, isn't that what teaching is all about?

Pulling Your Energy Back "The Young Man"

During the time that I was working at the acupuncture clinic, a young man came in for a Reiki session. Before starting any session I go over with my clients what to expect. He was very excited about Reiki. We ended up having a longer discussion than usual about energy and how it worked. He had a lot of questions. While we were talking, I felt myself begin to shake and my energy wobbled. Quickly taking note of what was going on, I did an assessment of my body and energy field. As I went through my own body looking for the source of my reaction I noted that I was being invaded. I found a strong energy that was pushing on me like it was trying to shove me against the wall. I felt a nervous energy in my field that wasn't mine. As I searched the room, I discovered that it seemed to be beaming from the young man's energy field. "Good," I thought, not having to deal with an attachment.

I stopped our conversation as I came to realize what was going on and asked the young man to pull his energy back. He seemed stunned by my comment but asked, "How?" I explained to him how to feel as though he was sucking his energy from the room back into his body. I told him to wrap a pair of angel wings around himself so he could feel secure. As soon as he did as I asked, I felt the tension in my body release. I was becoming exhausted just holding him back. The shakiness left immediately, and I was able to breathe a sigh of relief.

The young man looked at me with surprise. His eyes were saying he could feel his energy come back to him when he called it. I could see he was excited about the experience and he wanted to know more about pulling back the energy. I asked if he was okay, and then we talked about how our energy can push into someone else's energy field. I explained that this can happen without us knowing and is often caused by fear. It happens as we send out energy from our inner core to see if things are all right in our environment.

Energy works like sonar would on a submarine, but when we send out our energy towards another person, they often feel invaded. Most people wonder what is going on as they experience it, which may cause an upset in their personal field. By learning how to control our own energy, we can use it as a tool to understand others, to see if the environment is safe, or to pull it back to make others more comfortable.

People who are empathic are really good at this. They often use it as a safeguard, but it can backfire. On some occasions, an empath can pick up the energy of physical ailments from the person they are scanning without knowing it. This leads the empath to thinking that the symptoms of the other person are their own. This can also happen with emotional trauma coming from the other person's energy field that can stick to the empath. The empath then believes the trauma is theirs.

This happened to me one day when I was cleaning house. A friend of mine Terry popped into my thoughts, and I started to wonder how she was. At the time she had been dealing with clinical depression. All at once, out of the blue, I was hit with a deep depression like I have never experienced before. I could sense her in the room with me as I felt this overwhelming despair and complete hopelessness. The feeling was overwhelming as it consumed me. I quickly did a scan of myself and confirmed it wasn't mine, but I couldn't shake it off, no matter what I did. I finally sat down on a chair and let myself be aware of the experience. After about ten minutes, it lifted off of me like someone had picked it up and taken it away. I sat there for a few minutes processing what had just happened. I never forgot the experience. I get sad and depressed like everyone else, but this was like nothing I had ever experienced before. I told my friend Terry about it, and she confirmed that is what she experiences when she gets depressed. She is now being treated and is doing better.

Energy Medicine

One day while I was working at the clinic, I was invited to come into a private session that my acupuncturist friend Pam was conducting with a client. She wanted to see if I could help by seeing the client's energy field. I described what I saw and she smiled, thanking me. I went on with my day, not thinking much of it. As it turned out, it was the beginning of us working together as a team with clients.

One of the things I do is see energy as patterns as it moves or gets stuck in the energy fields. I had never really known what to do with that skill. I had some working knowledge of the colors that I saw and understood the basics of movement, although I had no real knowledge of energy medicine. As I worked with my friend every day, I developed a stronger connection with my spirit guides and record keepers on a more conscious level. The doorway to the connection that I used then was the Akashic Records. During that time, I began to comprehend what I was seeing. I learned and understood how different patterns of energy affected the clients' health.

I worked more closely with my spirit guides and record keepers. I used the gifts of hearing, seeing and feeling as tools when working with clients under the supervision of my acupuncturist friend. Sometimes the record keepers and spirit guides would tell me or instruct me what was going on. Often they would show me through something like a day dream that would enter my mind's eye. Under the direction of my friend Pam, who had a working knowledge of energy medicine in the body, I was able to learn how to ask specific questions to the record keepers and the spirit guides. I would repeat the answer that I was hearing from them verbatim to her and to the client. Sometimes I was describing what I was seeing. Pam would then use her knowledge to confirm what I was repeating from the record keepers and spirit guides.

On occasions the answer was not at all what I expected after opening the records of the client. Words and descriptions of images would flow out of my mouth, and Pam would then translate what I was repeating from the record keepers. Most of the time I didn't understand what I was saying, but she understood the energy language and could explain. The process was strange for me at first, but as we worked together I began to learn more and more about how energy operated on a broader basis. The work we were doing not only sparked my enthusiasm; it also caused an excitement in me about what I was learning.

One evening I was exploring the concept of using acupuncture without needles or tuning forks. My spirit guides were in agreement, showing me that the tools were not really necessary. I decided to look to see if anyone else was getting this information and maybe putting it out there on the web. To my surprise, I found a master teacher by the name of Mikio Sankey, an acupuncturist who taught something called esoteric acupuncture. I found him speaking on YouTube, and as I watched him, I felt a great connection. I understood what he was saying. It was all very refreshing to find someone speaking the same language as my spirit guides and record keepers. I discovered that he had also written several books on the subject. I ordered the first book, "Esoteric Acupuncture: Gateway to Expanded Healing" [10] and bought his DVD's containing some of his lectures about it. Excited about the whole experience, I couldn't wait to tell Pam.

The next day I walked into the clinic and announced my amazing discovery. I told Pam about the teacher and his books. She only laughed at me and took me over to her shelf in her office, showing me that she already had the books and had read most of them. She told me that she went to his lectures and did her thesis paper on esoteric acupuncture when she was getting her licenses. We had never talked about it before, and I rarely went into her office because I worked with clients in the treatment rooms, so I hadn't noticed the books on her shelf.

After that day, we used many of the esoteric techniques with our clients, but my Pam still felt that people would want to have the physical tools used on them so that they knew something was happening. I continued to feel drawn to the esoteric acupuncture, but found only a small handful of clients who felt okay using the techniques without the physical tools. It was truly gratifying to work in these sessions and people really enjoyed the new way of applying acupuncture. They experienced amazing results when we got to use the esoteric techniques. We were able to achieve more healing work in less time.

Later, when I finally decided to go deep with my study in energy medicine, I was stopped and told by my inner guidance that it wasn't really what I was here to do in this lifetime. Other things were calling me. I knew this was true, and as I put the books away, I could feel that something would be coming down the road. When it was time for me to leave the clinic, I was sad, but I understood that I had gotten an education about energy medicine. I was thankful for my friend Pam who took the time to teach me. I learned from that experience how to ask better questions, which was valuable for me to learn and go deeper into my own healing work.

Jumping Into Cancer

My husband and I had the opportunity to take the weekend off to travel to Taos a few months before I stopped working at the acupuncture clinic. We left late on a Thursday night after meeting at a family gathering in Frisco, Texas. On our drive that evening, I received a frantic call from Pam, the acupuncturist, who was helping another friend named Joy in healing her cancer. Pam was asking me to connect into Joy's energy to see if I could help. It had been a long day and a busy night with family. I found that I was too tired to really plug into her energy. I asked if we could try later or even work with my spirit guides when I was in twilight. Pam said yes, and we hung up as my husband drove us into Bowie, Texas, to find a hotel.

We found a place on the road and settled in for the night. I slept like a log, without much interruption to my sleep. The next morning I was awakened by my husband getting up and taking a shower. As I began to regain consciousness, I had for a few seconds an out-of-body experience. Spontaneously, I did a full body jump into Joy's cancer cells.

Later, when I was telling my husband about how the information was downloaded into me in those few seconds, I heard very clearly from my spirit guides to give him an example. I instantly saw what they meant. I explained to my husband that, for example, when you are flying on an airplane and it hits an air pocket, the plane seems to fall for a few seconds, and an electrical shock wave moves through your body, charged with fear. You may see your life flash before your eyes. In those few seconds, you are able to bring back a myriad of information from your entire experience. That is what happened to me.

In the body jump I was fully aware of where I was as I merged into the cellular energy of the cancer cells and experienced their vibration. I was instantly downloaded with information that really confused me. What I felt, saw, and understood was that the vibration of her cancer cells was pure, unconditional love. Now tell me, is that what we would usually think about cancer? I came back to my own body in a complete state of confusion. The rest of the information soon followed as I began grounding myself back into my physical form.

I was surprised. I had a short opportunity once to work with Joy weeks ago and was told in her Akashic Records that she had a choice to live or move on. When I conveyed that message, she promptly told me that she understood and already knew that. Joy said she wanted to live. In the weeks that followed, she became weaker and was not doing well at all. Why? I had wondered, when Joy said she chose life but I was told it was her choice that she was dying.

The unconditional love was highly confusing, as it was not in line with what we believe that cancer is about. When I merged with the cancer cells, I understood that she had many troubles and extreme emotional fears that she was attached to. She was having trouble letting go of the extreme anger and fear which had subsequently triggered the cancer.

What I understood was that the beautiful energy that is now emerging and changing our world in the universe is so much more refined to allow the body to hold on to negative energy within the cells and still sustain life. The cells of the body were creating a toxin with the negative emotional energy that would not survive unless released. The cancer therefore was triggered to bring the whole body back into balance. It was there to remind the body from where it had originated, which was in unconditional love. The cancer was to help her release the toxins that took over the mental emotional fields of the physical form to bring her back into balance.

I was told again by my spirit guides that she had a choice: to live or to die. It was up to her to deal with and release the mental emotional energy that had reprogrammed her cells into toxins that would no longer be able to sustain life. Treatment would ensure the release of negative energy on a whole vibrational level if she were willing to let go of the anger, fear, and blame of others for her fate in life. Recovery was about forgivingness, grace and gratitude. This was written in her soul contract, that she had a choice, to exit the earth plane, or to remain. But she had to bring back the balance to continue life.

The other part, which I understand more from my own experience, is like when you are on a diet and you have decided that nothing will bend your will to change your diet. You have to reach that certain state to flip the switch to lose the weight, or it is just not going to happen.

Again, I would like to point out it was a choice, in her case, to flip that switch to create absolute healing to move into remission. The biggest part of treatment is facing yourself and your worst fears, as you begin to purge toxic energy, which allows the cells to be reprogrammed into a more sustainable energy to heal and to bring the body back into balance.

I called Pam and wished her luck. It was more about her relaying the message to her friend, reminding her to make a choice to let those old programs go. The work that I could see ahead would certainly not be an easy road to travel, but it could be done. In this case, with the help and expertise of my friend, who is well-versed in vibrational medicine, the change could reverse.

I ended up talking to another friend who asked if that scenario is true with all cancer. Do people always have a choice? The answer I got back from the spirit guides was that it is different for each individual. It is written in their soul contract. This was, however, the case for her.

Internships

Internships can be an incredible experience if the match between the student and teacher is aligned. Trust is huge when finding a teacher to do an internship because it is all about the relationship.

A memory that comes to mind is when I was a child and my father was taking a martial arts class, he thought it would be good if I learned too. The instructor was an older man who was a jujitsu master teacher. One of the things that stood out in the class was when he would ask us to get in a stance, then he would try to throw us off balance by leaning or pushing on us. What I learned was that when we fell over, he corrected us, explaining how to hold our chi in center. He did this without losing his patience, taking the extra time with us to explain why we were losing our balance. Questions were always welcomed on any level about what we were all doing to improve our stances and what we were learning. It was incredible to watch people change within a few classes, seeing their confidence build within themselves.

Even in my own experience with internships, I find that my teachers test me. Though it is not always on the physical form, they find where my weakness is that throws me off balance. Sometimes the test is painful, and I have to take a breath. Other times it is joyful to move in the moment. I have found that when it is done in love, it still might hurt, but there is a sense of trust that the teacher is working with me and not against me. This in turn inspires the student to try even harder to learn. Trust is huge when it comes to internships. Also knowing that you are working with someone who has your best interests at heart and not their own agenda, when it comes down to it.

Cells and The Body - Cell Memory

Cell memory is something I think that we all need to know about because it can affect every one of us even in our relationships with others. One of the best examples I can think of can be found when there is physical or verbal abuse. The trauma is recorded in the cellular structure of the body. It doesn't matter what actually happened, it is all the same as far as the body is concerned, which puts out a signal of "fight or flight."

This means that a person who suffered any kind of trauma will often exhibit that feeling of "fight or flight" when a trigger goes off in the body. By trigger, I mean that if a person, often without conscious awareness, feels as though they are put in a similar situation to their previous trauma, they will react. The body, which has recorded that pattern of trauma, sends out a signal that there is danger, which causes a chemical reaction throughout the body. The body then recognizes the signal in the cells as a warning and reacts to the trigger.

This can mean that one minute you are having a lovely time with someone and then the next minute that person may be upset, angry, or wanting to leave. The key to treating this lasting effect is finding what caused the trigger to go off and learning more about the trauma. Once this is established, it can help both parties as a basis to work through the trauma, helping to strengthen a relationship without feeling helpless.

I had a personal experience like this while I was visiting Italy one summer with my husband and family. We were in Venice, and I found myself surrounded by pigeons. Lucky for me, my husband and I had discussed before we went to Italy, that this event may happen. I was then prepared to deal with it as it came. He even picked the word "pancakes" as a code word in case I needed to leave or if he felt that I needed to go.

Now that sounds funny when we look back on it, but it wasn't then. I couldn't remember what caused the reaction. As an adult I had always known that I was a little nervous around birds when friends had them as pets. Often they would ask if I wanted to hold their birds. I always refused. It wasn't until I was talking to my mom on the phone one day that a memory popped up of an incident that happened when I was three and we were in Italy.

I remembered my mother used to take me to Rome to do some of her shopping. While she was looking at the beautiful merchandise, which was often outside on the plaza, I would let go of her hand to run around and play with my toys. The pigeons would swarm all around me as they did with everyone else, but I was only three. They would land on me in large numbers, and I couldn't see. All I remember was screaming in a sea of birds that covered me, and my mother running to help me.

Looking back, I realized that because of the patience and caring of my husband, I was able to walk around the plaza and confront a childhood terror. I could enjoy just being with my family while moving through my fear, even though I was still feeling some of the old feeling of flight. I had to break an old pattern that no longer served me. I was now an adult and could have a different experience. Now, I talk to the birds and they don't bother me anymore when they gather around me. I can even hold them.

A lot has changed since that summer. I never used the code word, but knowing that someone else understood and there was help if I needed it was a great comfort. I also learned from this experience to recognize the signal that moves through my body when I am facing a fear. Now with my awareness I see fear as a gauge, which allows me to make decisions for changing things in my life. Fear is a wonderful tool to understand when we learn how to use it as a guide.

The Child - In The Heart Of Wounds

I have found it to be true that we all have a wounded child living within us, on a mental or energy level. I am sure many of you already know about the inner child, and some may have done healing work in this area of your life.

If you have ever been having an adult conversation with someone, then all of a sudden the other person reacts from somewhere off in left field, you may have touched a trigger point by accident, which takes that other person back somewhere into their childhood, when they experienced a wound. That means that the person you are talking to is no longer the adult, but is the child nursing an open wound.

You then experience a reaction from a child's point of view, because the adult has never healed and doesn't understand that the open wound still exists. Your conversation has poured salt on the wound, and the reaction is dramatic. Now you are having a conversation with a two year old, a five year old, a thirteen year old, or whatever age that person was when they had the traumatic experience.

This is where your compassion comes in if you are able to recognize that the other person is no longer with you but is reliving an experience from their past. The first and foremost rule is not to take anything they say personally. They are speaking from the heart of their own wounds, and if your intentions were not to wound, then you are on solid ground. Take a step back and analyze your own feelings, with the understanding that they may say something to spark your own inner trauma or inner child.

Allow yourself to take a time out if you need to, and know that what the other person is experiencing is very real to them. Take care of yourself by being gentle with your feelings and emotions, as they are not thinking but reacting from a trigger. You may not be in a position to bring it to their attention or make things right. However, you are in a position to understand where you yourself are.

So many of us have these wounds. We often, without thinking, speak from them, not realizing the damage that we are causing in ourselves and our relationships with others. As we each become aware of these traumas, we begin to realize that we have choices and that we can heal from those painful experiences while granting grace to others. This is another small step towards healing and understanding those around us. If we all took such a small step, it would change the world.

DNA

One afternoon I was visiting a book store with my daughter and enjoying myself as I went down the aisles, touching the books, and reading all the titles. One book in particular kept catching my attention. I picked it up to look at it and its cover. I placed it back on the shelf after deciding that it was too much for me to pay just to satisfy my mere curiosity. I then went to the bargain book section to see what was there. Once again I started to sort through books and titles when the same book appeared on the bargain shelf. Surprised to find it there on the marked down shelf, I picked it up. That was too much of a coincidence, so I went through it to see what I was missing. I had a few dollars in my pocket, and the book had been marked down numerous times. I had just enough to pay for it with the tax. Thrilled at my find, I took it home and started to read.

The book was about a curandera discussing some of the dreaming aspects of finding the spirit world. As I read, I recalled an experience when a friend committed suicide by jumping off the Rio Grande Gorge Bridge in Taos, NM. He was missing for days before his body was found. My mom had called me to ask for help. I went into a day dream and saw him lying in a cave. As I tried to wake him, three lightning bolts struck the ground around us. The light was so bright I was startled back into my body.

I called my mother and reported that I saw him in a cave. I thought he might be sleeping in a cave somewhere in the Gorge. Later that evening, I was washing my hair, and when I leaned back, laying my head in the tub of water, I saw the bottom of the Gorge Bridge. Floating in the tub made me feel like I was floating in the river, looking up. They found his body a few days later with his eyes open, on his back, not far from the bridge. It was a shock. Grief hit me like a ton of bricks.

Later I ran into the cave again when I was learning about curanderas. I was interested in the subject because of my Mexican background. I found a book called "A War of Witches" by Timothy J. Knab. [11] In it was a description of the cave with the lightning, which was one of the openings used to enter the underworld. The soul enters into a cave in the North where the lightning is kept. The description was like what I saw in that day dream those many years ago. I realized then that I had seen where he could cross but didn't know what I was witnessing at that time.

What I found fascinating was that this knowledge of the cave was passed down in the old Aztec wisdom. It was validation for me to know that I wasn't the only one who had this experience. I now know that the roadmap to the cave was a memory that may have been coded in my friend's DNA, which would mean that the soul of my friend knew of this opening to the other side. This could have been something he carried in his DNA that downloaded to his soul, or he could have used it to cross in other lifetimes. I had the same coded information. When I went to find him, it was as easy as matching up the energy frequency to the cave, which took me to him.

I wanted to see if a friend of mine, who also did dream work, knew about what I had just learned. I called her up and let her know what happened and what I had discovered in the book. She listened with great interest. I left the DNA part out and waited for her response. She knew that I was adopted. Without any information about the DNA, she quickly zeroed in on me being adopted and told me that there was something in my DNA that helped me make the connection with my friend who died. This made me wonder if we pass on our spiritual gifts to the next generation through our DNA. Why are we not teaching the younger generation how to use those amazing gifts for connecting to each other and to Spirit?

I have learned that we are very complicated as human beings. We not only have soul contracts, gifts of the spirit, and memories from the other side, but we also have some sort of ancient wisdom that is passed down through our DNA. Life just gets more curious.

Other Dimensions

Imagine my surprise when I was working with a client at the Acupuncture clinic and found an open door into her chakras. Quickly I asked my client's permission to enter, and with her consent, I went in. On that journey I discovered that there were open pathways leading into other dimensions from the chakras. An angel came as soon as I entered and escorted me into a sea of water. I felt like I was in a wave, in an undertow, as I moved into the energy of the chakra. I experienced a feeling of losing all control, but I knew my spirit guide was with me. I was finally spat out into another part of the universe. As I rolled, recovering from my plight, I was met by three other angels. My spirit guide coaxed me toward the angels for help because I was a little in shock from what just happened. We were taken to a place where I could find a piece of the person's soul, that I had been looking for. The soul had been hiding in that dimension.

Dimensional doorways don't just exist in other parts of the universe. They can be found just about anywhere. I think what surprised me the most from that experience was that we have these doors and pathways, even within our own bodies. This includes the physical and spiritual bodies, as everything opens up into energy. In the material world, if you are sensitive to these portals, you can either see them or feel a slight shift in energy field. Most of the time, they are moving and changing with the energy shifts of the universe, however they are there just the same.

You can find them closed, and other times they are open. It is just the way the universe works. You have heard that old saying, "So below as above." It can also be said, "So outside as inside." Again remember that we are created by tiny atoms and particles of light that bump into each other, creating vibration. That movement creates our gases, solids, and liquids. With that knowledge and the understanding that we are all created out of energy, as is everything else in the universe, we are starting to understand with Quantum Physics that we are also a reflection of the universe within ourselves. I run into doorways even in people's homes when we are doing spirit rescue in clearing houses. Once, my dear friend Robin asked me to come into her home. She was being awakened by a spirit who was bothering her as she tried to sleep. I invited another friend Veronica to come along to help. She was surprised when we found an open portal next to the bed that led into the bathroom. When we started we only thought we were dealing with spirits. We found out that the portal was on Robin's side of the bed. She had never told us which side of the bed she slept on. When I stepped into the space, the energy changed, shifting with the visual of looking out of a hole in a wall open to the universe with all the darkness and planets. Grateful Veronica was there with me, we closed the hole together. Later I described what I saw to Robin who asked us to clear the house. She was so excited; it was exactly what she saw and had experienced herself. She couldn't believe that we saw the same things, as she had not told anyone.

My friend who helped also likes to work with earth ley lines. She has the gift of clairvoyance and can see doorways opening and closing at different times and locations on the earth. In my own experiences I have discovered that there is a lot you can do with working with the different dimensions and these ley lines. I did learn, however, not to go through an open doorway without my spirit guide or spirt animal. I learned from teachers that often people can get trapped and not be able to get back to this dimension. They get lost in another world and leave their bodies in a comatose or in a daze state. It is really important to take the precautions of going with a guide when you plan a trip to explore these other realms.

Light & Color Healing

I have always loved color, and as an artist I have used it in many forms in different mediums of work. But when I started to see colors around people, it really began to get interesting. At first it was just a fascination. I tried to understand what I was seeing. Then one day a University of Texas at Arlington

Continuing Education magazine came in the mail. I found a course on color which caught my interest. Liking what I read in the course description I signed up to attend the class, although I was not really sure what I would learn.

I ended up being very pleased because Dr. Sarai who taught the class was my old meditation teacher. It was not an ordinary class on color like you would expect. She did an excellent job covering the basics in a few classes on energy and color. After that I was hooked. I loved working with color, and I started to read up on the subject of how it related to energy. To my surprise, my guides came to me in twilight, and we began to work with healing energies and light. It wasn't until years later looking back that I understood that my guides were beginning to awaken my understanding that the universal language of the universe was vibration and light.

What I did come to understand at that time was that we as multi-dimensional beings can be experienced as pure energy or light vibrations on many levels. When we are depleted of energy in certain areas of our body or our energy field, we naturally gravitate toward people who have a strong energy field of light coming from a chakra or astral field that attracts us. In this case, it is important to take care not to become energy vampires. We need to learn how to clear our own energy fields so that we can connect back into that flow of energy that keeps our bodies and astral fields healthy, which only comes from the Source.

In one of my past experiences, I had a dear friend Terri who used to come visit when she was in town. I always had to take a nap after one of her visits. I would be so exhausted when she left. We never did much except go out to lunch to catch up with our busy lives. Without fail, halfway through her visit I would always find myself trying desperately to stay awake. It was all I could do not to be rude; I loved my friend and really enjoyed my personal time with her.

One day she came over, and I noticed that I was starting to get sleepy. I didn't want to cut our visit short, so when she left the room to get a new tea bag, I pulled my energy in and centered myself. I had the thought to use my Reiki, so I brought in a golden light of protection around me, added a few Reiki symbols in my heart chakra, then expanded it out through my body. When she came back, I discovered that I was fine, not feeling tired, and starting to feel like my old self. She made her tea and talked for a few minutes, then she paused to say that she was getting tired and needed to cut our visit short. I could see that she was not being fed from my energy field and would not be able to hold her own during the rest of our visit. She quickly excused herself and went home.

We are always receiving some form of light vibration as we live and walk around this earth. It is everywhere. We send our energy out into the room and others take that energy to use it. We use our energy fields to see how people feel, to get hunches and ideas. If you can see energy, the world surrounding you becomes a moving collage of colors, dancing in the room, around and inside people who are participating in ordinary activities. It is beautiful! When you are not aware of it, it's still going on. Some artists like to draw or paint this. I have also learned that the color of energy changes with the mood or the vibrational atmosphere of the room. You may be an orange person one day and a purple person another, according to your emotions and what is happening around you.

Energy & Spirits In The House - The Link

Another kind of experience that happened to me was right after a trip to visit my mother in Taos one summer. I was exhausted from having spent twelve hours on the road driving back home to Texas. Once I got home that afternoon, I decided to take a nap. My daughter was reading, so I asked if it was all right if she read in the same room while I was napping. For some reason that I can't explain, I was feeling like I needed someone to be in the room with me. She wanted to continue reading and was happy to keep me company. She told me to go ahead, relax, and go to sleep.

My dream was what most would call a nightmare. I am not going into detail about it, but I do want to bring up that I experienced a murder and an explosion in my brain with a great amount of massive pain in my forehead. I awoke disoriented, shaking from the trauma. I looked over to where my daughter was sitting and noticed that she had also fallen asleep but was also awakening.

As I became more adjusted to my surroundings, I told her I was glad she was there, as I was waking from a nightmare and I was still shaking. I pointed to my forehead and opened my mouth to tell her about it when she stopped me. She asked if I had felt an explosion in my brain. When she saw my mouth gaping open, she continued. She pointed to the same spot on her head and said that she felt it explode in her own brain. She described in detail her dream, which matched the same the experience that I had had in my dream state.

We sat there blinking at each other, trying to grasp what had happened to us both. I realized that there was someone else in the room. A deep feeling of emotion caught me in the throat, and I understood that we were both shown how someone had died. It was such a traumatic experience to have the details and know that this soul was in pain. We both knew that whoever it was wanted us to know what happened to them.

At the time I was still learning the basics of communicating with the other side, so I didn't know how to help this poor soul. Later, I started to work with others who are gifted in working with spirit rescue. I discovered how to help those who, for some reason, can't find the light or are afraid of the light, to cross after death. I have found that by helping those on the other side with love and understanding, we find healing for those on this side and on the other side. Sometimes I don't think that people realize how closely linked we really are to the spiritual realm.

In the beginning of my journey in spirit rescue, I didn't understand how to work with the really dark force entities. My teacher at the time was more versed in opening a portal and having the entities sucked into it, then closing the doorway to seal it. Sometimes the portals that were already open were also used in banishing the dark forces. After several of my experiences, this method didn't seem to resonate with me. I felt like there must be another way to work with these entities. For a while, I stopped doing any crossings or clearings. I wasn't feeling right about it. At that time I didn't know there was another way to handle these dark forces.

It wasn't until I got a phone call from my mom, who told me about a book that she ordered from Amazon "by accident." The reason she was calling was that she had sent it to me to help with the spirit rescue, and she wanted me to be on the lookout for the book.

I received the book that week. It was by William J. Baldwin, Ph.D.: "Healing Lost Souls: Releasing Unwanted Spirits from your Energy Body." [12]

As I read, I came upon the subject of crossing dark force entities. It all started to come together, and it really resonated with me. One of the things that had bothered me was that I could feel the dark entities' pain as they were exiled into the portals. In Dr. Baldwin's book he talks about how everything is connected to the Creator, as we are all one; therefore even in the dark forces there is a spark of light that they have forgotten. This light can be ignited inside of them in remembering from where they first came. This means that instead of casting them out into oblivion, through a portal, they can be crossed over into the light. This is not an easy task, but it has been done successfully, and there are people who do this type of work. It all made so much sense to me that I started to incorporate it into my work and teachings. I rarely come across dark forces, but they seem to know that my intention is to help them cross into the light.

Dark Night Of The Soul

Usually the dark night of the soul comes at a point in your life when you and your soul are making a major transition. During this time, you may feel like you have been abandoned by everyone, including God. Often people are not able to sleep and become depressed because they feel completely alone. Really, it is a time of trial and reflection within your own being. It is a great time of inspiration and creativity. I call it a rebirth, or reboot. Life seems to blossom out of the ashes of the experience.

I was talking to my spirit teachers and heard "Ana, think about this: It is like when you go into a sweat lodge and you are in the dark, pulling out all your impurities, by the fire. When you spend your time reflecting and praying, that is the time when true inspiration will hit. When you leave the darkness of the lodge and return to the outside, the sun hitting you in the face, you feel connected to all that is. It is a time of inner reflection. It is a feeling of being new again because you have faced your deepest fears."

When you look at it that way, facing our fears in our lives that we carry deep within our souls is not a bad thing but a way of remembering that even when we feel completely alone, God never abandons us. We are always a part of unconditional love. We will always be cherished, even as a spark of inspiration, in the dark nights of the soul.

Energy Cords

Many people don't know that energy cords exist. This is something that is important to know as they can affect your day-to-day life. Energy cords can be attached to your solar plexus, running from you to someone else's solar plexus. They can plug into other places in the body, but it seems to happen most often in the solar plexus. Strong human emotions, such as neediness or fear, tend to send out energy cords. Most people have no idea that they are sending out and plugging into someone else's energy. Some people plug in out of curiosity. For others, it may be a survival technique and they know what they are getting into.

If you have the gift of sight, you can see these cords attached to people. If you are a feeler, then you may have noticed a feeling of being pulled or you can feel your energy being drained. As you become more in tune with your own gifts, you will become more aware of these kinds of attachments. You will start to experience energy being stolen or given by those around you. You may start to notice this process happening in your own energy field.

In cases of obsessive love, you may experience losing yourself in that person. A huge warning sign is when you can't tell where they begin and you end. Loving the person may feel fine, but being obsessed is detrimental to your health and the person you are obsessed with. Energy cords are not just about people in love. They can affect all different kinds of relationships such as friends, marriages, coworkers, and family relations.

As you read this, someone may be coming to mind. You might even have known someone who has a child, and their world seems to revolve around that child. In that case, everyone knows, except the two involved, that the child is overly needy or being drained. The sad thing is that someone in this kind of relationship is always giving, and the other is always taking. It is a human tug-of-war between the two energy fields. The balance is off because the cords are looking for something outside, instead of plugging into the Source, where there is no shortage of energy.

The one taking believes that this is just how it is and will sometimes push things to the limits as proof of the commitment from the other person. The giver gives until they are all used up and depleted, feeling tired or stressed. In these cases it is hopeful when the one being drained realizes that they have not been appreciated, moves out of the harmful relationship, and seeks help.

I have met people in my life who have said that life was all about what the other person wanted. As long as the other person was happy or content, their own life was good. That leaves a lot of responsibility for the other person to be happy all the time. Often the taker will retaliate by telling others how unhappy they are with the people pleaser.

If you discover that you have an energy cord attached to another person, then it is time to rid yourself of it and become free. You are not doing them any favors by trying to live your life through them, or by trying to please them. In fact, you are only a hindrance because you keep them from growing. Yes, the other person will know when the cord has been removed and will want you back. Why wouldn't they?

I took a class one weekend, and the teacher reminded us of the energy cords. She had us look for cords that we had attached to other people. She talked about how the they grow in thickness as the relationship gets stronger, but not in a healthy way. This makes it harder to sever or let go.

When I am ridding myself of the cords that I have attached or someone else has attached to me, I find it very helpful to ask my spirit guides to help me remove them. Once the cords are removed, I ask for the wound that is left from the attachment to be healed. Always ask for healing when you remove them. You don't want open wounds flying around when you have them cut. When energy is taken out of one place, it is important to fill up the empty space with love or ask for healing, so that it is not filled up with whatever is out there that may drift by.

I have had some interesting experiences with energy cords. In one case, a friend who was empathic had a lot of trauma when she was growing up. One day, as we were visiting, she asked me why she felt other people's physical pain when she was talking to them, even though she put up protection, severing all cords and attachments. The answer that came from the spirit guides was that, because of her past trauma, she sent out energy cords to people to see how they felt and if she could trust them. She was doing this unconsciously to protect herself. What happened when she attached to a person who was sick or in pain was that she ended up pulling their energy into her own body, suffering as though the pain or sickness were her own. She had to learn not to cord others and to trust her inner guidance, without using the cords.

Learning about energy cords can help you distinguish what energy is really yours and what is someone else's. Remember that getting in touch with yourself may reveal some things that need to be worked on. If you can learn to identify the cords and where they are coming from, the road to healing is like putting a stopper in the unplugged drain.

The Attachment

My friend Erin was doing chair massages at a Wellness Expo in Addison, TX in 2008 and invited me to spend the day with her to keep her company. It had been a while since I had attended an Expo, so I agreed to go. I thought it would be fun to look around and meet people in the different exhibits. I had a great time while I was there and enjoyed watching how she worked on people. Afterwards, we grabbed a bite to eat for dinner and visited for a while, then I went on my merry way home. During the drive, I noticed the smell of cigarette smoke. Having been at an Expo and out to dinner, I decided it was just one of those things, being out in public, so I didn't think much about it. I have never smoked myself and I am allergic to the smoke, so I try to avoid it.

I washed my hair and my clothes that night so I wouldn't have to smell it later. For days though, no matter where I was, in the house or in my car, I smelled smoke. It was not a faint whiff, but more like someone was lighting up right there blowing smoke in my face. I was starting to have reactions to it, feeling grumpy.

My family could also smell the smoke. On top of it, I was starting to dress differently and feeling the need to go out to have a drink. I was having flashes of myself in the mirror that I was a tall blonde with blue eyes. I am a brunette with dark brown eyes and a petite build.

I found myself doing things out of character for me, such as craving cigarettes and wanting to stop in at bars. Finally I complained to Erin and one of my spiritual teachers about this weird behavior. I felt like I was either having a midlife crisis or going crazy. Both my mentor and my teacher asked me to stop to take an assessment of my energy field. I did. As I went through the exercises, I discovered I had a rip in my energy field, and a visitor. I went on, wanting to know the name of the person that I had picked up at the Expo. By this time I was having urges to chain smoke. It was starting to become an obsession.

I discovered her name was Constance. She died in the 70's from lung cancer. She saw my energy at the Expo and was attracted to it. The rip in my energy field made it easy for her to move in and make herself at home. Apparently she loved to party, smoke, and drink. It was the 70's! She enjoyed keeping the company of different men and died at the age of 48. I was 38 when she found me and decided to go for a ride.

I asked my teacher Lonna if she would help cross her over and remove her from my energy field. It took a lot of encouragement because Constance didn't want to go. She was enjoying making herself at home. Together with the help of angels that my teacher worked with, Constance let go and allowed them to escort her into the light. It was a beautiful process. When she crossed I felt a rush of peace flood my body and energy field. Then the angels worked on me, healing then sealing the rip in my field. Instantly I felt much lighter. The urges of wanting to smoke, drink and party went away. I was very much relieved.

I went back to my normal life. The smell of smoke went away, which was a huge relief. Later, friends of mine who didn't really know what was going on said that something had changed in me. They felt I was not really myself during that time. After it was over, they were glad that I was back to being myself.

Ghosts, entities, and dark energies will attach themselves to a person, place, or thing. Ghosts and dark energies are intelligent. Sometimes they attach themselves and try to hold on to life. They may even find others that resonate or remind them of their past life on this earth. They can be attracted to people that give off a certain life force energy that indicates that the person can communicate with them in some way. A rip or tear in the host's energy field makes it easy for energies to climb on board and hang out.

Dark Ones

My husband and I wanted to take our children on a summer trip to London in 2004, so we saved up and planned a family vacation. It was a wonderful trip. We did lots of sightseeing, taking them to castles, a wax museum, St. Paul's Cathedral, the Tower of London, and Westminster Abbey. We even went so far as to venture to Stonehenge.

My husband Steve is one of those people who reads every plaque and documents everything by taking lots of pictures. Our children Cameron and Mason were young and patience was limited, including my own. Often they would wander off with me behind them. While we were in Westminster Abbey, Steve stopped to read something when Mason the youngest took off, with me on his heels. He wanted to see what all the commotion was around a part of the tour a few sections down. We discovered that it was Queen Elizabeth I's tomb that people were crowding around. As soon as we learned what it was, he was off again, and I followed, keeping him in my sight.

While I was tagging along after him, I got this feeling that I was going to be sick and needed to find a bathroom quickly. I felt faint, clammy, and was about to throw up as my stomach tied itself in knots. It came on so fast that I had to sit down to find my bearings, feeling somewhat confused. Mason noticed that I wasn't behind him and came running to my side, asking if he could help. I begged him to go back and find his father. I was feeling like I was turning green and would pass out if I did not lose all my bodily functions before that. Steve and Cameron came hastily back with Mason. My husband, seeing that I was ill, sized up the situation and left me there with the children to watch me as he tried to find the bathroom or some help. As I waited there, I thought maybe I could walk a little further to ask someone myself and get the ball rolling a little faster. The children helped me up, and as we took a few steps into another part of the Abbey, I was immediately starting to feel better. My thoughts cleared up, the stomach business and the dizziness went away. It was a miracle! I just needed to walk it out and I would be good as new. As we walked further, the symptoms went away and I was fine. By that time my husband had found the bathrooms. I was better, so we continued on our tour.

As we started to regroup, Steve asked if we could go back and retrace our steps so he could catch up and see Queen Elizabeth's tomb. With a little protest from my son, we walked back. Right before I got to her tomb, my stomach seized up again with the same feeling of being sick. I encouraged them to go on without me. I needed to find a bathroom. I went back in the other direction, only to find that as soon as I started to walk away, the feeling of sickness disappeared. I turned around to join them, and as I came back to that same spot, my stomach seized up and I got lightheaded. I turned around, once again walking away, but this time, it hit me that I was walking into an energy.

Just to make sure, I slowly walked back to that same area where I felt sick and, sure enough, I had the same severe reaction. I decided to leave and see if it would go away. I did this a few more times, letting myself understand that I was not sick, but my body and energy field were picking up on an energy. I noted what was around me, and I spotted a tomb. I had no idea who it was. All I knew was that when I came close to it, I became very ill. Finally we left and had a wonderful day without any more incidents.

Years later I was in a book store with Steve and was looking at a book that had photographs taken by people who had captured ghosts on film. I loved the book, as it was one of the few times I could show him what I saw with my eyes and he could see it too. A picture caught my attention, of a tomb at Westminster Abbey with a dark shadow of a ghost who was walking through the picture. Immediately my body tensed up. The memories of the whole experience on the grounds of the Abbey came flooding in. I knew without a doubt that, even though I didn't see the dark spirit, I had felt and experienced its presence when we were there in 2004. It was preying upon unsuspecting people.

I learned from that experience that, even though I had other encounters with dark spirits, I had more of an understanding of what happened when I couldn't see it to identify it. Later I learned that these dark energies feed off of people's energy fields, as they are completely disconnected from Source, needing to find a way to keep existing. This creates sickness in the host's body. I must have had a rip or opening in my energy field, making me a perfect target for it to latch on to. Lucky for me, this one didn't decide to go home with me and was happy to stay in one place where it could find unlimited fuel to feed on.

I learned very quickly about attachments, as I was now having more experience with them. I see beings around people all the time. In other chapters I have discussed angels, spirit guides, spirit animals, and loved ones who have crossed over. These beautiful spirits are the ones who are completely connected to the Source and have no need to feed off of people's energy fields. They are sustained by the unlimited energy from the Creator. But there are dark entities who hang out or are lost that haven't crossed over into the light. They are searching for hosts to help them exist between worlds where they are caught in their own hell.

After a few experiences with attachments and dark ones, I take extra care to keep my fields clear and check for any rips or tears in my energy field making sure that my vibration is raised so I am no longer on their radar. It is better to be safe than pick up a hitchhiker.

Dark Forces & Demons

The darker forces are those who have lost their way and have moved into the darkness, because they are separating themselves from the light of the Creator. They were once human and tend to have extremely evil intentions. They can be found just about anywhere. We are more aware of them when our vibration is on a lower level. Lower vibrations can be caused by different things. Exhaustion, stress, fear, or other strong negative emotions cause our frequencies to drop to where we can be seen by the dark entities. Our vibrations go up and down, depending on what is going on as we live our daily lives.

The pitch black spirit with a human silhouette is one that most people encounter. It gives off a pure sense of evil. Dark entities are attracted to fear or anger, feeding off the energy that is emitted by emotional bodies. They will do their best to create fear or lower emotional trauma, which will sustain their life presence. They often prey on those who have holes or weak energy fields where they can move in and attach to a human host. Dark forces can be extremely aggressive. These are the entities that people report holding them down when they are trying to sleep. A person might feel as if the dark force is trying to enter their body. One thing to remember is that you are always in control. They cannot enter your body without consent. You also have the power to evict them if they attach to your aura field.

Demons are non-human entities. Encounters with them are few and far between because they exist in lower dimensions. They detest human beings and are known to be intelligent. They can be attracted to a person when that person is in fear or experiencing lower levels of energy frequencies. The best advice in handling demons is to find someone who is trained to cast them out. You can find quite a lot of research about them on the internet or in books from different cultures.

I have found that fear can open doorways, leaving you vulnerable, whether you are working on crossing dark entities and demons, or stumbling upon them by accident. Your biggest asset and defense is keeping your frequency at a higher vibration where you are invisible to them. Protection and working with a team of angels, spirit guides, and spirit animals is always a good idea. In spirit rescue, we encourage the dark entity to find the light connecting them to the Creator so that they can also be crossed into the light. Grace is for all things. I have had my moments with angry ghosts and dark entities. Mostly this occurs when I am doing house clearings. In those moments when I feel fear creep up, it is always nice to know that I am well protected and being guarded. Fear will melt away because I have checked my fields, done my protection, and called in my Spirit teams.

Shadow People

One type of dark entity you may have caught a glimpse of is the shadow people. They can be described as dark silhouettes moving across the walls or ceilings, or fleeing off into another room. These entities can range from harmless to very aggressive, depending on each encounter. I have learned that they don't hang around or see you when you are in a higher vibration such as love, joy, and happiness.

The dark ones are what I call ghosts who for some reason haven't crossed into the light. They are still trying to exist on the earth plane. Sometimes they feel attached to someone or something. Often they may stay if they have unfinished business or just want to help the living. Still others have trouble coming to terms that they are no longer in a physical body because their death was so violent or sudden. Some feel that they are not worthy of the light or that they may be punished when and if they do cross. Then there are those who are addicted to the lower level emotions, like a perfume which attracts them to the darker side of the living. When this happens it places them in a place where they feel stuck and disconnected. The longer they are disconnected by turning away from Source, the more they can become angry and confused. They may lash out at the living and other ghosts who are in their space of existence.

It has been my experience that the longer they stay stuck, lost, or live in the in-between world of existence, they become darker as they become more separated from the light. This is one of the reasons I practice spirit rescue. I believe that if you have the ability to communicate with the other side, it is important to use your gift as a service to help those on both sides of the veil. I have asked my friends who do spirit rescue to help me, if for any reason I got stuck.

Spirit Rescue

I know that I have mentioned spirit rescue in other parts of this book but really haven't taken the time to explain what it is. I guess what comes to my mind is a service that helps those who are stuck in-between worlds that need help in crossing over. The work is done out of pure compassion and unconditional love.

Spirit rescue is also working with a team of angels, spirit guides, and spirit animals that want to help those who are lost. It has been my experience that no one is denied access to the Source if they want to be connected. Judgement comes from the physical world and doesn't exist in the vibrational frequency of unconditional love in the higher realms. There is care and help on the other side for those who want to move into that frequency that have been caught between the physical world and Source.

The other thing I would like to mention is that free will plays a huge part of spirit rescue, and since spirits are intelligent they have the right to make that choice. No one is crossed or made to do anything without their consent. Moving back into the light can only happen by choice. Loved ones and the spirit team come to help, encourage, or show where to find the doorway back into the light.

When I was first learning about spirit rescue, my friend Amy wanted me to help someone they knew who was having trouble with a spirit. At the time I really wanted to work in this field, so I agreed to go. When I got to the house, I searched it, expanding my energy fields out to look for the ghost. I finally found a young girl that appeared to be a teenager hiding in the den area of the house. I asked her if she was okay and sat down on one of the chairs. I talked to her as I would any other teenager. I could see that she was upset. Her sorrow and anger was so strong that it seemed to resonate right through me. I kept encouraging her to talk, wanting to know what had happened to her. After a while, she answered my question of how old she was. She was seventeen. I waited patiently for her to open up. Sometime in the communication she realized that I could see her and wasn't going away. That seemed to break the ice and, she started to open up a little more. She shared her story of being so depressed that she had committed suicide by slitting her wrists and then falling asleep. When she woke up, she realized what she had done, but it was too late. She saw her body lying there on the floor, not moving. She watched her family grieve over her, but there was nothing she could do. She was afraid of the light and of being punished for what she had done. So she hid from it. She was Catholic and believed that God would condemn her. She cried, and I cried for her. It touched my heart to know that this young person was lost and terrified for so long.

My spirit guides were there with me and were in communication with her spirit guides at the same time. They let me know that it might be a good time for us to call in an archangel. When the angel arrived, the room filled up with light, which confused the ghost. The angel brought other angels and the girl's grandmother, who had already passed on. Together they explained that she didn't have to worry about being punished; there was help on the other side. They encouraged her to go with them back into the light. They would help her, explaining that she wouldn't be condemned. There was nothing but unconditional love and grace in the light. She would be welcomed and they would be there with her every step of the way.

After a while, she finally agreed to let go and went with them into the light. When they all left, there was a slight pressure in the air as the bright light went with them. The room was empty, and I noticed a lightness in the atmosphere of the room as the ghost's energy had left. The owner of the home noticed it too when they returned. They had no more incidences with the ghost after that.

Spirit rescue is an amazing service. When people ask me about it, I like to recommend the book called "Spirit Rescue: A Simple Guide to Talking with Ghosts and Freeing Earthbound Spirits," by Wilma Davidson. [13] If you are able to communicate with the other side, this may be something you want to learn more about.

Chapter Twelve: Balance

Healing Stones

Many people have asked me how different types of stones have healing properties. The best way I know how to explain this regards the atomic makeup of the stones.

As most of you know from your science classes in school, everything is made up of atoms. Everything has its own way of being put together with the atoms so that it is created the way it is intended to be. With this simple idea you can then see that a piece of jade has a different atomic structure than a diamond.

Now, think of the ways the atoms move within each stone. You can't see them with your eyes, but you know they are there. Your energy field can pick up the movement because your energy field is also made out of the atoms that are constantly moving.

Remember too that emotions are energy. A person whose energy field is weak because of something they are going through has energy that is not vibrating as high as it would if they were happy or excited. For example, emotional trauma likes to settle in the heart area. (Ever have a heartache?) A stone like green Diopside resonates a healing vibration of atoms that helps sooth the heart as it fills in the gaps.

It is like a guitar in a music store where you can pluck a string, and the other guitars will resonate on the same string, even though you never touched them. They are in tune with the vibration of that note. You are no different from a fine-tuned instrument that can get out of balance or detuned. The things around you are also in line with your energies as you live on this earth. Don't forget that color also has a vibrational energy that can be measured and will also help with healing for the same reasons. Color can play a big part of why you reach for certain stones, as you need to be in sync or need that healing property in your energy field.

Healing The Three Parts Of Self

One of the experiences I had with self-healing was when I was working on an emotional block that seemed to hold me back in my life. At the time I was getting really frustrated, unable to identify what was making me feel a loss of my own personal power. When I started to do dream work with the intention of learning about my fear, it was revealed to me.

My biggest breakthrough began when I had a nightmare. This experience, like any dream of its kind, brought out my fears, causing me much distress in my dream. In the dream I was able to discern, that there were three obstacles in my life and that I was working on life lessons associated with one specific fear. I had been working to master two of the obstacles, but the third befuddled me. That fear was deeply rooted in my DNA.

After I awoke I had many questions, so when I had time during the day I went into the Akashic Records to find some answers about this fear.

I learned that, since we are both physical body and spirit beings, finding the root of our primal fears within ourselves is more complex than we realize. All of our experiences, in different parts of our being, are merged together in the human body.

We all have different experiences in this lifetime. The other lifetimes are not so apparent. One piece to the puzzle in finding those blocks can be from the soul's perspective, from a past life experience that was merged into the physical body, that created its own program within the living tissue and brain. Another part of the soul is what I call the "sins of the father," that are passed down through the DNA, from generation to generation. These really are not sins, but experiences that are inherited through DNA. It kind of reminds me of our appendix which is never used but for some reason we all have one. We also have the mind, which has to run through a process of understanding and changing the way we think, to dissolve any old baggage. We have to remember that we are multidimensional beings. To heal, we must treat our whole being on all levels, and see it all from a much larger perspective. Wonder why it takes so long to heal?

Prophesies

Many people attach a stigma to prophets or seeing the future. People's belief systems about this can make it a hard subject to approach. But people see the future all the time, often without a clue they are actually seeing it.

What I have come to understand is that prophesies can happen in several different ways. Sometimes seeing the future can be as easy as recognizing patterns or forecasting an event. My daughter likes to blurt out the endings to movies sometimes when she sees a certain pattern. Most of the time she is right on target but it ruins the movie for me. It is kind of like watching a movie for those who pick up on the behavioral energy or emotional patterns that we all tend to run.

In those cases it is important to understand that unlike a movie that is stuck in one plot, real people have a choice to change the outcome. That is what you might call free will. It is when a person acknowledges the pattern deciding to make changes in their behavior that lead to a certain outcomes which will change the energy patterns around them. This is what others will pick up on sensing something is different.

The future may come though dreams, a knowing, premonitions, visions, thoughts, symbols, or signs. There is a multitude of ways that we experience the possibilities of future events by gathering information that inspires us to forecast what may come about in our lives.

Prophesies about the future can be hard to predict as often you will see people set their sights and become fixated on a particular outcome from the prophecy, when they can actually make decisions that will move them to higher states of achievement in their lives. Some people, when you tell them the possibilities they could reach, still decide that they don't want to move in a particular direction, as it is too much work. These people may not fulfill their soul contracts in their lifetimes on this earth. Sometimes you can explain to people that they are heading for a disaster and what the outcome is, and they just refuse to change their behavior.

The kicker is that those who give predictions seem to get the bum deal. They can be branded as not being true to an outcome if it doesn't completely match what was forecasted. Zoe Hagon said that, "A prophet is only of value in telling people what could happen unless they change their ways. If what a prophet prophesies doesn't happen, he has actually fulfilled his mission." [14]

I learned from all of this that sometimes the best lessons in life are learned through a person's own experiences. From the higher perspective, it is neither good nor bad to be judged. I must admit that I find myself gritting my teeth sometimes when I see the possibilities of the outcome, but in those cases, I send out lots of love. If someone asks, I can look at the different directions they may choose to go, but that is all I can do. The outcomes are really up to the person, based on how they wish to pursue the information that is shared. The truth is that no one can mess with free will!

The Movies

A dear friend of mine asked me once if I was really scared when I watched scary movies. I explained that I understood the difference between what was real and what was not real. Working in the spirit world is a lot like watching a scary movie about outer space. You know that it doesn't apply to your world, so you don't have a panic attack about it happening when you watch it. The same goes with ghost movies, although lately the movie people are getting close to the real deal in some of the movies I have seen.

A while ago I had the opportunity to ask someone in the movie business about why the movies are starting to get close to what is really going on out there in the spirit world. He told me that many writers were doing their research to find out more about the supernatural and make the movies more believable. Even though they do this, I still find that they throw in a lot of Hollywood effects for the thrill of the movie experience.

Friends & Family

One of the hardest things that I have encountered in this journey of healing is being called to be completely accountable by the Spirit to follow the path of ascension toward a higher vibration. This accountable part of us wakes up realizing the sweetness of knowing what it is all about and doesn't want to go back into the darkness that kept us shackled to our old realities. As the chains fall away and we begin to realize that there is more to life than we ever could imagine, we can move one foot in front of the other.

Oh, we still feel the sting of life that teaches us about the lessons of this world, but we no longer feel held in bondage as we learn to forgive and release those emotions that caused harm or sickness in our bodies and energy fields. Still, there is a mourning process as we let go of those old energy patterns and allow others to be where they need to be as they go along in their own evaluation.

Sometimes we grieve the loss of those we have loved as life takes them in another direction. Later we find that we will meet others following our same path, and we find common ground in our life journey. On a larger perspective, life is like running a race, knowing where everyone is on the track, but also knowing it isn't about who finishes first. We all get there one way or another. I know the perfect scenario is that we all run together at the same pace, but that is not the reality that we face. We learn to move up or change lanes. Our life journey is not about holding our breath as others pass us by or even staying behind. The journey is about moving on and continuing to learn.

However many people there are on this earth, we each have our own timing when we race across the finish line. That principle in itself is perfect, as it was set by the divine for the purpose of our soul's evolution.

So take heart when watching others fall behind or speed up, as the journey is not about comparing who we are to others, but rather learning how to remain focused on our own soul contract. As for those who are in the same vibration as yourself the company is only an added benefit. For those who break off and follow their own path, they teach a lesson of knowing we are still all in the life journey together.

Only Opportunities

I was working with a client one day, and she told me that she had made some big mistakes that caused her a lot of misery in her life. The mistakes made her shrink from herself, causing great fear. I must admit that the word "mistakes" always makes my ears perk up when I hear it. There are none, but that is hard to tell someone when they are stuck.

When we investigated the incident, looking in detail at what had happened to her, she discovered that she could change a pattern that was being replicated in her life. By exploring the experience, which she called a "mistake," she realized that, without a doubt, she would continue to choose those kinds of situations just out of pure habit. Of course she had fear. It was only by exploring the lessons that she allowed herself to step back into her life and into her personal power. I watched her transform from a victim into a person who could learn and make choices that changed her life.

If there are no accidents in the universe or God makes no mistakes, then there is something to learn from every experience. Looking back from where we are now, maybe we wouldn't make the same choices we have made. But, to know this is to also know that we choose things in our lives when we are ready for those lessons. If we learn the lesson, we move on; if we don't, we continue to choose the same lesson over and over, until we do learn. Our evolution in our life journey is about where we are at the time and where we go from there.

One of the things my grandfather used to say that always stuck in my mind was, "There are no mistakes. There are only opportunities." When we look at those around us who learn instead of being afraid to move on, we see that they have just as many opportunities as the rest of us.

A Lesson From a Ghost

My husband Steve was complaining of nightmares one day, feeling he wasn't getting the rest that he needed to be productive at his work. We didn't know why that was happening, so we spent some time exploring what his dreams might mean. We weren't able to make a connection and ended up letting it go, not knowing what to do next.

A few days later I woke up and noticed a tall man with a big belly standing next to my husband's side of the bed. I knew immediately that the man was a ghost because I could see through him. At the time, I was delighted that I could see him so clearly. I could even see that he was dressed in blue jeans with a plaid button-down shirt that was left untucked. He was that clear. He was so intent on staring at my sleeping husband that he was a bit startled when he finally noticed me watching him. He then quickly faded away.

I told Steve about my amazing encounter when he woke up. He told me again that he was still upset with his dreams. We still couldn't find any connection to what they might mean.

Knowing he needed his sleep, I suggested we trade sides of the bed, thinking that a change of location might help.

I didn't know that I was in for a night of terror. It all happened right after we went to bed. I started to have these very strange nightmares. I woke up in a panic, calming myself only to fall asleep into another disturbing dream. Finally, after repeating this process a few times, I became lucid enough to know to ask for help from my spirit guides. They told me that the dreams I was having were from an outside source. Then they said that someone was sharing their experiences with me through my dreams. I knew in that moment that the ghost who had been visiting my husband had been giving him those dreams that kept him awake.

I willed myself to open my eyes and found the ghost standing right next to me by the bed. Once again he seemed to be surprised that it was me instead of my husband. In that instant the connection broke from the energy that he was using to share his experiences. Without hesitation, once released, I quickly locked in on him, holding his energy with my intentions, and I called for the archangel Michael to come to help cross this poor man. The angel Michael and other angels came to assist in the crossing, allowing me to let go.

Freed from the connection, I was able to think about what my husband had gone through all those nights experiencing the nightmares that the ghost was sharing with him. After the whole experience, my husband no longer had any nightmares and was able to rest peacefully.

Food - The Circle Of Life

In the past I have not really given a lot of thought to the food that I have placed in my mouth. I did know that vegetables and lower-fat food are much better for maintenance. I understood that the body knows how to break down the food I eat and make it into fuel.

Then there is the understanding that the food that we put in our bodies might not provide the right nutrients, and that when it breaks down, the body throws it out because it can't use it. Therefore, by not eating the right food, we can starve ourselves, even if we eat massive amounts of it.

Of course we all know that things we put in our mouths have preservatives, hormones, and pesticides in them, so we need to be aware of what we are ingesting. A lot of us go organic and watch where we buy our meat. Even with all the research and new ways to keep food preserved, we are still learning how it works.

Once, I was enjoying a nice glass of white wine with my friends at a dinner party and there in the middle of eating during a discussion, I raised my glass up to my lips to take a sip, and suddenly, time stopped for just a few seconds. I heard my spirit guide say that,"The sip I was about to take was more than just a sip of wine. It was a form of liquid energy that would merge into my body and into my whole life force beyond."

What followed was a thought that if I took that sip, whatever energy the wine held is what I would become. I was suddenly aware that, whether good or bad, that energy is what I would put into my body and energy field.

My attention went to my plate, where I witnessed a scene of the meat being prepared. The fear that the animal experienced came rushing into my body. I looked up to see if anyone was watching.

I could not only see it; I felt it. I pushed my plate aside as fast as this happened. I was able to distract myself, so I was not as aware of what was going on with the food as we continued to talk and moved on with the meal.

It wasn't until a few days later, that I was reminded yet again of what I was placing in my mouth and was able to reflect on what had happened. In some way this was a lesson for me to pay attention to what I was eating.

As a lesson goes, this was what I learned from the experience that food is not just fuel. It is far more important than that. It is a merging of a person's energy and the energy that the food carries. This energy is not just the physical form that breaks down in our stomach. It is also a life force of energy, surrounding us and merging with our whole being.

The movie "Like Water for Chocolate" [15] comes to mind.i The story is about a young woman who is in love and is forbidden to marry, so she turns to food as a release for her passion. As she creates and prepares the food, she puts into it everything that she feels for her beloved. This causes quite a stir as people who eat her cuisine find that they begin to feel her desires.

It has been years since I saw this movie but being reminded of it helped me to understand that the person who is creating your meal puts their own energy into it. The animal or vegetable has its own energy. It is no wonder we have so much trouble with our stomachs and digestion, when we put so much emotional energy into our mouths.

We are finding that not only do we have our physical bodies but we also have emotional energy that can play a big part in our health, and affect us mentally, emotionally, or physically. So what happens when we add everyone else's emotional energy to the pot?

Please, know that energy can also be changed with intention so prayer is huge.

Choices

One of the things that most of us forget when we are going through our own trials and tribulations is that we have choices. A lot of us beat ourselves up over and over, not giving ourselves a break, until we are exhausted. Energy follows thought, and if we change our thoughts we can change our energy. The first time one of my teachers said that, I wasn't sure what he was talking about. I remembered after I was in a situation where I learned I could change my thought patterns and move my energy to a much higher ground. I was excited when I did this. My circumstances seemed to change in a big way.

Don't get me wrong: Changing your energy is not about ignoring a situation or denying yourself the experience. The truth is that looking at a situation in your mind helps to allow yourself to see it from all different angles, perspectives, patterns, and solutions, and to change the outcome. If you are in a position that you can't change the outcome, you can change the way you experience or feel something. The choice is really up to you. You have the ability to shift your focus and relieve yourself of extra stress and anguish that gets recorded in your body, cells, and energy field.

Often our emotions get the better of us. When we speak from raw emotions, we discover they can take over. In many cases we end up spouting things that don't help the situation. By allowing ourselves to stay in the raw emotional state, we bring our energy down into a lower frequency and more dense energy.

In the end, our emotional state is up to us. We have the power to make choices. We can allow ourselves to experience an emotional thought, honoring what we feel, without being destructive to ourselves and others. We can move into that space of looking at it as we learn what we need to do to change our behaviors that create that fear or pain within. We have the choice to move out of something that seems hopeless or painful and move into a state of grace and personal power.

A Time Of Change

As we move into this time of change, we are remembering, as we merge back into an alignment of our true selves and our Creator. For some of us, it is unnerving, and for others, it is a great adventure. As epiphanies and feelings of connection reemerge back into our lives, we will suddenly begin to recognize a knowing deep within us. Once we cross over into a state of true knowing, we will understand that there is a greater presence intermingled outside and inside of ourselves. We are all a part of everything. We will come into that understanding, without question, that everything is not only made out of the atoms that we know from our science classes but everything is created out of and held together by the one thought of our Creator, unconditional love.

In this state of knowing, there is no room for violence, fear, hatred, or anger as this is something we have created in our own lives when we forget where we come from and believe we are separate. From this experience, we will understand that this separation is an illusion within the third dimensional experience that we fall into, thinking that we are lost. It is a shift of focus to remember that brings you back into that state of grace and understanding. This is only half of it as it takes the experience of completely letting go to merge into full alignment.

This is that part where you release all your fears without judgment within yourself, which will create an experience where you completely let go to merge. It can be that simple. Yet like the experience that was mentioned about jumping into cancer in an earlier chapter, it can be difficult unless we let go completely. The choice is up to you as each experience is as unique to each person as their own life lessons.

Also, it can also be as simple as spontaneously bursting into that state of connection because others have remembered. Your energy field may pick it up when you come into contact with those who remember the pattern from merging into that state of being. The key is knowing what is happening and understanding that you are having a taste of your true self in full connection with the Creator, as you see and experience yourself and the whole universe coming together, both from within and outside of oneself.

Self Healing With Help From The Angels

In the summer of 2011, I discovered a teacher right under my nose. Kristi BlueFeather was someone I knew when I worked at the clinic. We had always talked about our families and our own paths of personal healing, but that was all. So when I heard that she was a teacher, I was surprised.

When I discovered that Kristi was a Qigong teacher and also taught a form of energy work that was assisted by her spirit guides, I was intrigued. She explained to me that she had been treated by a woman in Canada and had some good results in releasing her fears that helped her to heal some old wounds. Because of the success of the treatment, she became excited about the techniques and interned with that healer to become a practitioner and teacher. After spending some time talking about it, I wanted to learn how she worked in her field. Understanding how to release is a big deal because our old energy patterns that are no longer healthy in our bodies or outer fields can hinder us from progressing, on many different healing and spiritual levels. Learning how to release old baggage that is trapped in us can help us heal faster and help us stop replaying old emotional tapes that keep us stuck.

I contacted her to ask if she would take me as a student. She was most gracious to say yes. I started soon after, and we began at 5 in the morning. She would call me on the phone in those early hours and guide me through a protection grid, then discuss how to identify what I wanted to work on to clear my energy fields. I have mentioned this adventure before but wanted to go more into what we did when we ventured into the other side.

We always met with our spirit guides when we went exploring the body grid. For a while, I was only allowed to observe and ask questions. Then later, I was carefully supervised while Kristi's spirit guides tutored me, to help with what was being released. As I went through the process with her and the spirit guides, I learned the different techniques that were being applied. After about an hour, we would come back to the physical plane, where she would review what happened. Our sessions always ended with a homework assignment for the next time we would meet.

On our weekly visits, we always started off in a journey and worked together in the body's energy fields. Sometimes we worked together on the same plane, or sometimes she sent me off with my spirit guides to work on other things that needed to be reviewed or released. At first I was surprised by how much I noticed the difference in my body after we worked together in my energy field. Emotional and physical releases would happen in between sessions and during the day. These could get a little intense. Tears or strong emotions would erupt as past memories surfaced and I worked on releasing those old programs that were recorded in my cells or energy bodies.

I was to call Kristi at any time if I needed help or got stuck during the day and couldn't release on my own with my spirit guides. My family was warned during that period in my life, I might be a little unstable emotionally, while I was bringing up old memories and feelings that had been buried deep within me. My reactions were not all emotional, though; my body went through its own release. Lucky for me, I only had to call a few times. I could usually work through it with my spirit guides helping me move my emotional state and body, bringing it all back into balance until the next time.

Learning how to release and work on myself was amazing. No longer was I at the mercy of someone else's schedule. I could do this work on my own with my spirit guides. I had instant access to them if I got myself into too much release. It was all quite freeing. (Don't get me wrong: I still enjoy working with others in the physical plane who understand healing on a deeper level.) If I can't reach anyone when I need relief, I use this technique. As we finished the class, I felt very well taken care of, and I felt a deeper respect for work with the spirit guides.

Listening To That Voice Of Reason

When I talk to others about my experiences, I let them know that in the beginning I had my doubts until it happened to me personally. I understand when others don't get it. I know what it is like to be left out of the loop. I also know what it is like to be swept up into something that I can't deny really happened. I have questioned my own experiences, and yet I can't prove to myself that it was all a dream or didn't happen. Too much information from each experience has been recorded in the memory of all of my senses to ignore the fact that these experiences really did happen.

There is also a still, quiet voice that comes from all around, resonating inside of me, which stands out from everything else. My whole being, on all levels, responds when I hear this voice. It is not the usual chatter in my head. When I hear it state my name, I know it will be followed by a teaching or a lesson. It will always be from a broader view allowing me to see into experiencing a situation, person, or teaching on a larger perspective. I call this voice the "Voice of Reason," and I associate it with my spirit guides. The "Voice of Reason" always comes through as stern and loving, often reminding me how to see without judging myself or others.

When I get stuck in a state of fear and I recognize that I am working out my own emotional blocks, I ask for guidance. Sometimes I don't get an answer right away if the answer is not meant for me to know. Then there are those times that I am to learn from an experience. Still other times it may take a while to get an answer, as I may block the spirit guides with my own fears, so I have to center myself in order to receive the information when it does come. If I am still blocked, I will go into twilight, as I am less likely to obstruct the information in that state.

Often, however, I get the answer right there on the spot, and the information comes flooding in, either as a vision or someone explaining what is happening. Other times, when I think that I didn't receive an answer, I find out later that my question was answered in a different way than what I expected. Whether I know the answer right away or I need to have more life experience before I learn it, really all depends on what is for my own highest good. I must admit that I do like it when it is instant as I am human.

At times I feel the physical presence of strong energies, standing by me or behind me, waiting to be recognized, often when I am working with someone or speaking to a group. When this happens, I let others know that there will be personal information coming through from the other side. I then let the information come in from the loved ones, spirit guides, spirit animals, or record keepers, who also have a great deal of respect for the process of communication and each other. They don't try to take over or order me around. They wait, and then, if asked, they will share.

One thing to remember is that spirit guides and guardian angels are with you ever since your birth or incarnation into this physical world. Often you will know them already and recognize the way they feel when you start to work with them on a conscious level. They are here to help guide and fulfill the sacred contracts that you have with your soul and others on this plane of existence. They are here to lovingly help us understand why we get stuck and what we need to experience for our soul's own evaluation. All you have to do is ask.

Expansion

I was working with my teacher Kristi, who was teaching me about healing energies. She was very clear that this was not the end-all and be-all of healing. There were many other things in the universe that help. We, as a collective, only know a small thimbleful of wisdom or knowledge of the universe. Learning is always progressing and expanding ourselves. As long as we are willing to learn, we will be blessed with lessons and teachings in our life.

This goes back to what the medicine man in Taos said when I told him I was learning how to heal myself and would be finished by the end of the week.

I remember how he looked at me, speaking with a small grin. "Ana, You know that you are learning now how to allow yourself to heal, and you will continue to heal in this life, on the other side and in other lifetimes. Healing does not happen with a one-time-fix. You are going to grow, as you are now opening to understanding and learning. You are in the somewhere-in-between with what you have learned. You still have a great deal to learn."

"Oh," I said. That was news to me; I thought it would be an easy, quick fix.

I know that sometimes we have experiences that we consider really bad or that we wish had never happened. On the physical side, we live through great tragedies, but on the other side they are just that – "experiences." By moving through these life lessons in the physical realm, we can learn to step into our own evolution in valuing the lessons and changes within ourselves, which affect not only us but all those around us.

Another Trip To Taos, The Book

My husband and I decided to take a quick trip to Taos on his birthday in 2012. We thought we would drive up on Friday, spend the weekend, and drive back on Sunday, so we could start work that following Monday. My mom had told me about the Mable Dodge Luhan house so we got on the Internet and booked the solarium room that was all glass. It was beautiful and lived up to all the things we had heard about it.

Our eleven-hour drive was relaxing, and we really delighted in visiting with each other. We took our time, stopping for breaks, eating, and enjoying just being on the road. It all felt so freeing as we appreciated everything around us. We arrived in Taos around 6:15 in the evening and checked into the lodge. As we were filling out the paperwork, the hostess told us about a book signing that started at 7:00 that evening. They were having a weekend conference all day on Saturday, celebrating women authors who were going to talk about their books and discuss the industry. I was excited, so we decided to go to the signing that night.

When we arrived to the room where they were going to have the conference, they were still setting up. A woman told us that they would be open at 7:00, but we were welcome to look around and check out the books that were being launched that evening.

As I spoke with the lady, my husband was already reading the cover of a book and laughed out loud. I looked at him, somewhat annoyed, as I was trying to have a short conversation with the woman that was setting up, when he said, "Look who wrote the book." I immediately recognized the name of the author,

Mirabai Starr as a memory came rushing in of her behind the desk when I first went to Taos to grieve for my soul at Golden Willow. She was the one who checked me in to see Ted and later on spent a day listening to me as I tried to put things together. Afterwards she introduced me to my heart chakra by leading me on my first guided meditation. There in that sacred space of the heart I discovered a spark only to recognize the connection that had been forgotten. Surprised, I stood there thinking what good fortune it was to be here when she was launching her book.

My husband and I decided to leave and come back to see her and hear her presentation. When we returned, the conference room had only a few seats left at the very back. As we sat there enjoying Mirabai's talk about her new book, she announced it was her seventh. She mentioned there was a chapter on the counselor from Golden Willow, Ted, who was also there in the room that night, and she wanted to honor him. She pointed with her finger in my direction. Behind me sat my counselor Ted and his lovely wife, whom we all had come to respect and love. I felt joy in my heart to see these beautiful souls again in one room, who had so much to share about helping others. I got to visit for only a few minutes afterwards before Ted was swallowed up in a human ball of those trying to talk to him. Mirabai was also surrounded by people at the gathering. My husband and I were both tired from the long drive that day. We needed rest, so we left and made our way out to our room.

The next day we returned to the Women's Book Conference. I looked forward to seeing more friends. As I listened to the different authors and took notes, I started to feel inspired. This is when I heard laughing. I knew that it was not coming from the crowd that had gathered that day. It was more from the angelic realm, as all my senses felt the laughter move through me. Finally I asked, "What is all the laughter about?" I heard several voices chime in to tell me that it was not a mistake that I was there. My presence at the conference had been arranged long ago with my spirit guides, to inspire me to write a book. So here I was making the full circle in my journey returning to be greeted by the very ones who had helped set me back on my path. It was then that I remembered once again that, "There are no accidents in the Universe."

The summer before, I knew in my heart that I was going to write a book, but never took the time to sit down to do it. The funny part was that while I was vacationing with my family that fateful December in New York City, I sat down one day and within a few hours wrote an outline of the book that I was to write. When I got home I filed it away, not giving it a second thought.

After we left Taos, my husband asked what things needed to be done to make this book happen. I was happy to tell him that most of it was already done.

All that was needed was for me to actually sit down and fill in the stories. I already had the outline, table of contents, and knew the form of how it was to flow.

I learned from this adventure in Taos that sometimes, when we don't want to take the extra time to do something that is important for us to accomplish, we often get a little help from our friends. Isn't it wonderful that the spirit guides and loved ones are still looking out for our welfare so that we will honor soul contracts? They even help us move into a space where we are inspired so that we can fulfill what we need to do.

Attachments

For me, in 2012 when I looked back on some of my experiences I could see on a much larger perspective that my journey had brought me back to completing the circle. I started the journey of healing making my pilgrimage to Taos with the spiritual crisis and ended back where I began inspired to write about my adventures.

What I learned by following the path into the sacred heart was that we are all connected and no one is ever left out.

Something to add is a statement that my father used to say to me all the time. "People don't own things; things own people." I remember thinking, what did that mean? As I grew older, I saw that we as human beings can quickly get attached to things – not only physical things, but other things such as images, ideas, thoughts, power, control, religious beliefs, or even addictions. I began to notice a pattern in which I saw myself. I also saw others who were shaping their lives around whatever it is that we don't want to let go of. Then, without realizing it, I soon discovered that whatever it was, it started to define who we were.

I know that the energies have now shifted on this planet and the whole universe in the last few decades. We were in a world of belief, and now we are in a world of knowing. This means that we don't just have faith that something exists; we are now moving into full knowing and understanding with our whole being that it does.

Recall the story that I call the "knitting experience," where I merged out of my body, sloughing off old worries and beliefs like dirty laundry. I was able to merge because I was able to let go of everything from this earth that separates me from other people and our Creator. I was able to let completely go and trust the journey as I merged back as a soul into spirit and then into the ocean of our

Creator. There I was met with the understanding that the only thing that separates us is us. Our beliefs, our prejudices, our fears, our control, our addictions, our idea of being separate, all hold us captive to the physical world, where we forget from where we once came.

These things that we hold onto that separate us from who we really are and from each other, only distort what we have come to learn and remember. We define ourselves as separated from each other and our Creator. The fact is that we are never separated. In truth, it is a bad habit or an addiction to this world which keeps us glued to it.

Some people, when it is time to exit the physical world, which we call dying, have every opportunity to let go of this one, yet make the choice to hold on to it. If you decide, you can move on and are welcomed into the sea of unconditional love. Many who have become attached to the material things that belong in this world become stuck. They refuse to let go and continue to vibrate within the lower levels of the physical world. In such cases, they cause great anguish and grief to themselves.

It is love that fuels the power of rescuing those who are lost. Love continues to exist, opening pathways into the higher vibrational levels. Things like judgement, hate, anger, and fear have no place in the realm where only unconditional love exists. They simply don't exist. Unconditional love is just that: unconditional. No limits! When you merge into that energy, you soon discover that you can only reach those realms of existence by letting go and letting God. Let go!

Everything else that is not unconditional love only separates us from each other, limiting us from our full potential. I know that the rest is a part of this physical world. If we want to achieve that which is whole, forgiveness and unconditional love play a big part in returning home.

Akashic Library: A spiritual library that holds the "Book of Life" where every thought, action, and deed is recorded in the collective consciousness.

Akashic Records: Also known as the "Book of Life"; Contains every thought, word, deed, or action experienced in the past, present, or future since the conception of a soul.

Angels: Angelic beings who guard and aid human beings in completing their soul contracts and life lessons.

Astral Projection: The conscious practice of an out of body experience.

Body Jumping: The merging of two consciousnesses into the physical mind of one body.

Bodywork: Any kind of energy or physical body work that helps bring the body back into balance

Chakra: Spinning wheels, or energy centers, that carry energy through the physical body.

Clearing process: When we begin to release all the dense energy that is stuck in our bodies and energy fields.

Curandera: Latin American folk healer

Dense Energy: Lower vibrational energy that draws on the lower emotions and lower self.

The Field: Interconnected Universe

Grokking: another term used for body jumping.

Journeying: When a person leaves their body by astral traveling to other worlds and dimensions. The person is also accompanied by an animal spirit who serves as a guide and protector on the other side. Usually journeying is used by a Shaman or Shaman Practitioner who is trained in entering the supernatural realms and working with the spirits on the other side.

Knowing: When knowledge comes directly from the higher self, Spirit, or Universal mind into the physical mind.

Kundalini: A rush of spiritual energy that begins at the base of the first chakra and moves through all the primary seven chakras, out of the crown, creating spiritual enlightenment and bliss.

Master Teacher: A person or spirit being who has mastered one or more modalities in the physical and spiritual planes.

Medicine Drum: A rawhide drum that is used to create a theta beat that aids a person to move into a twilight trance in order to spirit walk or connect to the other side.

Meridians: Energy pathways located in the physical body that help move energy to bring the body into alignment to aid with healing.

Modality: A practice or set of skills and tools used by a practitioner to aid the mind, body, and soul in healing.

Reiki: A laying of hands on a person, animal, plant etc... Channeling a healing energy from Source to clear all pathways while bringing the physical body, energy centers, and spiritual energy into balance.

Shaman: A person who has the ability to move from the physical world into the supernatural world and other dimensions to help aid with healing and balancing the mind, body, and soul. The shaman has a keen knowledge and working relationship with the spirits and other entities on the other side.

Soul Contract: A contract between souls, and the Creator, before birth that determines the different parts that each soul will play in helping to learn life lessons in the physical world.

Soul Group: A group of souls that are connected on the spiritual and physical planes to help teach each other life lessons.

Soul Retrieval: When a shaman or practitioner "Spirit Walks" into other dimensions and supernatural realms to retrieve a part or parts of a soul that has splintered off from the original soul due to a trauma, bringing it back to reunite it with the person who lost it.

Source: God, Creator, Universal mind

Spirit: Holy Spirit

Spirit Animal: Spirit Animals or Animal Totems act as teachers, helpers, and guides to the person they are connected to. They also help in journeying to the supernatural realms to aid and protect the person they are working with.

Spirit Guides: Appointed spirit beings that are guardians for each person, who teach and help guide them in completing their soul contract.

Spirit Walking: The ability to astral walk in the different dimensions, energy centers, holographic blueprints, and ethers of other supernatural realms.

Twilight: The time and space of the transition between physical and spiritual worlds in which a person is about to wake from dreaming or fall into a dream state.

Aknowledgements

I want to thank my family who put up with me during this time of my spiritual progression and healing. They laughed and cried with me as my lessons were not always easy. A special thanks to my husband Steve and my two children Cameron and Mason. A big thanks to my mom Donna who edited this book and encouraged me to continue writing when I wanted to stop. Thank you to my little sister Angelique who not only encouraged me to learn about my spiritual gifts but reminded me that it was also a part of who I am. I also want to thank my dad and all my family and loved ones who love me and supported me in my work.

Thank you to all the teachers from the other side who show up in different times in my life when I need to learn a lesson or need help changing directions. Thank you to all my spirit guides, Spirit animals, Spirit teachers and the Spirit council.

I also wanted to thank all the teachers from the physical world who have shown up in my life and continue to show up. Jodi Lovoi - Akashic Records teacher, Ted Wiard - LPC Counselor & founder of Golden Willow retreat center, Holli Blackwell - C.Ht. Reiki Master Teacher, Martha Fiddes - CQM Qigong & Tai Chi Master Teacher, Medicine Man - Taos NM, Pam Durham - Acupuncturist & Acutonics teacher. Lonna Bartly - Akashic Records teacher, Daniel D'Neuville - Fire Walker, Christi BlueFeather - Energy healing teacher, John Holland - Psychic Medium & Spiritual teacher, Hank Wesselman - Shaman practitioner & Spiritual teacher, Mirabai Starr - healer, Jean Smith - healer & Reiki Master, Paula Schermerhorn - Psychic Medium, Dr Sarai Stuart, ND. - meditation coach & color teacher, Gail Carswell - Shaman Practitioner, Alyce Payne - Blessing Teacher, Kirby Cory - Grid Master.

Thank you to my Reiki and Healing Circle friends for all their support and help with the circles.

Carolyn King - Reiki buddy & Healing Circle, Amy Patterson - Reiki buddy & Healing Circle, Debra Rohlfing - Healing Circle, Terri - Healing Circle, Stella - Mentor & Healing Circle, Lynda - Healing Circle.

Thank you to my friends who were there for me when I was moving through my own transitions. Jenny McAllister, Robin Evens, Aishwarya Saigal, Christopher Cardin, Mary Burke-Kelly, Theresa Slagle, Kolton Webber, Sonya Wickman, and Veronica Zapata

Thank you to my friends who let me just hang out with them at their stores when I needed somewhere to go or just be in their healing energy. Thank you to Mary Harrison owner of the "The Artful Bead" in Fort Worth, TX. Tray, Pat, and Fall Owners of "The Power of the Rainbow" in Arlington, TX.

And last but not least a Thank you to my mother Donna who helped me edit my drafts countless of times before being edited by my editor Michelle Foster.

About the Author

Ana is an Usui and Karuna® Master Reiki Teacher. She is a certified Akashic Record consultant and Blessing giver. Ana earned her Bachelor of Science degree from North Texas State University in Textile Chemistry and Design. Later she pursued a Bachelor of Arts Degree in Education from the University of Texas at Arlington that she uses in facilitating circles and support groups for those looking to find others on the same path of healing and learning about their spiritual gifts.

Ana and her family currently reside in Richardson, Texas where she continues to write and takes time to work on her art.

End Notes

In the great scheme of things we are all here for a very special reason and all of our lives really do have meaning. The one aspect of the whole equation is whether we are willing to make the effort to find what it is all about. It is on that journey where we find ourselves venturing into the life essences of the sacred heart and what connects us to all things in discovering our true selves.

1. Tapping Into Your Inner Confidence & Personal Power. (2006). (A guided meditation to unleash your true potential) John Holland [CD Audio].

2. Reiki The Healing Touch, http://www.reikiwebstore.com/ProductPage.cfm?ProductID=52&CategoryID=2

3. Samuel Taylor Coleridge, The Rime of the Ancient Mariner, 1st Publication, 1798, Part II.

4. King, Serge Kahili PH.D. (1990). Urban Shaman. New York, NY: Fireside

5. Brennan, Barbara Ann (1987), Hands of Light : A Guide to Healing Through the Personal Energy Field. New York, NY: Bantam Books

6. Bulletproof Romance. (n.d.). Bulletproof romance. On [CD].

7. Revelation Song. (n.d.). [Music Score].

8. Judith, A. (1999). Wheels of life : A user's guide to the chakra system. St. Paul, Minn.: Llewellyn Publications.

9. Simpson, L. (1999). The Book of Chakra Healing. New York, NY: Sterling Publishing Company, Inc.

10. Sankey, M. (2003). Esoteric acupuncture: Gateway to expanded healing. Mountain Castle Pub. Retrieved from Google Scholar.

11. Knab, Timothy J. (1995). A War of Witches. New York, NY: Harper Collins Publishers.

12. Baldwin, William A. (2003). Healing Lost Souls: Releasing Unwanted Spirits From Your Energy Body. Charlottesville, VA.: Hampton Roads Publishing Company, Inc

13. Davidson, W. (2006). Spirit rescue : A simple guide to talking with ghosts and freeing earthbound spirits. Woodbury, Minn.: Llewellyn Publications. Retrieved from Library of Congress or OCLC Worldcat.

14. Hagon, Zoe (1989). Channeling, The Spiritual Connection. Garden City Park, NY: Avery Publishing Group, Inc.

15. Like Water for Chocolate. (1992). (A 1992 film in the style of magical realism based on the popular novel, published in 1989 by first-time Mexican novelist Laura Esquivel) [Motion Picture]. Mexico.

Made in the USA
San Bernardino, CA
14 February 2017